THE BOOK OF
Mr. Natural

THE BOOK OF
Mr. Natural

BY R. CRUMB

FANTAGRAPHICS BOOKS

SEATTLE, WASHINGTON

Fantagraphics Books
7563 Lake City Way NE
Seattle, WA 98115

Editor: Mark Thompson
Publishers: Gary Groth & Kim Thompson
Front cover coloring by R. Crumb; separations by Rayson Films.
Back cover color by Mary Woodring
Special Thanks to Ron Turner

First Fantagraphics Books edition: September, 1995.
1 2 3 4 5 6 7 8 9 10
ISBN: 1-56097-194-0

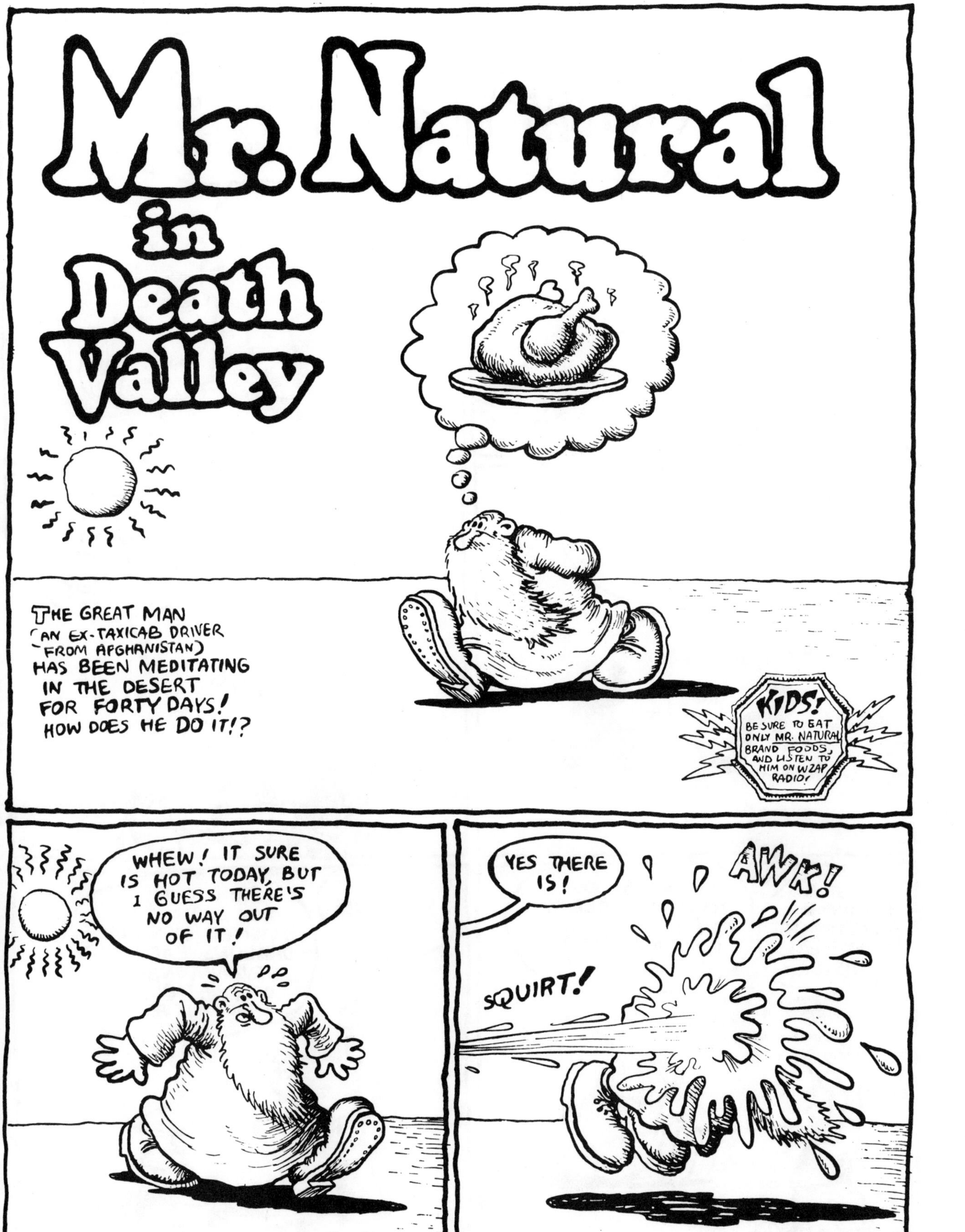
Mr. Natural in Death Valley
THE GREAT MAN (AN EX-TAXICAB DRIVER FROM AFGHANISTAN) HAS BEEN MEDITATING IN THE DESERT FOR FORTY DAYS! HOW DOES HE DO IT!?
KIDS! BE SURE TO EAT ONLY MR. NATURAL BRAND FOODS, AND LISTEN TO HIM ON WZAP RADIO!
WHEW! IT SURE IS HOT TODAY, BUT I GUESS THERE'S NO WAY OUT OF IT!
YES THERE IS!
AWK!
SQUIRT!

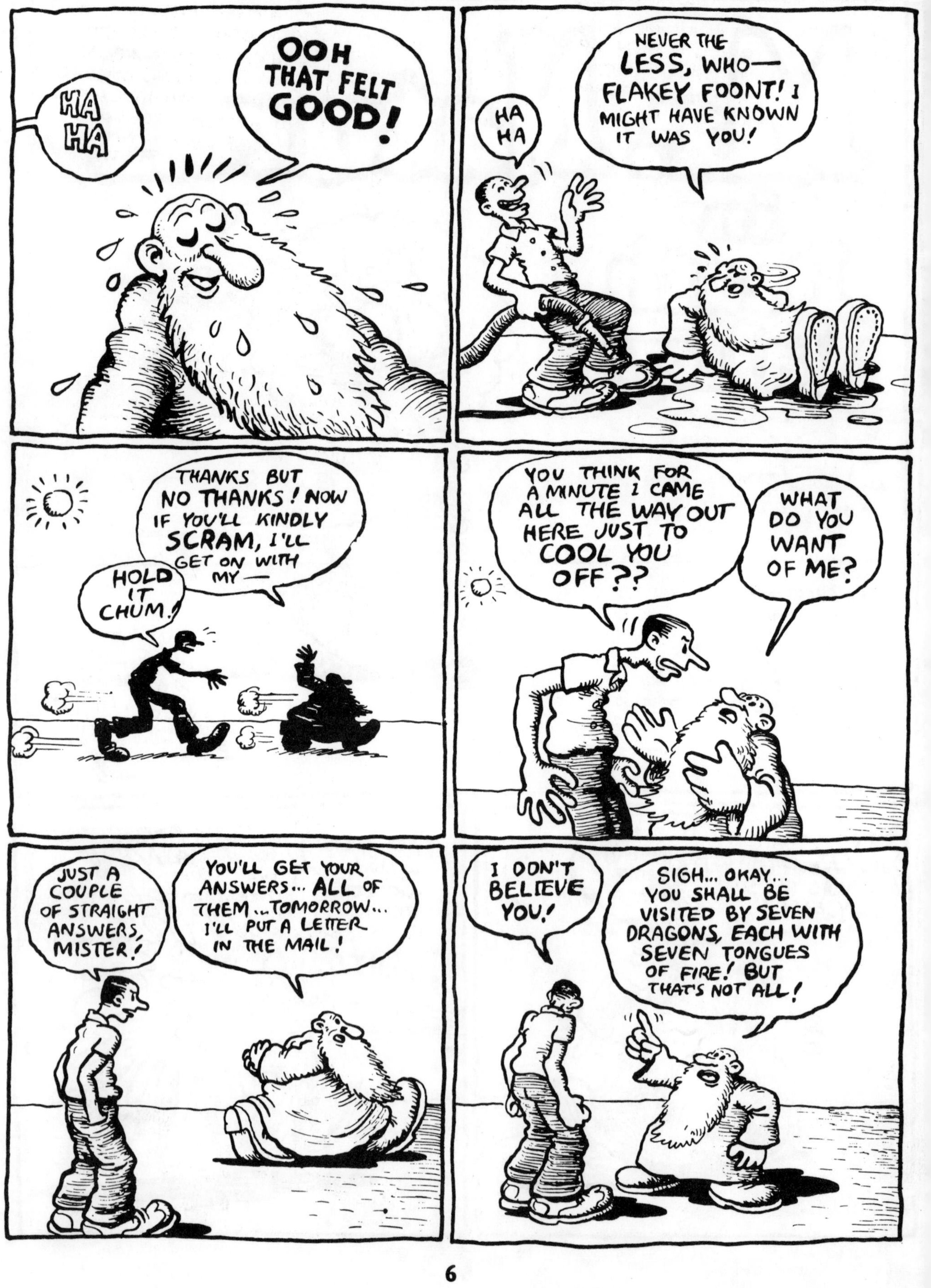
HA HA
OOH THAT FELT GOOD!
HA HA
NEVER THE LESS, WHO— FLAKEY FOONT! I MIGHT HAVE KNOWN IT WAS YOU!
THANKS BUT NO THANKS! NOW IF YOU'LL KINDLY SCRAM, I'LL GET ON WITH MY—
HOLD IT CHUM!
YOU THINK FOR A MINUTE I CAME ALL THE WAY OUT HERE JUST TO COOL YOU OFF??
WHAT DO YOU WANT OF ME?
JUST A COUPLE OF STRAIGHT ANSWERS, MISTER!
YOU'LL GET YOUR ANSWERS... ALL OF THEM...TOMORROW... I'LL PUT A LETTER IN THE MAIL!
I DON'T BELIEVE YOU!
SIGH... OKAY... YOU SHALL BE VISITED BY SEVEN DRAGONS, EACH WITH SEVEN TONGUES OF FIRE! BUT THAT'S NOT ALL!

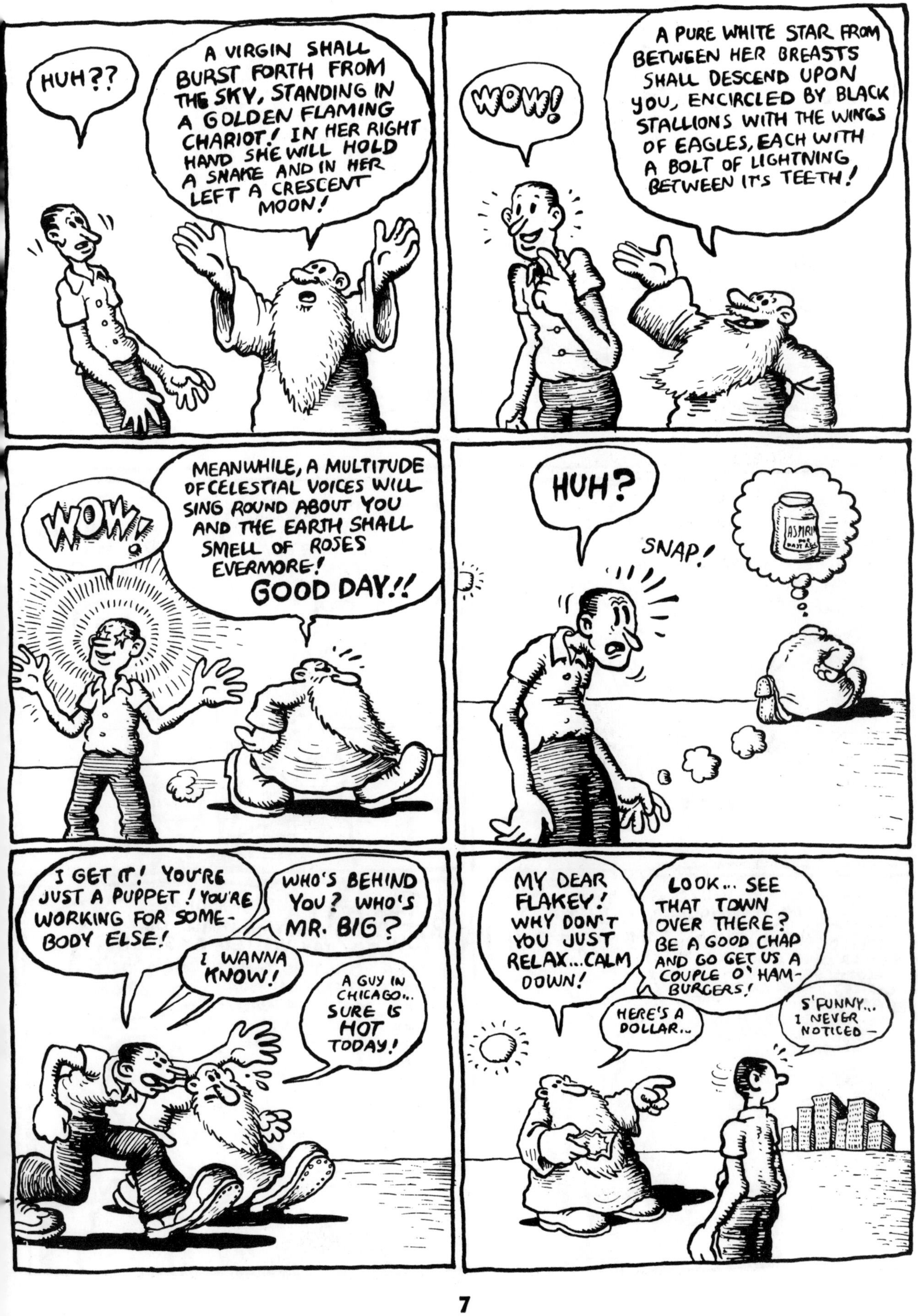
HUH??
A VIRGIN SHALL BURST FORTH FROM THE SKY, STANDING IN A GOLDEN FLAMING CHARIOT! IN HER RIGHT HAND SHE WILL HOLD A SNAKE AND IN HER LEFT A CRESCENT MOON!
WOW!
A PURE WHITE STAR FROM BETWEEN HER BREASTS SHALL DESCEND UPON YOU, ENCIRCLED BY BLACK STALLIONS WITH THE WINGS OF EAGLES, EACH WITH A BOLT OF LIGHTNING BETWEEN IT'S TEETH!
WOW!
MEANWHILE, A MULTITUDE OF CELESTIAL VOICES WILL SING ROUND ABOUT YOU AND THE EARTH SHALL SMELL OF ROSES EVERMORE!
GOOD DAY!!
HUH?
SNAP!
ASPIRIN
I GET IT! YOU'RE JUST A PUPPET! YOU'RE WORKING FOR SOMEBODY ELSE!
WHO'S BEHIND YOU? WHO'S MR. BIG?
I WANNA KNOW!
A GUY IN CHICAGO.. SURE IS HOT TODAY!
MY DEAR FLAKEY! WHY DON'T YOU JUST RELAX...CALM DOWN!
LOOK... SEE THAT TOWN OVER THERE? BE A GOOD CHAP AND GO GET US A COUPLE O' HAMBURGERS!
HERE'S A DOLLAR..
S'FUNNY... I NEVER NOTICED —

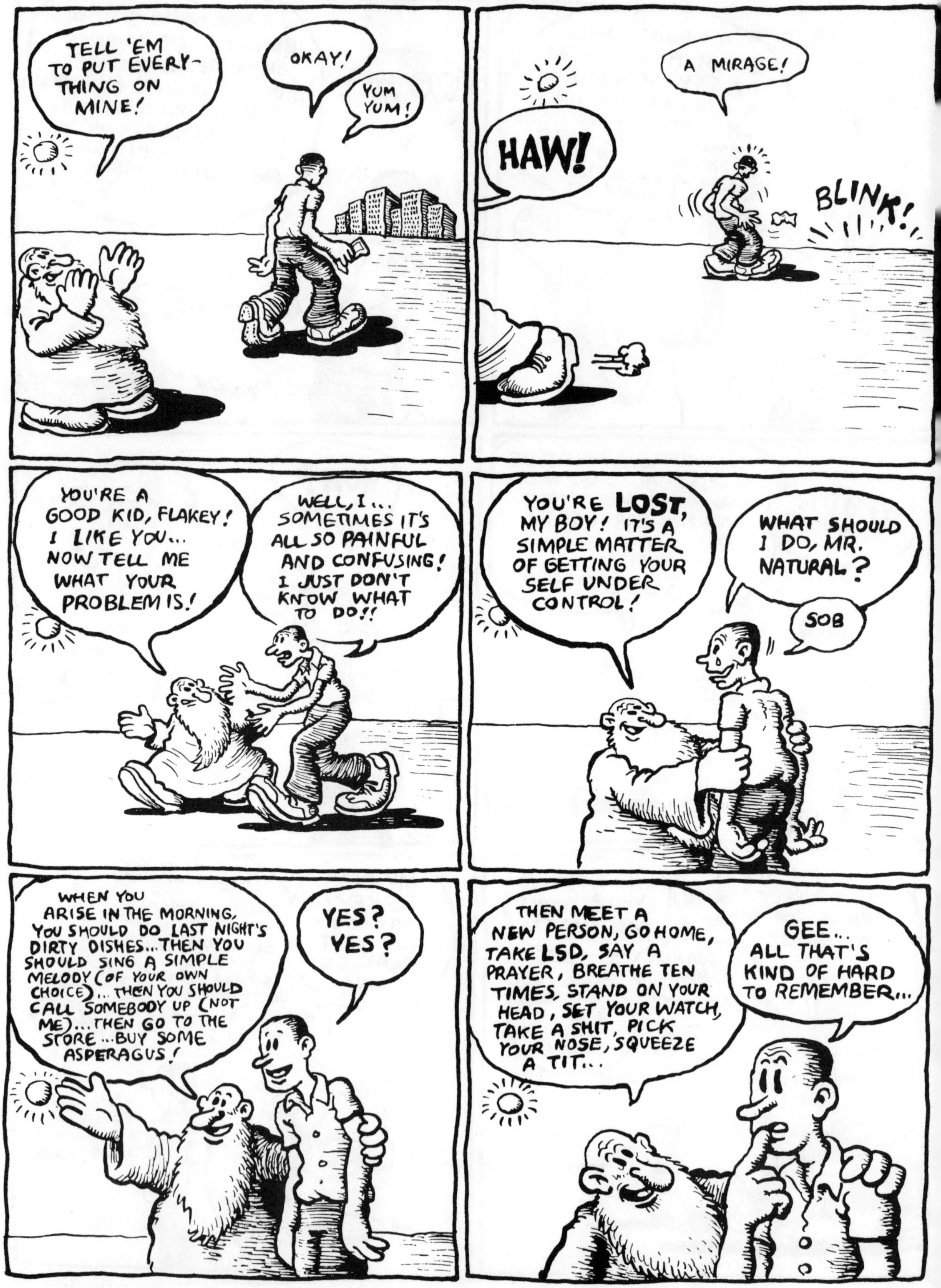
TELL 'EM TO PUT EVERY-THING ON MINE!
OKAY!
YUM YUM!
A MIRAGE!
HAW!
BLINK!
YOU'RE A GOOD KID, FLAKEY! I LIKE YOU... NOW TELL ME WHAT YOUR PROBLEM IS!
WELL, I... SOMETIMES IT'S ALL SO PAINFUL AND CONFUSING! I JUST DON'T KNOW WHAT TO DO!!
YOU'RE LOST, MY BOY! IT'S A SIMPLE MATTER OF GETTING YOUR SELF UNDER CONTROL!
WHAT SHOULD I DO, MR. NATURAL?
SOB
WHEN YOU ARISE IN THE MORNING, YOU SHOULD DO LAST NIGHT'S DIRTY DISHES... THEN YOU SHOULD SING A SIMPLE MELODY (OF YOUR OWN CHOICE)... THEN YOU SHOULD CALL SOMEBODY UP (NOT ME)... THEN GO TO THE STORE... BUY SOME ASPERAGUS!
YES? YES?
THEN MEET A NEW PERSON, GO HOME, TAKE LSD, SAY A PRAYER, BREATHE TEN TIMES, STAND ON YOUR HEAD, SET YOUR WATCH, TAKE A SHIT, PICK YOUR NOSE, SQUEEZE A TIT...
GEE... ALL THAT'S KIND OF HARD TO REMEMBER...

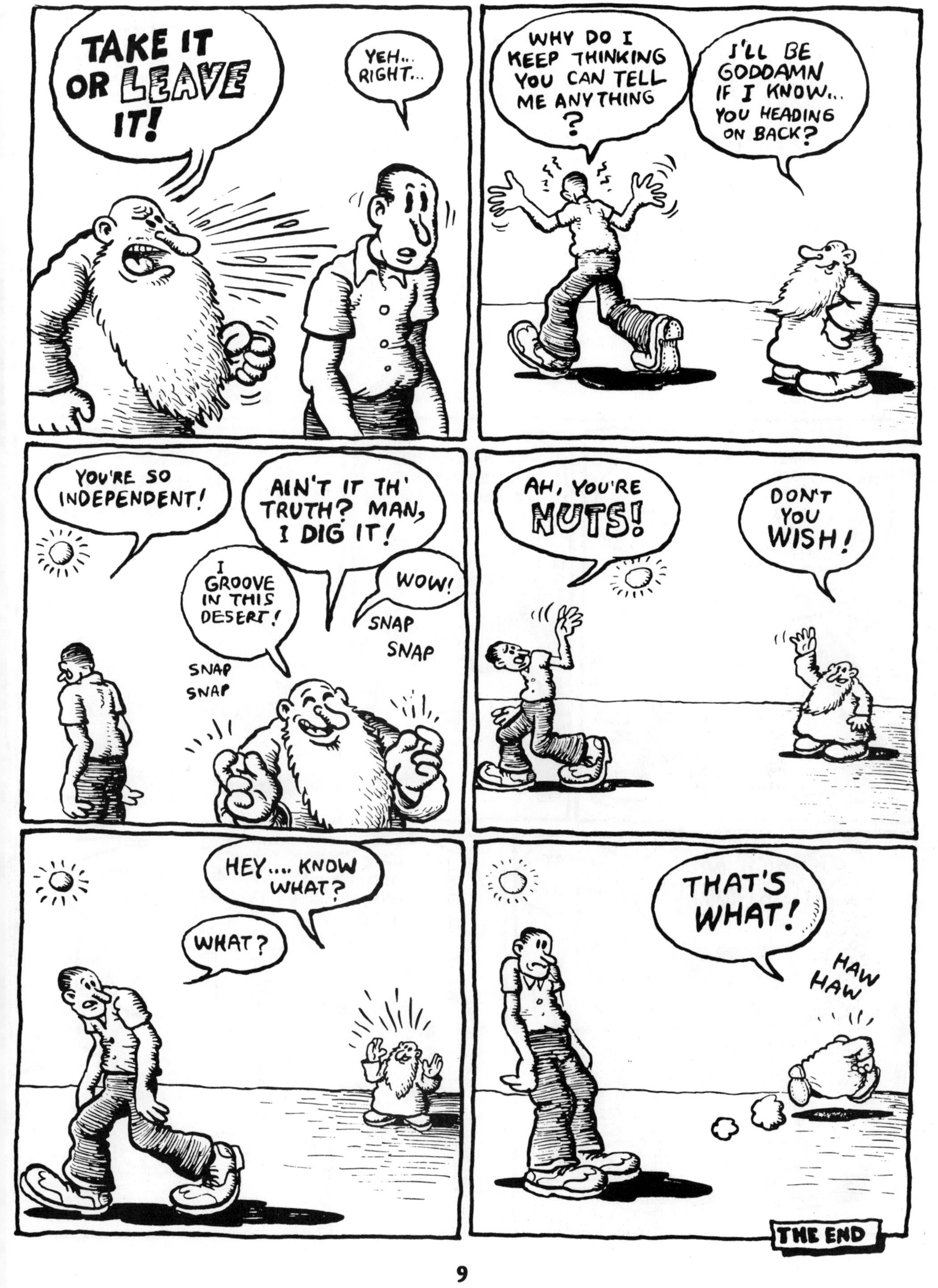
TAKE IT OR LEAVE IT!
YEH... RIGHT...
WHY DO I KEEP THINKING YOU CAN TELL ME ANYTHING?
I'LL BE GODDAMN IF I KNOW... YOU HEADING ON BACK?
YOU'RE SO INDEPENDENT!
AIN'T IT TH' TRUTH? MAN, I DIG IT!
I GROOVE IN THIS DESERT!
WOW!
SNAP SNAP
SNAP SNAP
AH, YOU'RE NUTS!
DON'T YOU WISH!
HEY.... KNOW WHAT?
WHAT?
THAT'S WHAT!
HAW HAW
THE END

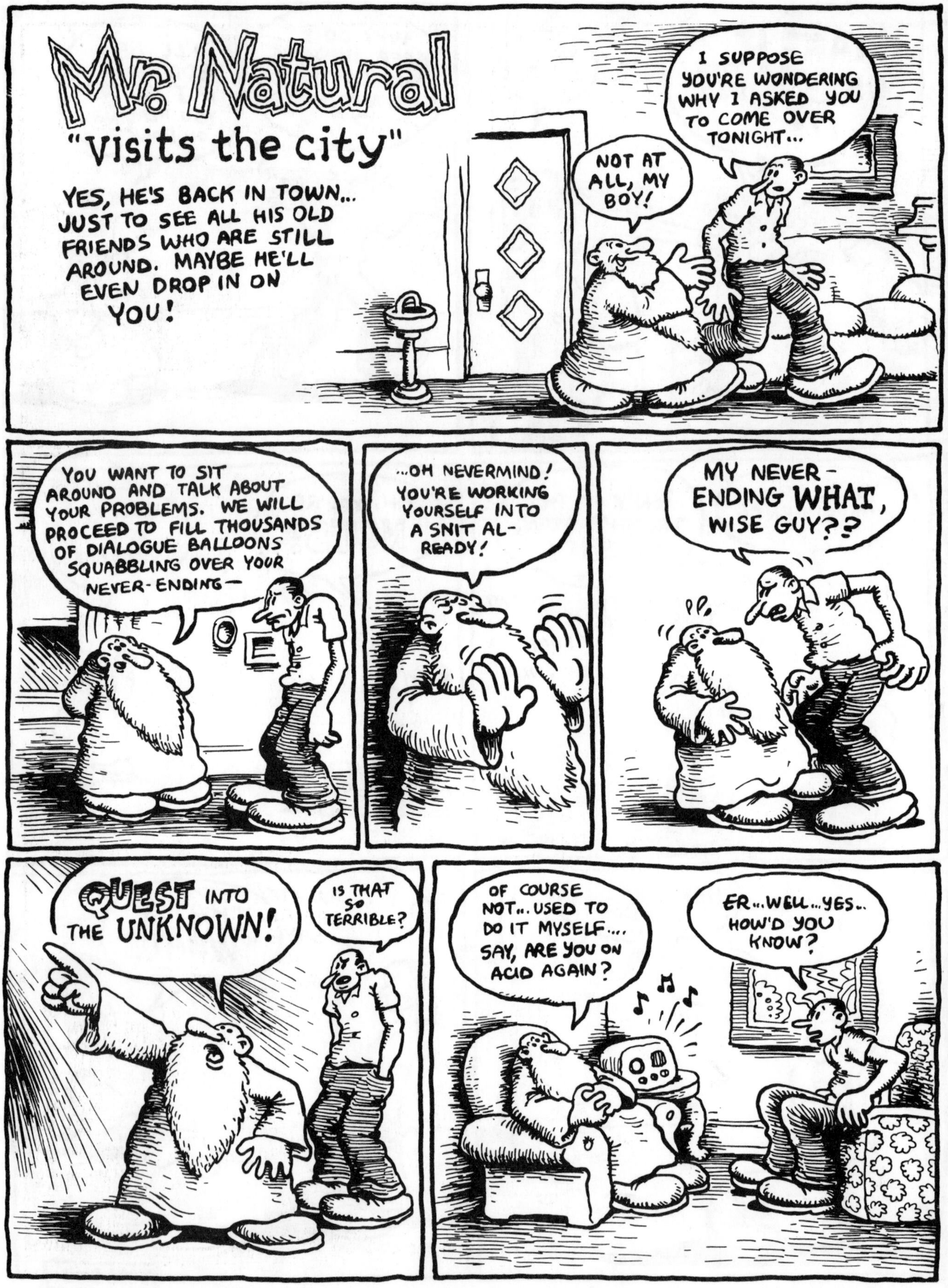
Mr. Natural
"visits the city"
YES, HE'S BACK IN TOWN... JUST TO SEE ALL HIS OLD FRIENDS WHO ARE STILL AROUND. MAYBE HE'LL EVEN DROP IN ON YOU!
I SUPPOSE YOU'RE WONDERING WHY I ASKED YOU TO COME OVER TONIGHT...
NOT AT ALL, MY BOY!
YOU WANT TO SIT AROUND AND TALK ABOUT YOUR PROBLEMS. WE WILL PROCEED TO FILL THOUSANDS OF DIALOGUE BALLOONS SQUABBLING OVER YOUR NEVER-ENDING—
...OH NEVERMIND! YOU'RE WORKING YOURSELF INTO A SNIT AL-READY!
MY NEVER-ENDING WHAT, WISE GUY??
QUEST INTO THE UNKNOWN!
IS THAT SO TERRIBLE?
OF COURSE NOT... USED TO DO IT MYSELF.... SAY, ARE YOU ON ACID AGAIN?
ER...WELL...YES.. HOW'D YOU KNOW?

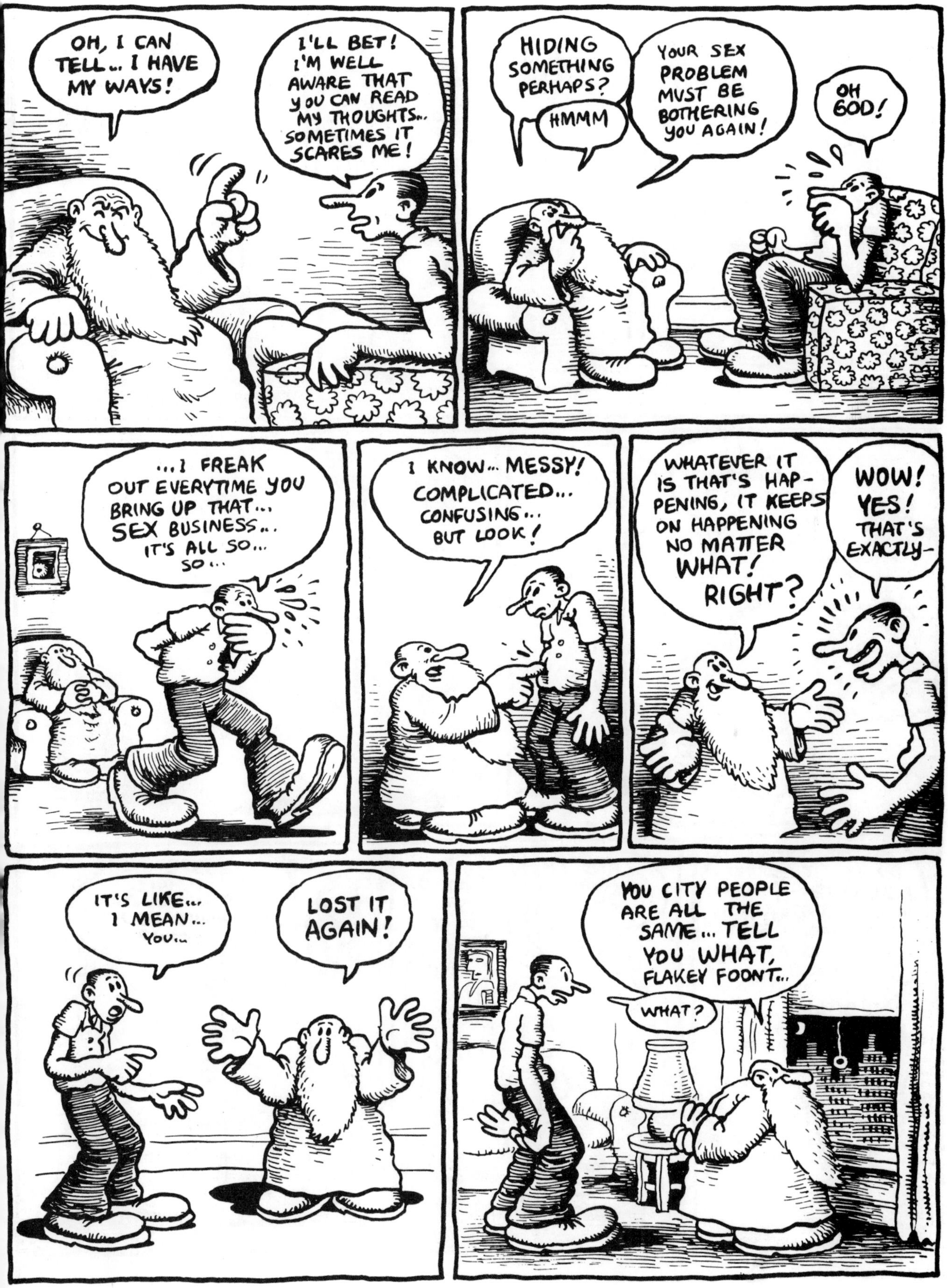
OH, I CAN TELL... I HAVE MY WAYS!
I'LL BET! I'M WELL AWARE THAT YOU CAN READ MY THOUGHTS... SOMETIMES IT SCARES ME!
HIDING SOMETHING PERHAPS?
HMMM
YOUR SEX PROBLEM MUST BE BOTHERING YOU AGAIN!
OH GOD!
...I FREAK OUT EVERYTIME YOU BRING UP THAT... SEX BUSINESS... IT'S ALL SO... SO...
I KNOW... MESSY! COMPLICATED... CONFUSING... BUT LOOK!
WHATEVER IT IS THAT'S HAPPENING, IT KEEPS ON HAPPENING NO MATTER WHAT! RIGHT?
WOW! YES! THAT'S EXACTLY-
IT'S LIKE... I MEAN... YOU...
LOST IT AGAIN!
YOU CITY PEOPLE ARE ALL THE SAME... TELL YOU WHAT, FLAKEY FOONT...
WHAT?

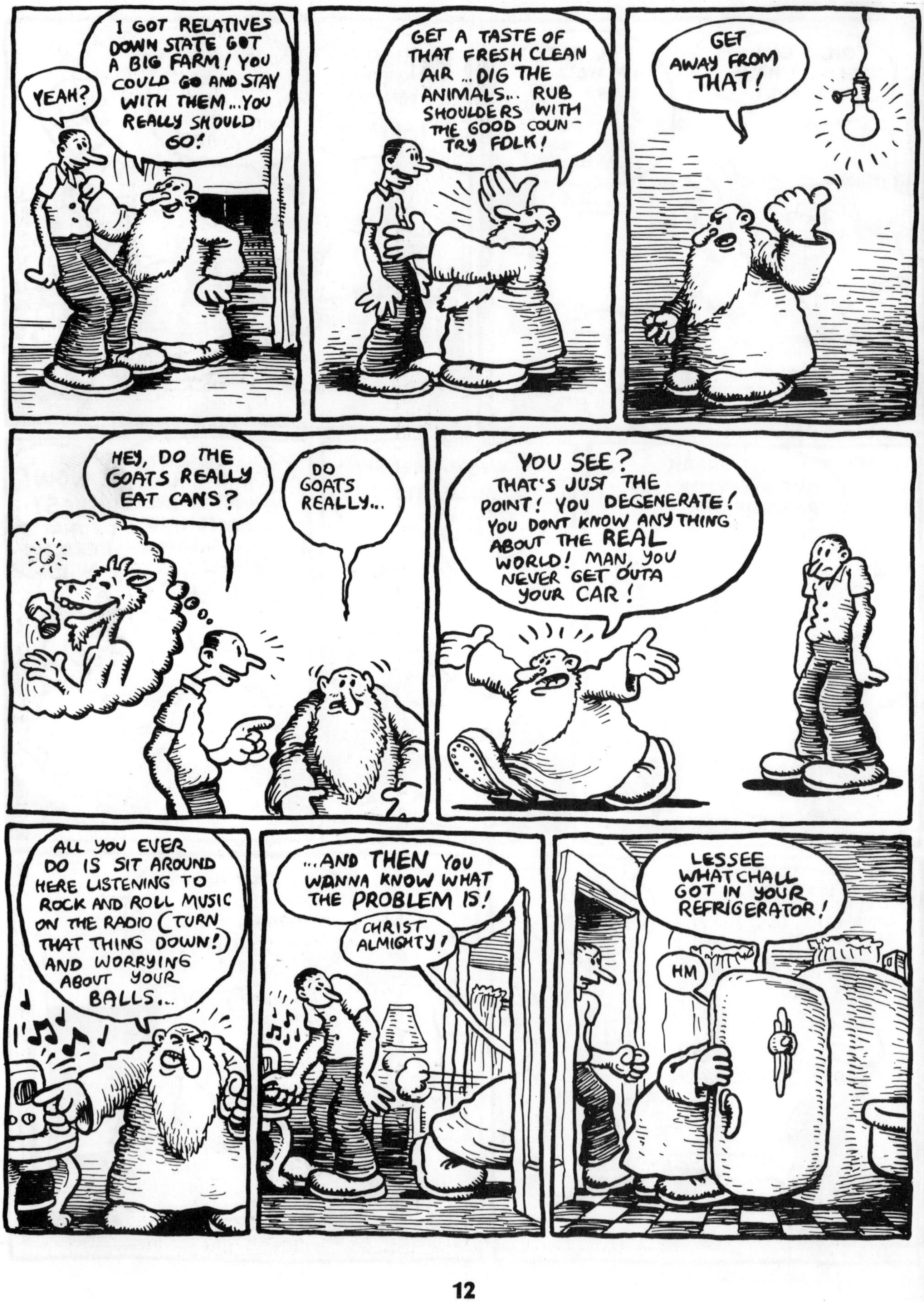
YEAH?
I GOT RELATIVES DOWN STATE GOT A BIG FARM! YOU COULD GO AND STAY WITH THEM...YOU REALLY SHOULD GO!
GET A TASTE OF THAT FRESH CLEAN AIR ...DIG THE ANIMALS... RUB SHOULDERS WITH THE GOOD COUN-TRY FOLK!
GET AWAY FROM THAT!
HEY, DO THE GOATS REALLY EAT CANS?
DO GOATS REALLY...
YOU SEE? THAT'S JUST THE POINT! YOU DEGENERATE! YOU DONT KNOW ANYTHING ABOUT THE REAL WORLD! MAN, YOU NEVER GET OUTA YOUR CAR!
ALL YOU EVER DO IS SIT AROUND HERE LISTENING TO ROCK AND ROLL MUSIC ON THE RADIO (TURN THAT THING DOWN!) AND WORRYING ABOUT YOUR BALLS...
...AND THEN YOU WANNA KNOW WHAT THE PROBLEM IS!
CHRIST ALMIGHTY!
LESSEE WHATCHALL GOT IN YOUR REFRIGERATOR!
HM

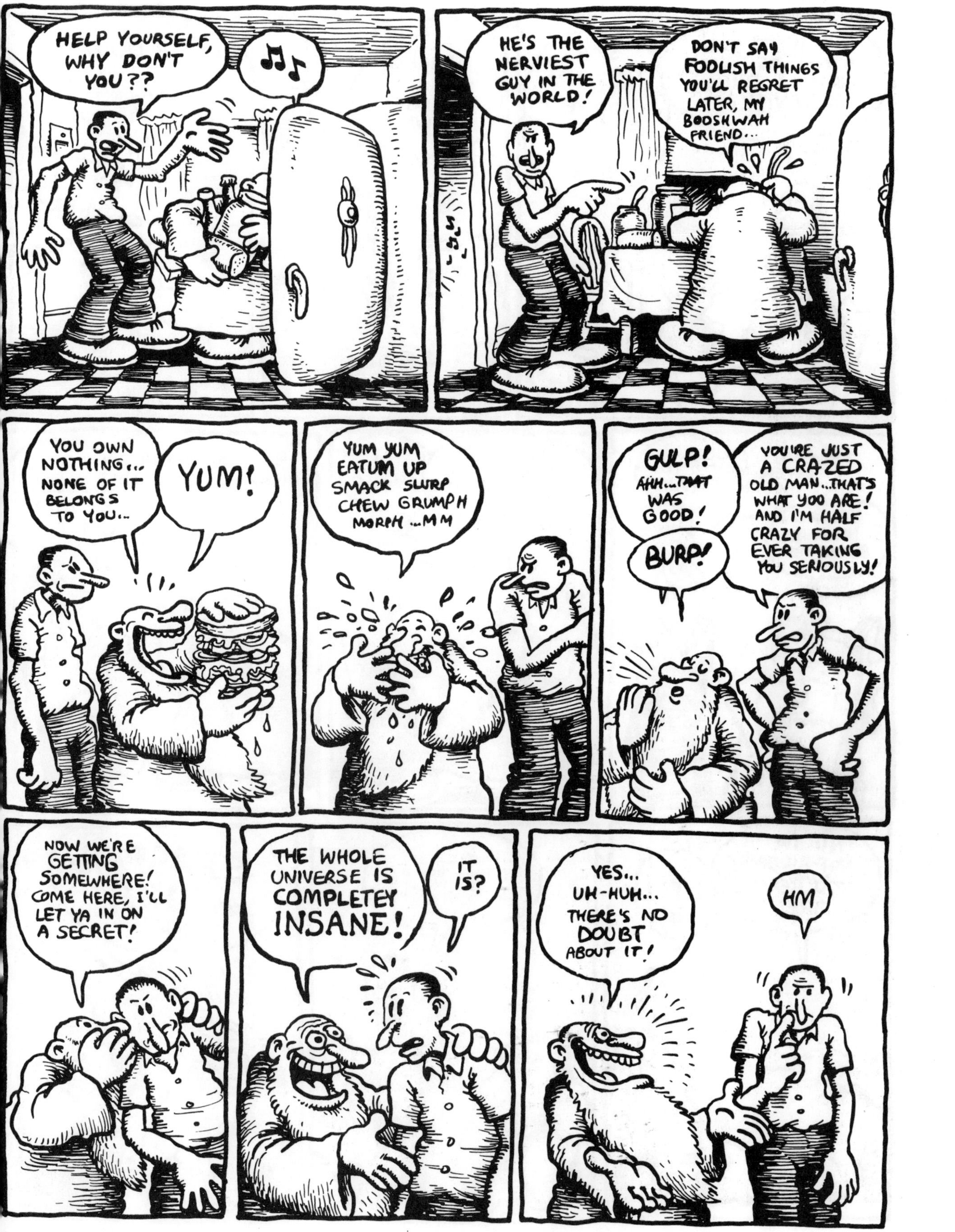
HELP YOURSELF, WHY DON'T YOU??
♫♪
HE'S THE NERVIEST GUY IN THE WORLD!
DON'T SAY FOOLISH THINGS YOU'LL REGRET LATER, MY BOOSHWAH FRIEND...
YOU OWN NOTHING... NONE OF IT BELONGS TO YOU..
YUM!
YUM YUM EATUM UP SMACK SLURP CHEW GRUMPH MORPH ...MM
GULP! AHH...THAT WAS GOOD!
BURP!
YOU'RE JUST A CRAZED OLD MAN...THAT'S WHAT YOO ARE! AND I'M HALF CRAZY FOR EVER TAKING YOU SERIOUSLY!
NOW WE'RE GETTING SOMEWHERE! COME HERE, I'LL LET YA IN ON A SECRET!
THE WHOLE UNIVERSE IS COMPLETEY INSANE!
IT IS?
YES... UH-HUH... THERE'S NO DOUBT ABOUT IT!
HM

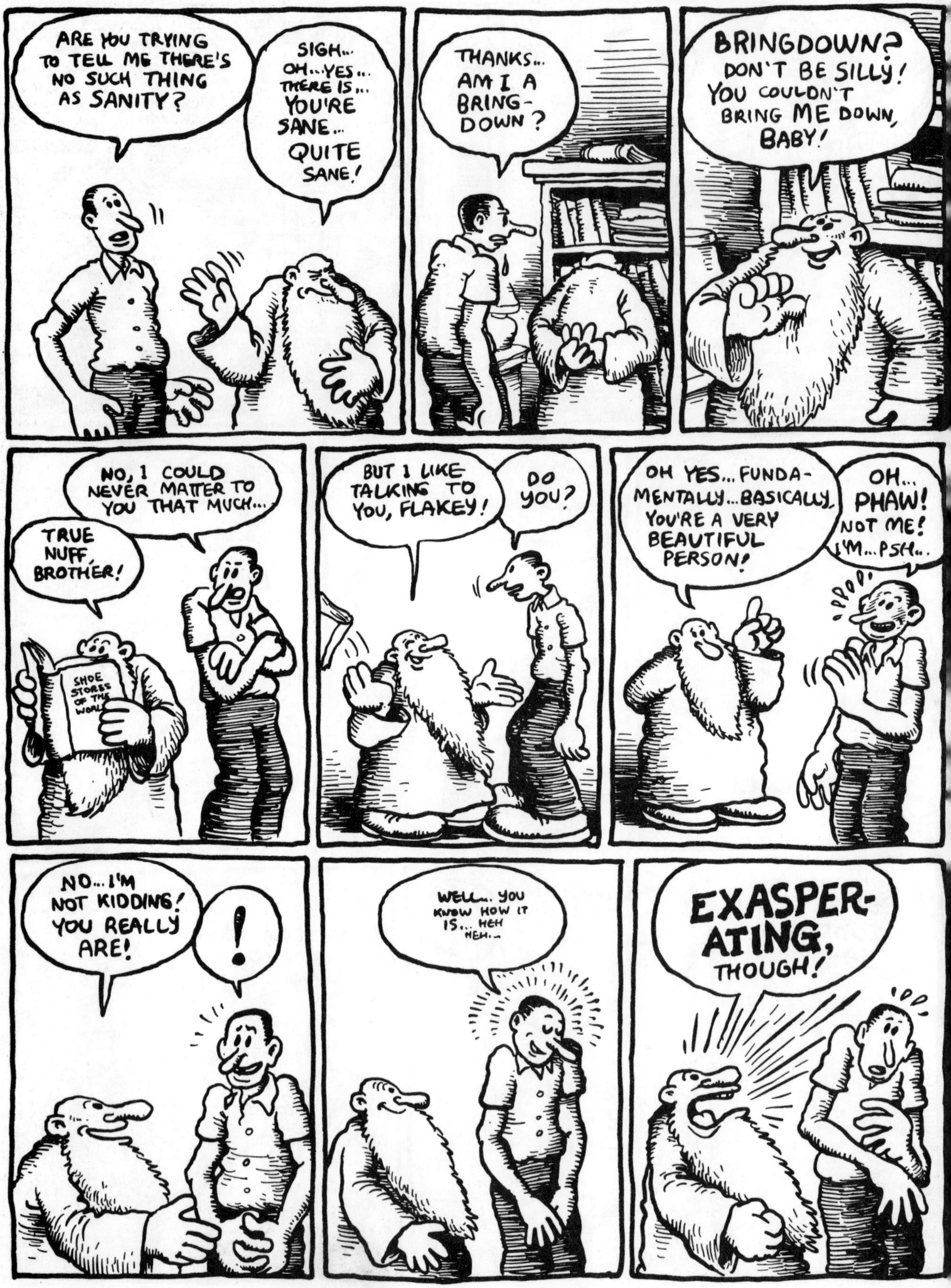
ARE YOU TRYING TO TELL ME THERE'S NO SUCH THING AS SANITY?
SIGH... OH...YES... THERE IS... YOU'RE SANE... QUITE SANE!
THANKS... AM I A BRING-DOWN?
BRINGDOWN? DON'T BE SILLY! YOU COULDN'T BRING ME DOWN, BABY!
NO, I COULD NEVER MATTER TO YOU THAT MUCH...
TRUE NUFF, BROTHER!
SHOE STORIES OF THE WORLD
BUT I LIKE TALKING TO YOU, FLAKEY!
DO YOU?
OH YES... FUNDA-MENTALLY... BASICALLY, YOU'RE A VERY BEAUTIFUL PERSON!
OH... PHAW! NOT ME! I'M... PSH...
NO... I'M NOT KIDDING! YOU REALLY ARE!
!
WELL... YOU KNOW HOW IT IS... HEH HEH...
EXASPER-ATING, THOUGH!

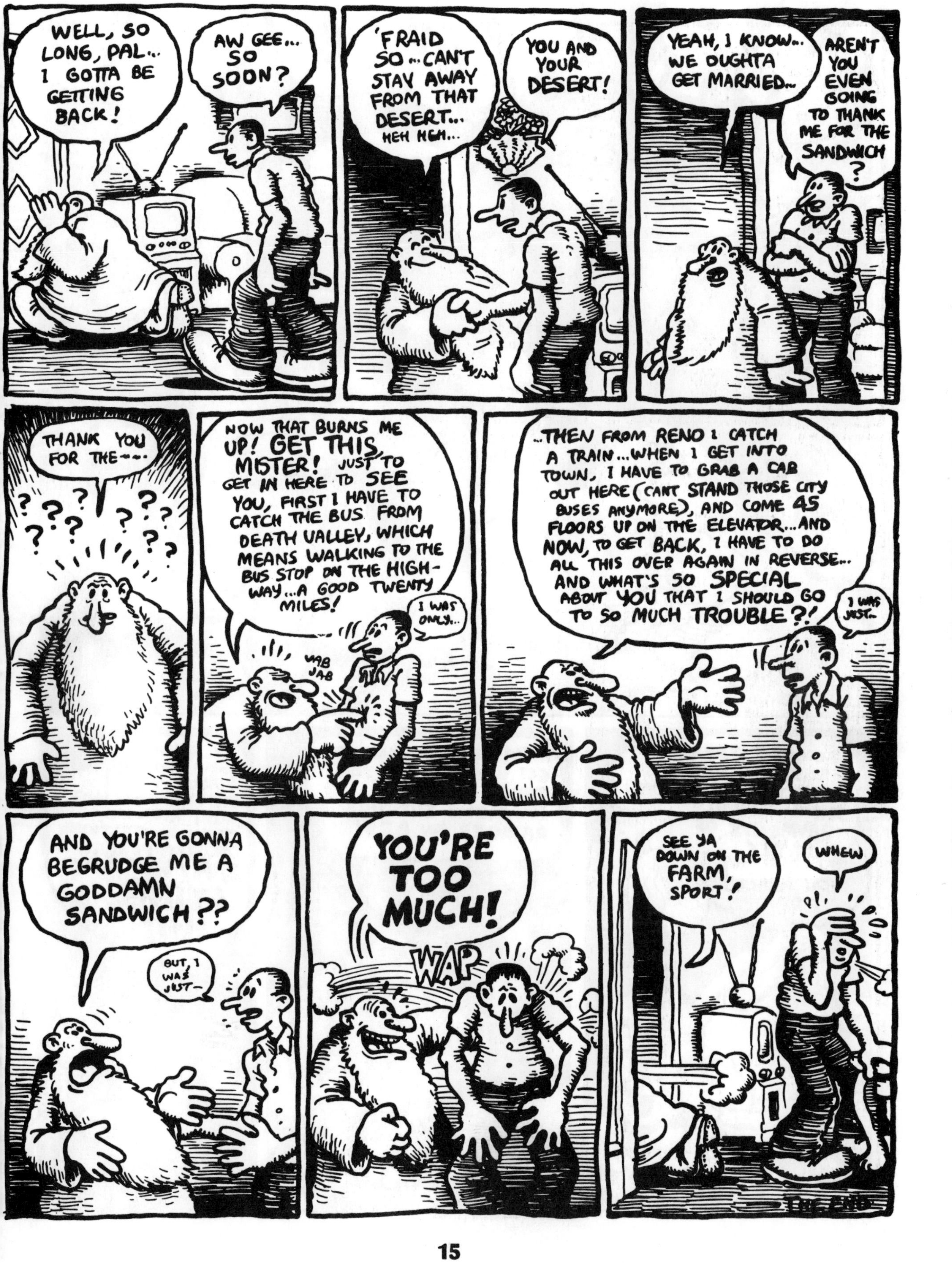
WELL, SO LONG, PAL... I GOTTA BE GETTING BACK!
AW GEE... SO SOON?
'FRAID SO... CAN'T STAY AWAY FROM THAT DESERT... HEH HEH...
YOU AND YOUR DESERT!
YEAH, I KNOW.. WE OUGHTA GET MARRIED...
AREN'T YOU EVEN GOING TO THANK ME FOR THE SANDWICH?
THANK YOU FOR THE---
NOW THAT BURNS ME UP! GET THIS, MISTER! JUST TO GET IN HERE TO SEE YOU, FIRST I HAVE TO CATCH THE BUS FROM DEATH VALLEY, WHICH MEANS WALKING TO THE BUS STOP ON THE HIGH-WAY... A GOOD TWENTY MILES!
I WAS ONLY...
JAB JAB
...THEN FROM RENO I CATCH A TRAIN... WHEN I GET INTO TOWN, I HAVE TO GRAB A CAB OUT HERE (CAN'T STAND THOSE CITY BUSES ANYMORE), AND COME 45 FLOORS UP ON THE ELEVATOR... AND NOW, TO GET BACK, I HAVE TO DO ALL THIS OVER AGAIN IN REVERSE... AND WHAT'S SO SPECIAL ABOUT YOU THAT I SHOULD GO TO SO MUCH TROUBLE?!
I WAS JUST...
AND YOU'RE GONNA BEGRUDGE ME A GODDAMN SANDWICH??
BUT, I WAS JUST—
YOU'RE TOO MUCH!
WAP
SEE YA DOWN ON THE FARM, SPORT!
WHEW
THE END

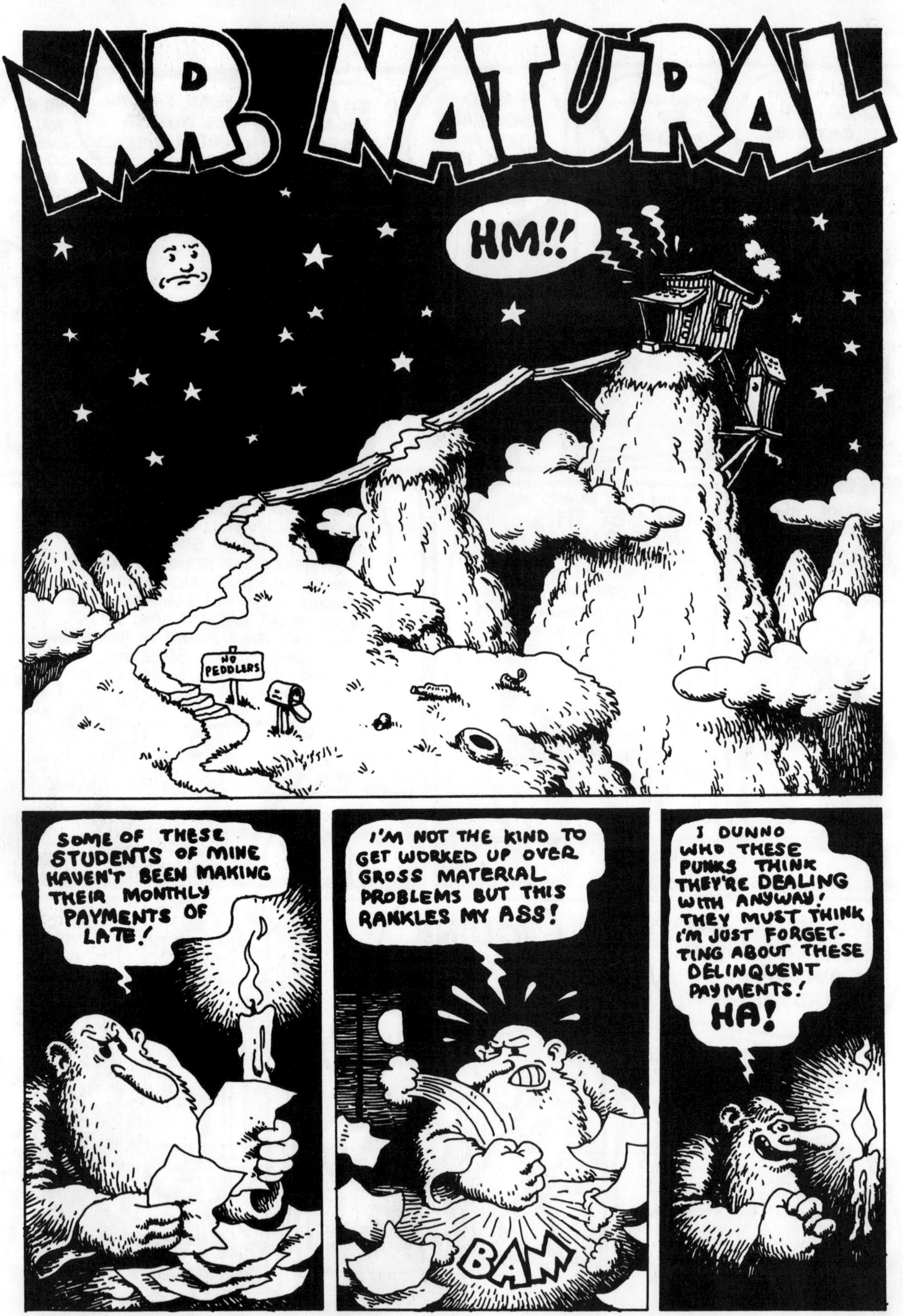
MR. NATURAL
HM!!
NO PEDDLERS
SOME OF THESE STUDENTS OF MINE HAVEN'T BEEN MAKING THEIR MONTHLY PAYMENTS OF LATE!
I'M NOT THE KIND TO GET WORKED UP OVER GROSS MATERIAL PROBLEMS BUT THIS RANKLES MY ASS!
BAM
I DUNNO WHO THESE PUNKS THINK THEY'RE DEALING WITH ANYWAY! THEY MUST THINK I'M JUST FORGET-TING ABOUT THESE DELINQUENT PAYMENTS! HA!

BOY! ARE THEY GONNA GET WISED UP PRETTY DAMN QUICK!

OUT TO LUNCH

I'LL SOCK IT TO 'EM WITH MY NEW "GET TOUGH" IMAGE!

By Morning

AH! THERE'S SHAM FRANCISCO, WHERE MOST OF THE DEADBEATS RESIDE!

IN FACT THERE'S FLAKEY FOONT ON HIS WAY TO WORK!

DRUGS

HEY FOONT! DROP OUT!

WHA—

MUNICIPAL RAILWAY

MR. NATURAL!

HEH HEH

F.R.

MY GOD! IT'S GREAT TA SEE YA, CHIEF!

DON'T GIVE ME THAT "CHIEF" CRAP!

YOU'RE 38.50 SHORT ON YOUR DUES, FOONT!

HMM... TRUE...

SIGH

SAY, I'VE GOT AN IDEA, GURU!, OL' BUDDY!

YEAH? WHAT?

WHERE'S MY 38.50?

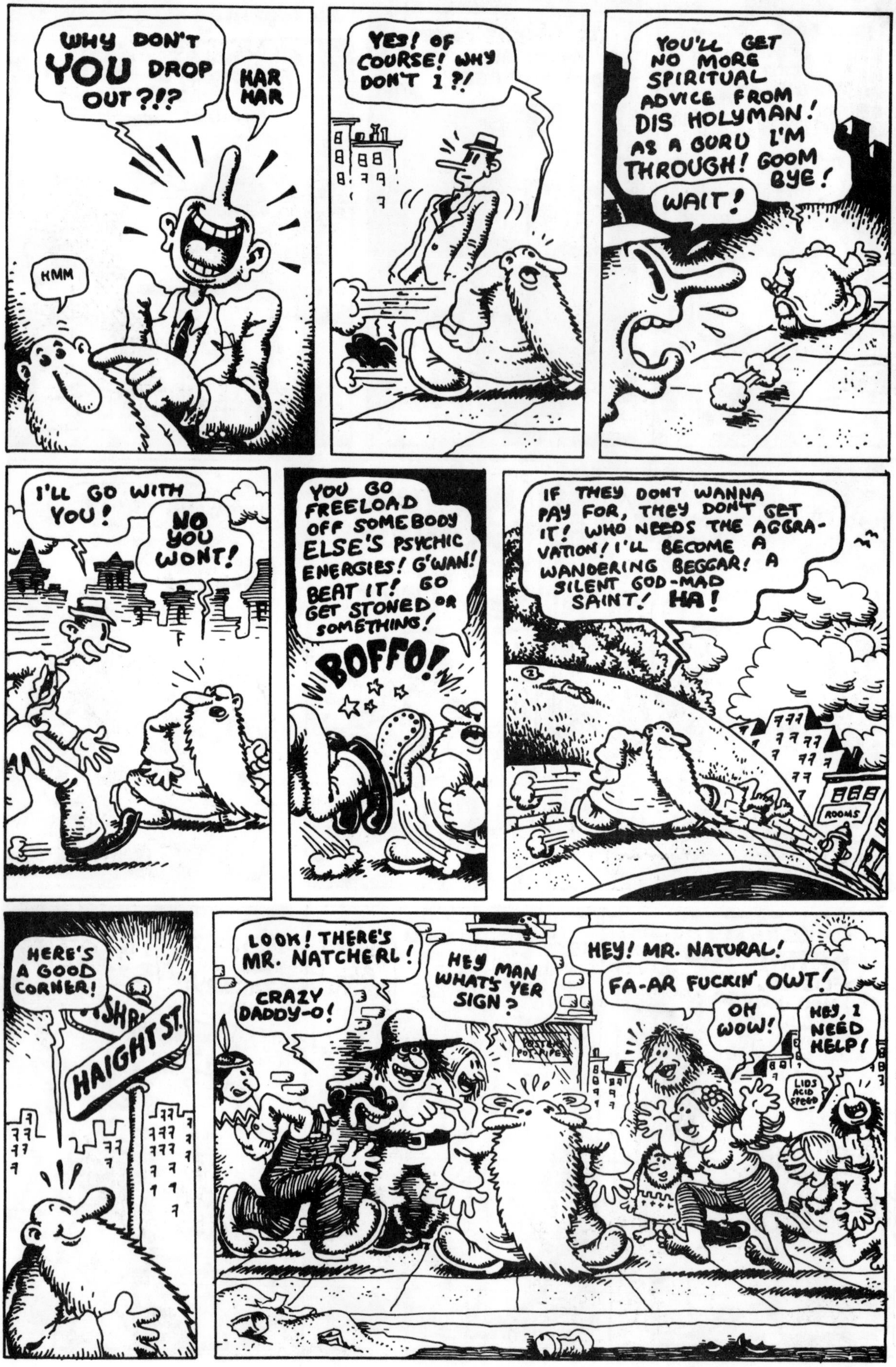

WHY DON'T YOU DROP OUT?!?
HAR HAR
HMM
YES! OF COURSE! WHY DON'T I?!
YOU'LL GET NO MORE SPIRITUAL ADVICE FROM DIS HOLYMAN! AS A GURU I'M THROUGH! GOOM BYE!
WAIT!
I'LL GO WITH YOU!
NO YOU WONT!
YOU GO FREELOAD OFF SOMEBODY ELSE'S PSYCHIC ENERGIES! G'WAN! BEAT IT! GO GET STONED OR SOMETHING!
BOFFO!
IF THEY DONT WANNA PAY FOR, THEY DON'T GET IT! WHO NEEDS THE AGGRAVATION! I'LL BECOME A WANDERING BEGGAR! A SILENT GOD-MAD SAINT! HA!
ROOMS
HERE'S A GOOD CORNER!
HAIGHT ST.
LOOK! THERE'S MR. NATCHERL!
CRAZY DADDY-O!
HEY MAN WHAT'S YER SIGN?
HEY! MR. NATURAL!
FA-AR FUCKIN' OWT!
OH WOW!
HEY, I NEED HELP!
LIDS ACID SPEED

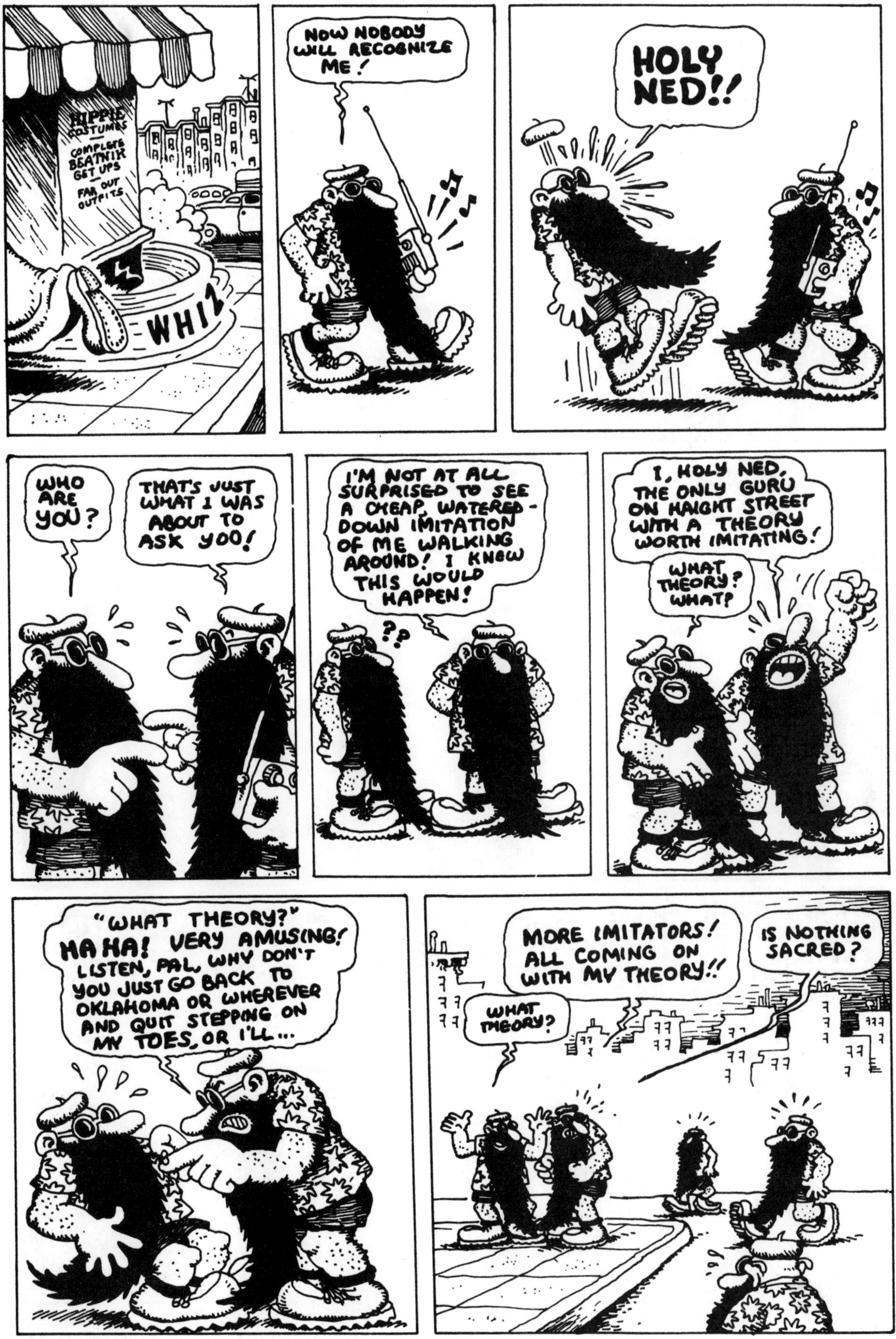
HIPPIE COSTUMES
COMPLETE BEATNIK GET UPS
FAR OUT OUTFITS
WHIZ
NOW NOBODY WILL RECOGNIZE ME!
HOLY NED!!
WHO ARE YOU?
THAT'S JUST WHAT I WAS ABOUT TO ASK YOO!
I'M NOT AT ALL SURPRISED TO SEE A CHEAP, WATERED-DOWN IMITATION OF ME WALKING AROUND! I KNEW THIS WOULD HAPPEN!
??
I, HOLY NED, THE ONLY GURU ON HAIGHT STREET WITH A THEORY WORTH IMITATING!
WHAT THEORY? WHAT?
"WHAT THEORY?" HA HA! VERY AMUSING! LISTEN, PAL, WHY DON'T YOU JUST GO BACK TO OKLAHOMA OR WHEREVER AND QUIT STEPPING ON MY TOES, OR I'LL...
MORE IMITATORS! ALL COMING ON WITH MY THEORY!!
IS NOTHING SACRED?
WHAT THEORY?

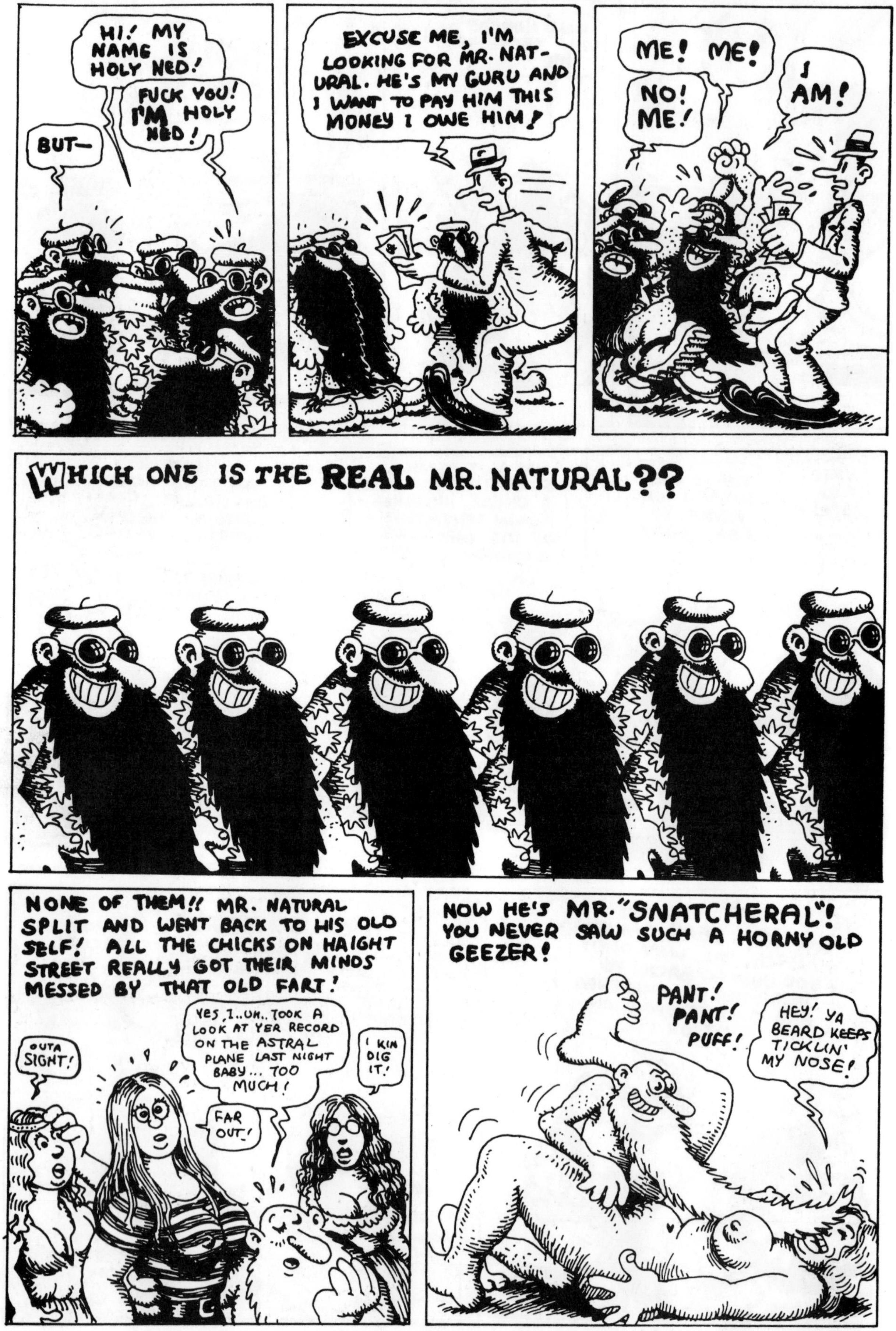
HI! MY NAME IS HOLY NED!
FUCK YOU! I'M HOLY NED!
BUT—
EXCUSE ME, I'M LOOKING FOR MR. NATURAL. HE'S MY GURU AND I WANT TO PAY HIM THIS MONEY I OWE HIM!
ME! ME!
NO! ME!
I AM!
WHICH ONE IS THE REAL MR. NATURAL??
NONE OF THEM!! MR. NATURAL SPLIT AND WENT BACK TO HIS OLD SELF! ALL THE CHICKS ON HAIGHT STREET REALLY GOT THEIR MINDS MESSED BY THAT OLD FART!
OUTA SIGHT!
YES, I..UH.. TOOK A LOOK AT YER RECORD ON THE ASTRAL PLANE LAST NIGHT BABY... TOO MUCH!
FAR OUT!
I KIN DIG IT!
NOW HE'S MR. "SNATCHERAL"! YOU NEVER SAW SUCH A HORNY OLD GEEZER!
PANT! PANT! PUFF!
HEY! YA BEARD KEEPS TICKLIN' MY NOSE!

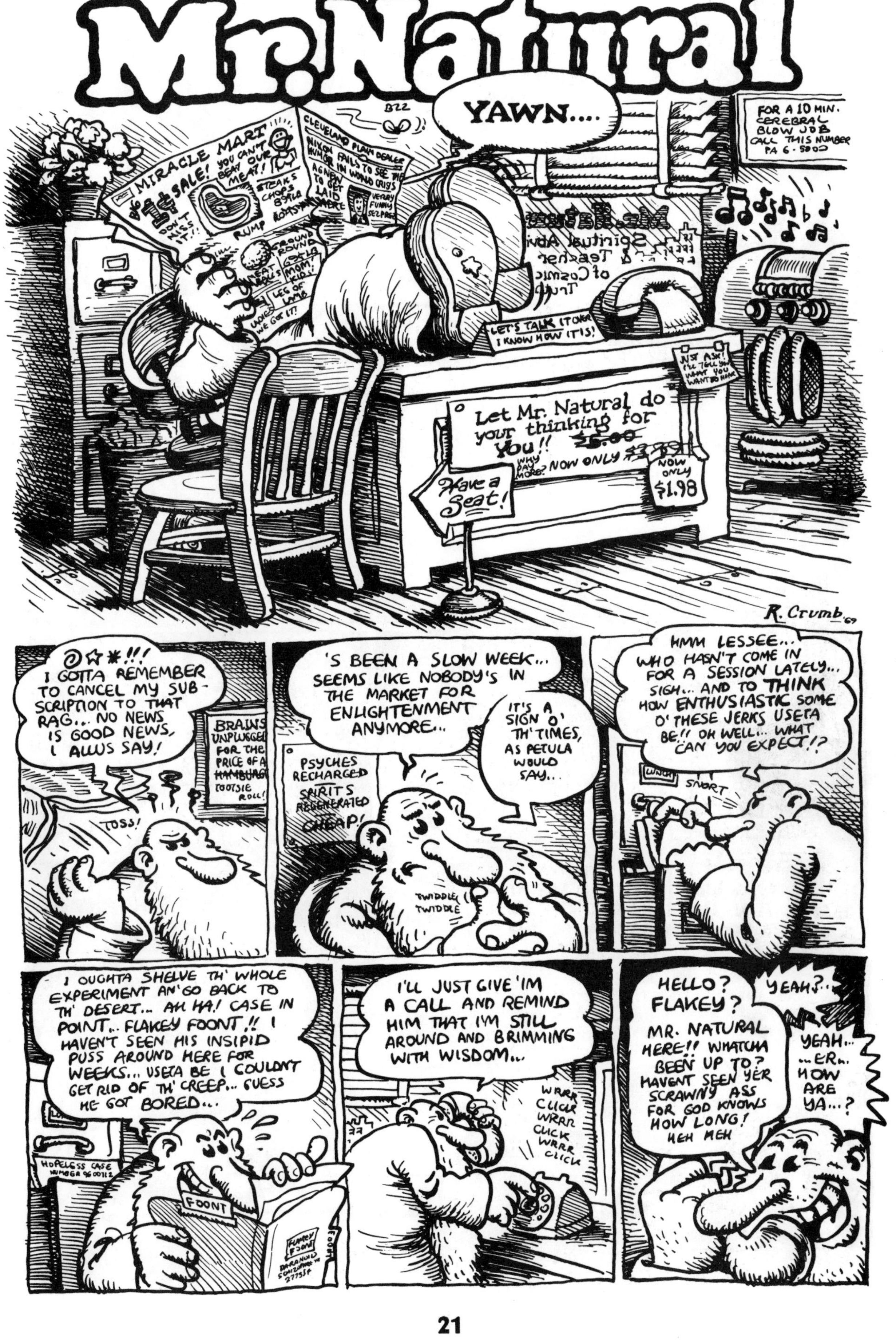

Mr. Natural
YAWN....
BZZ
MIRACLE MART 1¢ SALE! YOU CAN'T BEAT OUR MEAT! DON'T MISS IT!! STEAKS CHOPS RUMP ROAST GROUND ROUND MEAT BALLS MOM! KIDS! LEG OF LAMB LADIES WE GOT IT!
CLEVELAND PLAIN DEALER
NIXON FAILS TO SEE THE HUMOR IN WORLD CRISIS
AGNEW TO GET LAID THERE
VERRY FUNNY
FOR A 10 MIN. CEREBRAL BLOW JOB CALL THIS NUMBER PA 6-5002
LET'S TALK IT OVER I KNOW HOW IT IS!
JUST ASK! I'LL TELL YOU WHAT YOU WANT TO HEAR
Let Mr. Natural do your thinking for You!! $5.00 WHY PAY MORE? NOW ONLY
NOW ONLY $1.98
Have a Seat!
R. Crumb '69
@☆✱!!! I GOTTA REMEMBER TO CANCEL MY SUBSCRIPTION TO THAT RAG... NO NEWS IS GOOD NEWS, I ALLUS SAY!
BRAINS UNPLUGGED FOR THE PRICE OF A HAMBURGER TOOTSIE ROLL!
TOSS!
'S BEEN A SLOW WEEK... SEEMS LIKE NOBODY'S IN THE MARKET FOR ENLIGHTENMENT ANYMORE...
IT'S A SIGN 'O' TH' TIMES, AS PETULA WOULD SAY..
PSYCHES RECHARGED SPIRITS REGENERATED CHEAP!
TWIDDLE TWIDDLE
HMM LESSEE... WHO HASN'T COME IN FOR A SESSION LATELY... SIGH... AND TO THINK HOW ENTHUSIASTIC SOME O' THESE JERKS USETA BE!! OH WELL... WHAT CAN YOU EXPECT!?
SNORT
I OUGHTA SHELVE TH' WHOLE EXPERIMENT AN' GO BACK TO TH' DESERT... AH HA! CASE IN POINT.. FLAKEY FOONT!! I HAVEN'T SEEN HIS INSIPID PUSS AROUND HERE FOR WEEKS... USETA BE I COULDN'T GET RID OF TH' CREEP... GUESS HE GOT BORED...
HOPELESS CASE
FOONT
I'LL JUST GIVE 'IM A CALL AND REMIND HIM THAT I'M STILL AROUND AND BRIMMING WITH WISDOM...
WRRR CLICK WRRR CLICK WRRR CLICK
HELLO? FLAKEY? MR. NATURAL HERE!! WHATCHA BEEN UP TO? HAVENT SEEN YER SCRAWNY ASS FOR GOD KNOWS HOW LONG! HEH HEH
YEAH?..
YEAH... ...ER.. HOW ARE YA...?

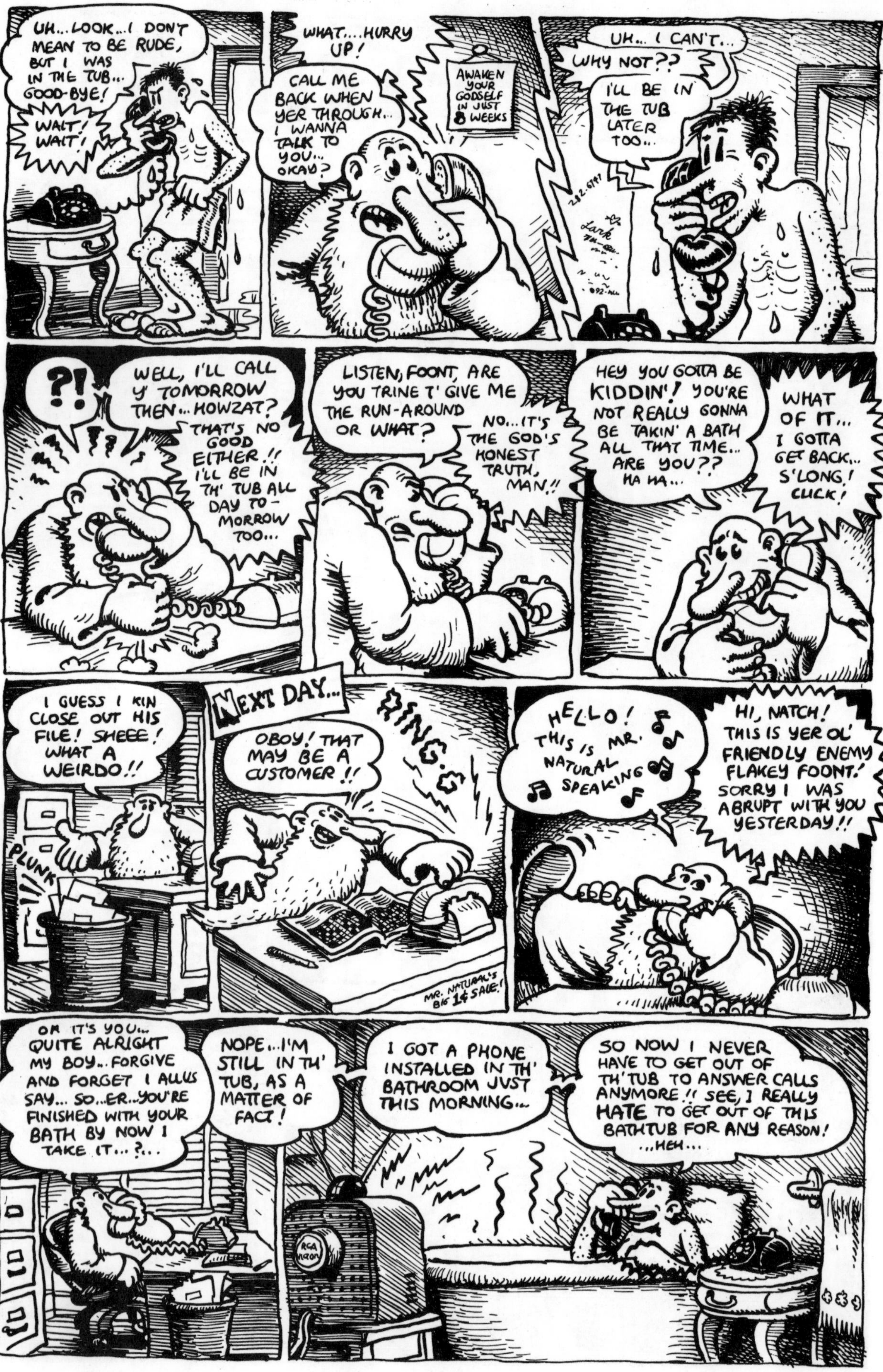
UH... LOOK... I DON'T MEAN TO BE RUDE, BUT I WAS IN THE TUB... GOOD-BYE!
WAIT! WAIT!
WHAT.... HURRY UP!
CALL ME BACK WHEN YER THROUGH... I WANNA TALK TO YOU... OKAY?
AWAKEN YOUR GODSELF IN JUST 8 WEEKS
UH... I CAN'T...
WHY NOT??
I'LL BE IN THE TUB LATER TOO...
?!
WELL, I'LL CALL Y' TOMORROW THEN... HOWZAT?
THAT'S NO GOOD EITHER!! I'LL BE IN TH' TUB ALL DAY TO-MORROW TOO...
LISTEN, FOONT, ARE YOU TRINE T' GIVE ME THE RUN-AROUND OR WHAT?
NO... IT'S THE GOD'S HONEST TRUTH, MAN!!
HEY YOU GOTTA BE KIDDIN'! YOU'RE NOT REALLY GONNA BE TAKIN' A BATH ALL THAT TIME... ARE YOU?? HA HA...
WHAT OF IT... I GOTTA GET BACK... S'LONG! CLICK!
I GUESS I KIN CLOSE OUT HIS FILE! SHEEE! WHAT A WEIRDO!!
PLUNK
NEXT DAY...
OBOY! THAT MAY BE A CUSTOMER!!
RING
MR. NATURAL'S BIG 1¢ SALE!
HELLO! THIS IS MR. NATURAL SPEAKING
HI, NATCH! THIS IS YER OL' FRIENDLY ENEMY FLAKEY FOONT! SORRY I WAS ABRUPT WITH YOU YESTERDAY!!
OH IT'S YOU... QUITE ALRIGHT MY BOY... FORGIVE AND FORGET I ALLUS SAY... SO...ER...YOU'RE FINISHED WITH YOUR BATH BY NOW I TAKE IT...?...
NOPE... I'M STILL IN TH' TUB, AS A MATTER OF FACT!
I GOT A PHONE INSTALLED IN TH' BATHROOM JUST THIS MORNING...
SO NOW I NEVER HAVE TO GET OUT OF TH' TUB TO ANSWER CALLS ANYMORE!! SEE, I REALLY HATE TO GET OUT OF THIS BATHTUB FOR ANY REASON! ...HEH...
RCA VICTOR

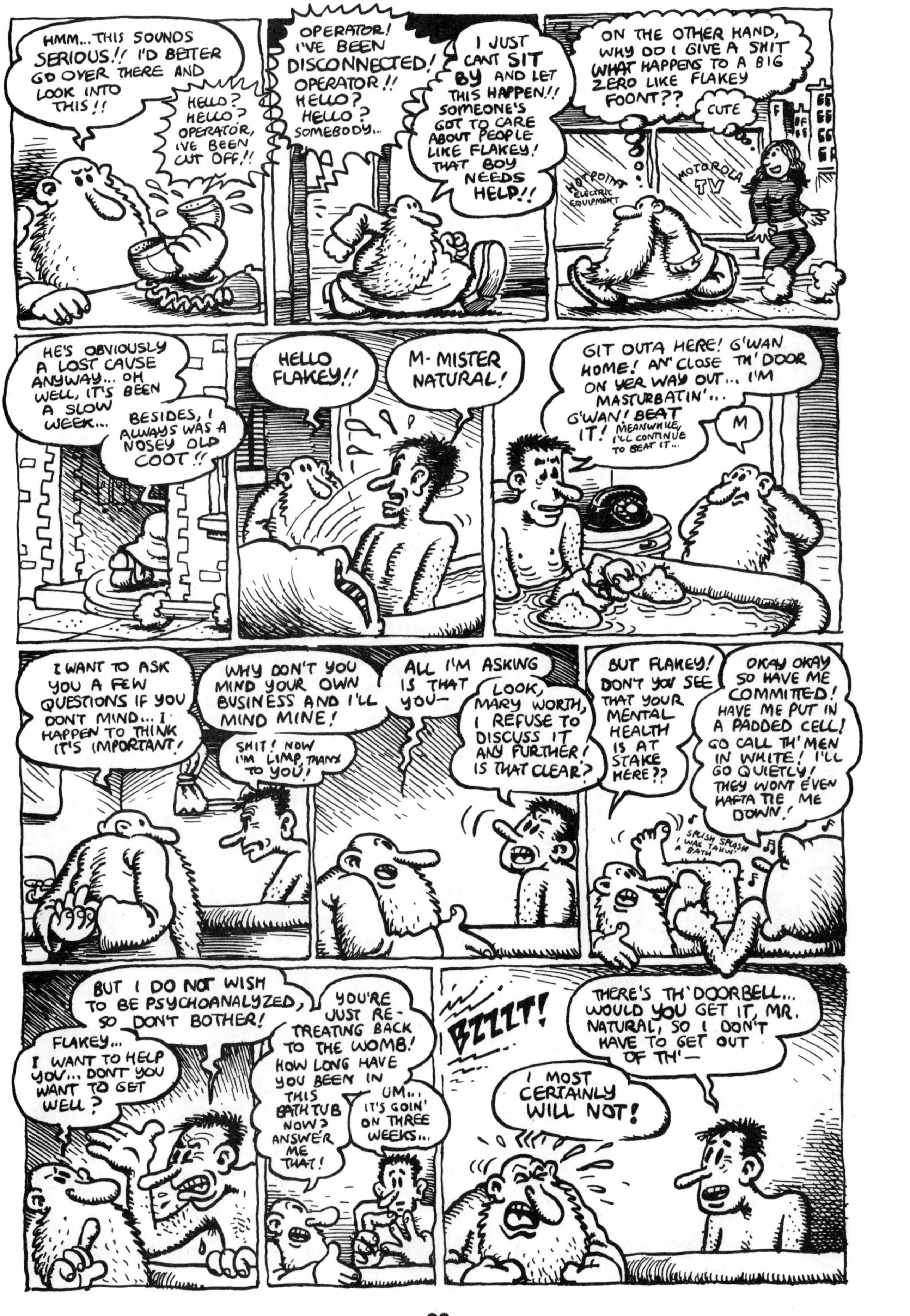
HMM... THIS SOUNDS SERIOUS!! I'D BETTER GO OVER THERE AND LOOK INTO THIS!!
HELLO? HELLO? OPERATOR, I'VE BEEN CUT OFF!!
OPERATOR! I'VE BEEN DISCONNECTED! OPERATOR!! HELLO? HELLO? SOMEBODY...
I JUST CANT SIT BY AND LET THIS HAPPEN!! SOMEONE'S GOT TO CARE ABOUT PEOPLE LIKE FLAKEY! THAT BOY NEEDS HELP!!
ON THE OTHER HAND, WHY DO I GIVE A SHIT WHAT HAPPENS TO A BIG ZERO LIKE FLAKEY FOONT??
CUTE
HOTPOINT ELECTRIC EQUIPMENT
MOTOROLA TV
HE'S OBVIOUSLY A LOST CAUSE ANYWAY... OH WELL, IT'S BEEN A SLOW WEEK...
BESIDES, I ALWAYS WAS A NOSEY OLD COOT!!
HELLO FLAKEY!!
M-MISTER NATURAL!
GIT OUTA HERE! G'WAN HOME! AN' CLOSE TH' DOOR ON YER WAY OUT... I'M MASTURBATIN'... G'WAN! BEAT IT! MEANWHILE, I'LL CONTINUE TO BEAT IT...
M
I WANT TO ASK YOU A FEW QUESTIONS IF YOU DON'T MIND... I HAPPEN TO THINK IT'S IMPORTANT!
WHY DON'T YOU MIND YOUR OWN BUSINESS AND I'LL MIND MINE!
SHIT! NOW I'M LIMP, THANX TO YOU!
ALL I'M ASKING IS THAT YOU—
LOOK, MARY WORTH, I REFUSE TO DISCUSS IT ANY FURTHER! IS THAT CLEAR?
BUT FLAKEY! DON'T YOU SEE THAT YOUR MENTAL HEALTH IS AT STAKE HERE??
OKAY OKAY SO HAVE ME COMMITTED! HAVE ME PUT IN A PADDED CELL! GO CALL TH' MEN IN WHITE! I'LL GO QUIETLY! THEY WONT EVEN HAFTA TIE ME DOWN!
SPLISH SPLASH I WAS TAKIN' A BATH
BUT I DO NOT WISH TO BE PSYCHOANALYZED, SO DON'T BOTHER!
FLAKEY... I WANT TO HELP YOU... DONT YOU WANT TO GET WELL?
YOU'RE JUST RE-TREATING BACK TO THE WOMB! HOW LONG HAVE YOU BEEN IN THIS BATHTUB NOW? ANSWER ME THAT!
UM... IT'S GOIN' ON THREE WEEKS...
BZZZT!
THERE'S TH' DOORBELL... WOULD YOU GET IT, MR. NATURAL, SO I DON'T HAVE TO GET OUT OF TH'—
I MOST CERTAINLY WILL NOT!

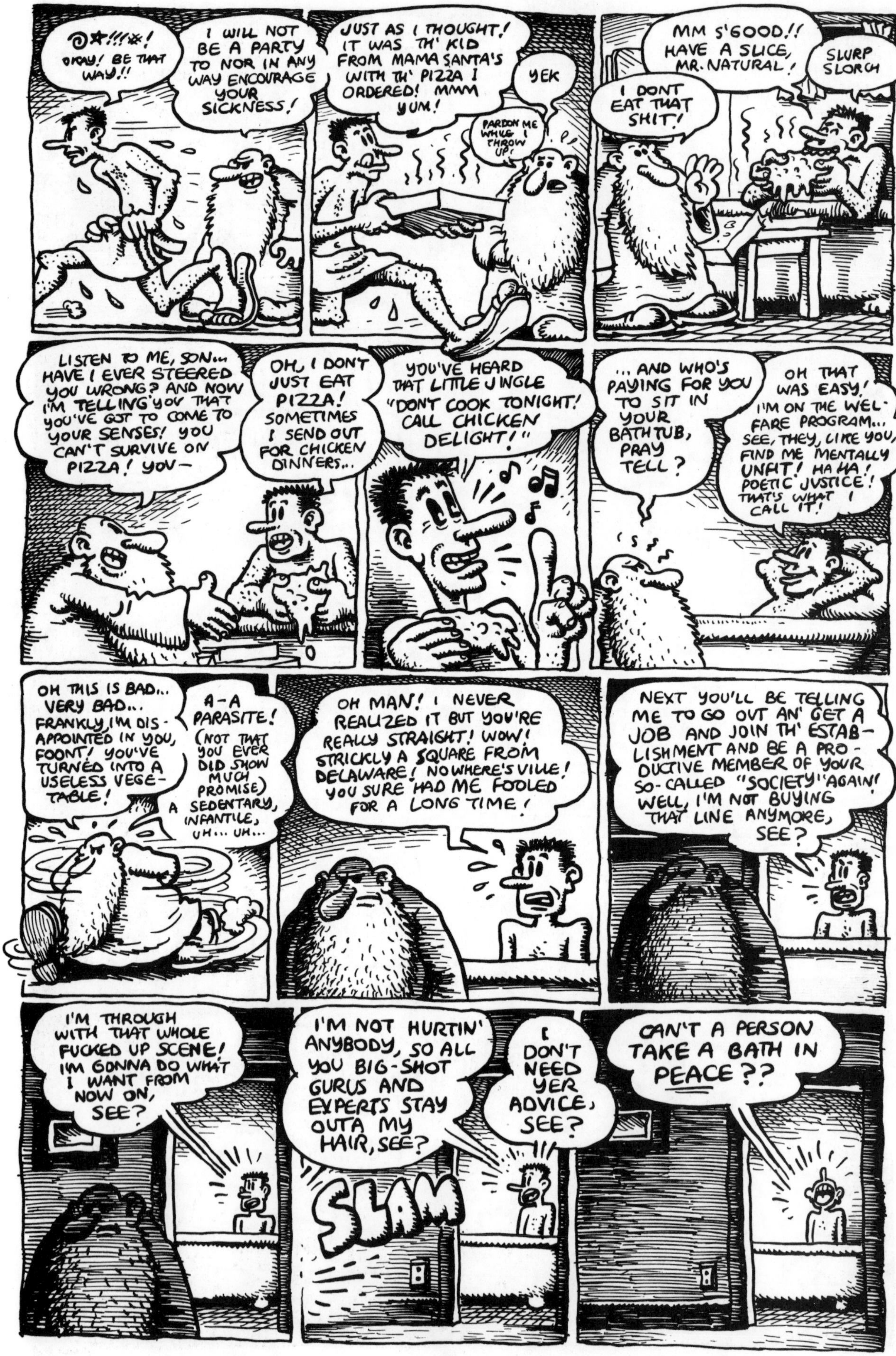
@☆!!!☆! OKAY! BE THAT WAY!!
I WILL NOT BE A PARTY TO NOR IN ANY WAY ENCOURAGE YOUR SICKNESS!
JUST AS I THOUGHT! IT WAS TH' KID FROM MAMA SANTA'S WITH TH' PIZZA I ORDERED! MMM YUM!
YEK
PARDON ME WHILE I THROW UP!
MM S'GOOD!! HAVE A SLICE, MR. NATURAL!
SLURP SLORCH
I DONT EAT THAT SHIT!
LISTEN TO ME, SON... HAVE I EVER STEERED YOU WRONG? AND NOW I'M TELLING YOU THAT YOU'VE GOT TO COME TO YOUR SENSES! YOU CAN'T SURVIVE ON PIZZA! YOU—
OH, I DON'T JUST EAT PIZZA! SOMETIMES I SEND OUT FOR CHICKEN DINNERS..
YOU'VE HEARD THAT LITTLE JINGLE "DON'T COOK TONIGHT! CALL CHICKEN DELIGHT!"
...AND WHO'S PAYING FOR YOU TO SIT IN YOUR BATHTUB, PRAY TELL?
OH THAT WAS EASY! I'M ON THE WELFARE PROGRAM... SEE, THEY, LIKE YOU, FIND ME MENTALLY UNFIT! HA HA! POETIC JUSTICE! THAT'S WHAT I CALL IT!
OH THIS IS BAD... VERY BAD... FRANKLY, I'M DISAPPOINTED IN YOU, FOONT! YOU'VE TURNED INTO A USELESS VEGETABLE!
A-A PARASITE! (NOT THAT YOU EVER DID SHOW MUCH PROMISE) A SEDENTARY, INFANTILE, UH... UH...
OH MAN! I NEVER REALIZED IT BUT YOU'RE REALLY STRAIGHT! WOW! STRICKLY A SQUARE FROM DELAWARE! NOWHERE'SVILLE! YOU SURE HAD ME FOOLED FOR A LONG TIME!
NEXT YOU'LL BE TELLING ME TO GO OUT AN' GET A JOB AND JOIN TH' ESTABLISHMENT AND BE A PRODUCTIVE MEMBER OF YOUR SO-CALLED "SOCIETY" AGAIN! WELL, I'M NOT BUYING THAT LINE ANYMORE, SEE?
I'M THROUGH WITH THAT WHOLE FUCKED UP SCENE! I'M GONNA DO WHAT I WANT FROM NOW ON, SEE?
I'M NOT HURTIN' ANYBODY, SO ALL YOU BIG-SHOT GURUS AND EXPERTS STAY OUTA MY HAIR, SEE?
SLAM
I DON'T NEED YER ADVICE, SEE?
CAN'T A PERSON TAKE A BATH IN PEACE??

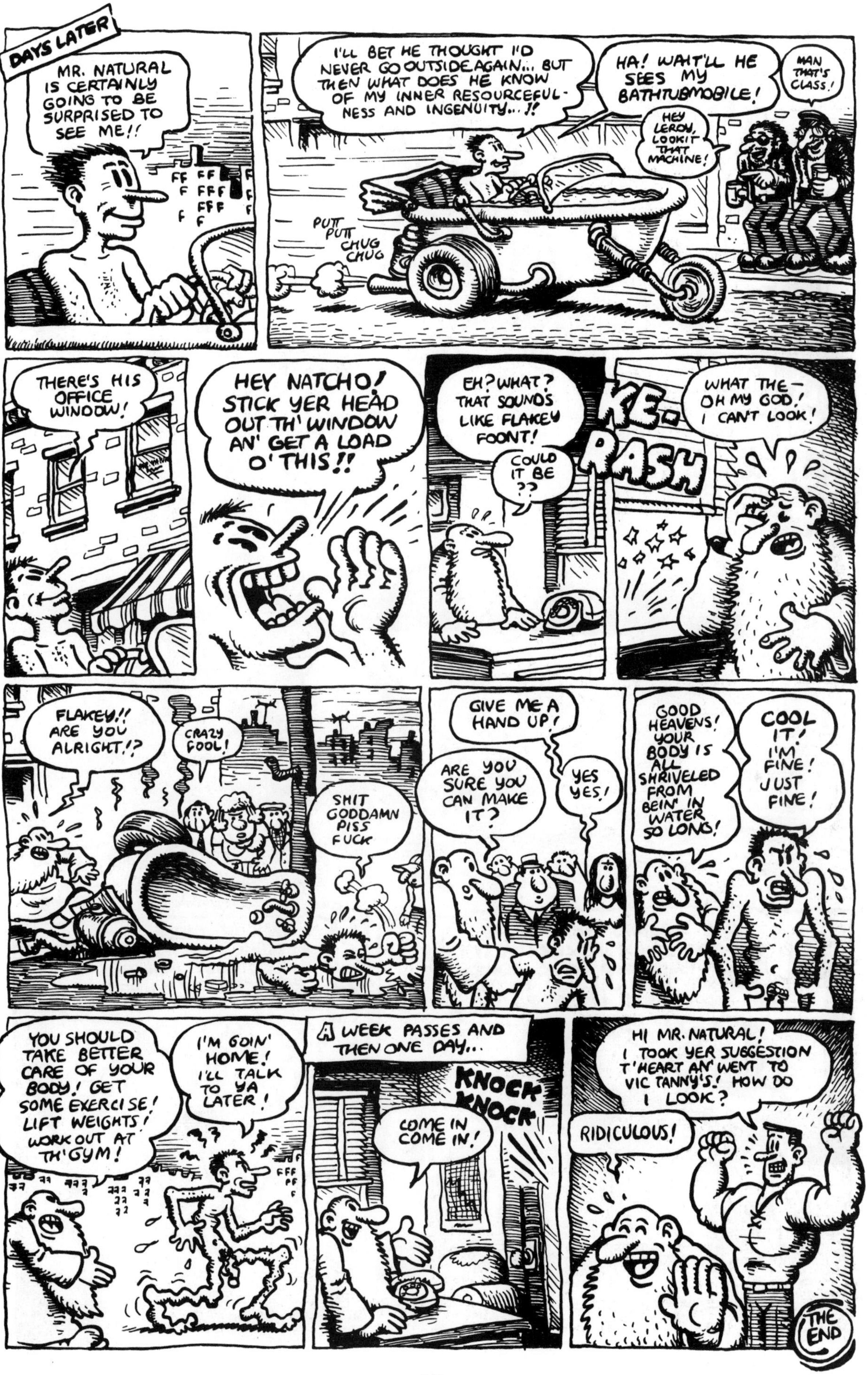
DAYS LATER
MR. NATURAL IS CERTAINLY GOING TO BE SURPRISED TO SEE ME!!
I'LL BET HE THOUGHT I'D NEVER GO OUTSIDE AGAIN... BUT THEN WHAT DOES HE KNOW OF MY INNER RESOURCEFULNESS AND INGENUITY...?!
HA! WAIT'LL HE SEES MY BATHTUBMOBILE!
MAN THAT'S CLASS!
HEY LEROY, LOOKIT THAT MACHINE!
PUTT PUTT CHUG CHUG
THERE'S HIS OFFICE WINDOW!
HEY NATCHO! STICK YER HEAD OUT TH' WINDOW AN' GET A LOAD O' THIS!!
EH? WHAT? THAT SOUNDS LIKE FLAKEY FOONT!
COULD IT BE ??
KE-RASH
WHAT THE— OH MY GOD! I CAN'T LOOK!
FLAKEY!! ARE YOU ALRIGHT!?
CRAZY FOOL!
SHIT GODDAMN PISS FUCK
GIVE ME A HAND UP!
ARE YOU SURE YOU CAN MAKE IT?
YES YES!
GOOD HEAVENS! YOUR BODY IS ALL SHRIVELED FROM BEIN' IN WATER SO LONG!
COOL IT! I'M FINE! JUST FINE!
YOU SHOULD TAKE BETTER CARE OF YOUR BODY! GET SOME EXERCISE! LIFT WEIGHTS! WORK OUT AT TH' GYM!
I'M GOIN' HOME! I'LL TALK TO YA LATER!
A WEEK PASSES AND THEN ONE DAY...
KNOCK KNOCK
COME IN COME IN!
HI MR. NATURAL! I TOOK YER SUGGESTION T'HEART AN' WENT TO VIC TANNY'S! HOW DO I LOOK?
RIDICULOUS!
THE END

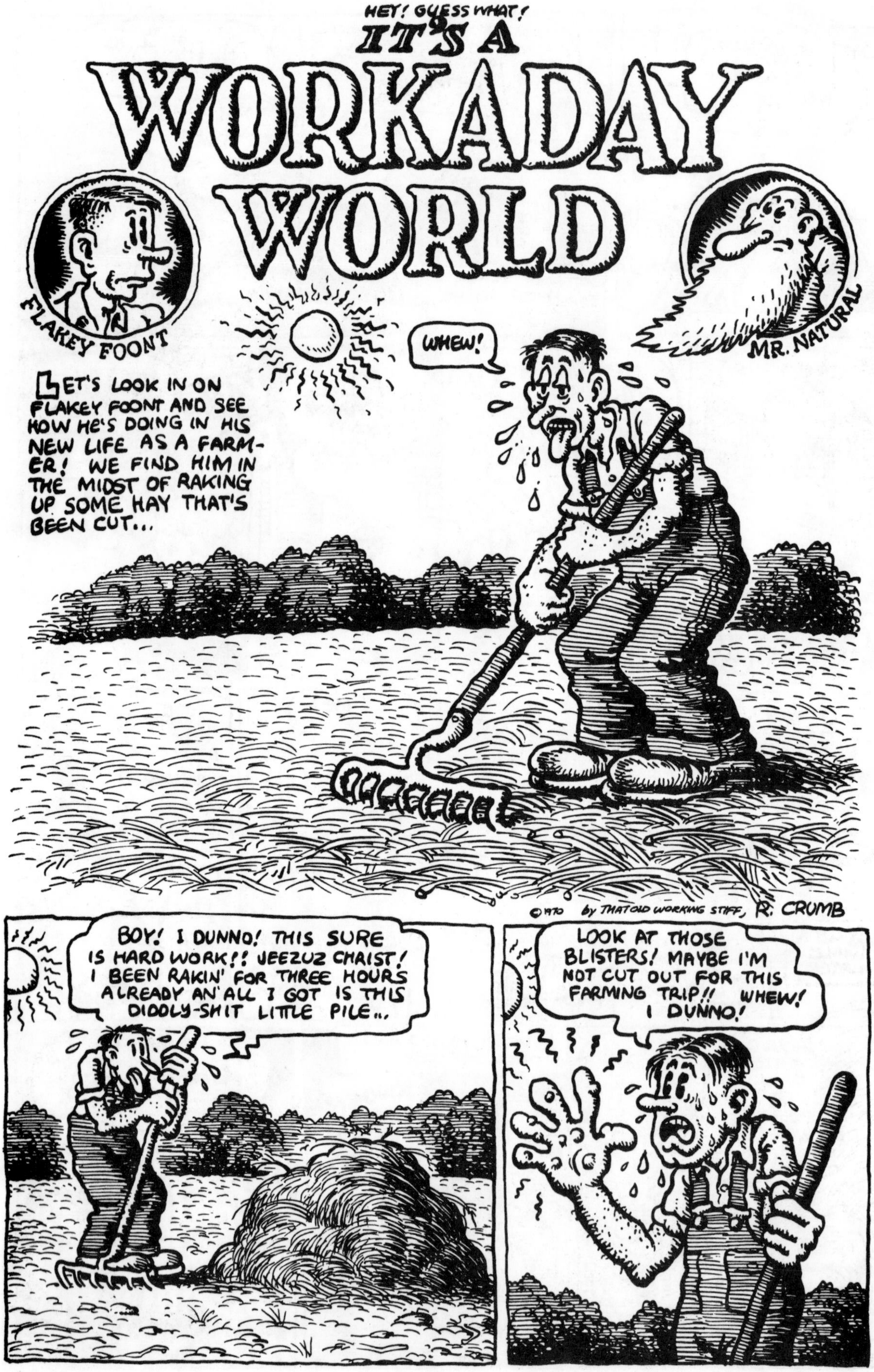
HEY! GUESS WHAT!
IT'S A WORKADAY WORLD
FLAKEY FOONT
MR. NATURAL
LET'S LOOK IN ON FLAKEY FOONT AND SEE HOW HE'S DOING IN HIS NEW LIFE AS A FARMER! WE FIND HIM IN THE MIDST OF RAKING UP SOME HAY THAT'S BEEN CUT...
WHEW!
©1970 by THAT OLD WORKING STIFF, R. CRUMB
BOY! I DUNNO! THIS SURE IS HARD WORK!! JEEZUZ CHRIST! I BEEN RAKIN' FOR THREE HOURS ALREADY AN' ALL I GOT IS THIS DIDDLY-SHIT LITTLE PILE...
LOOK AT THOSE BLISTERS! MAYBE I'M NOT CUT OUT FOR THIS FARMING TRIP!! WHEW! I DUNNO!

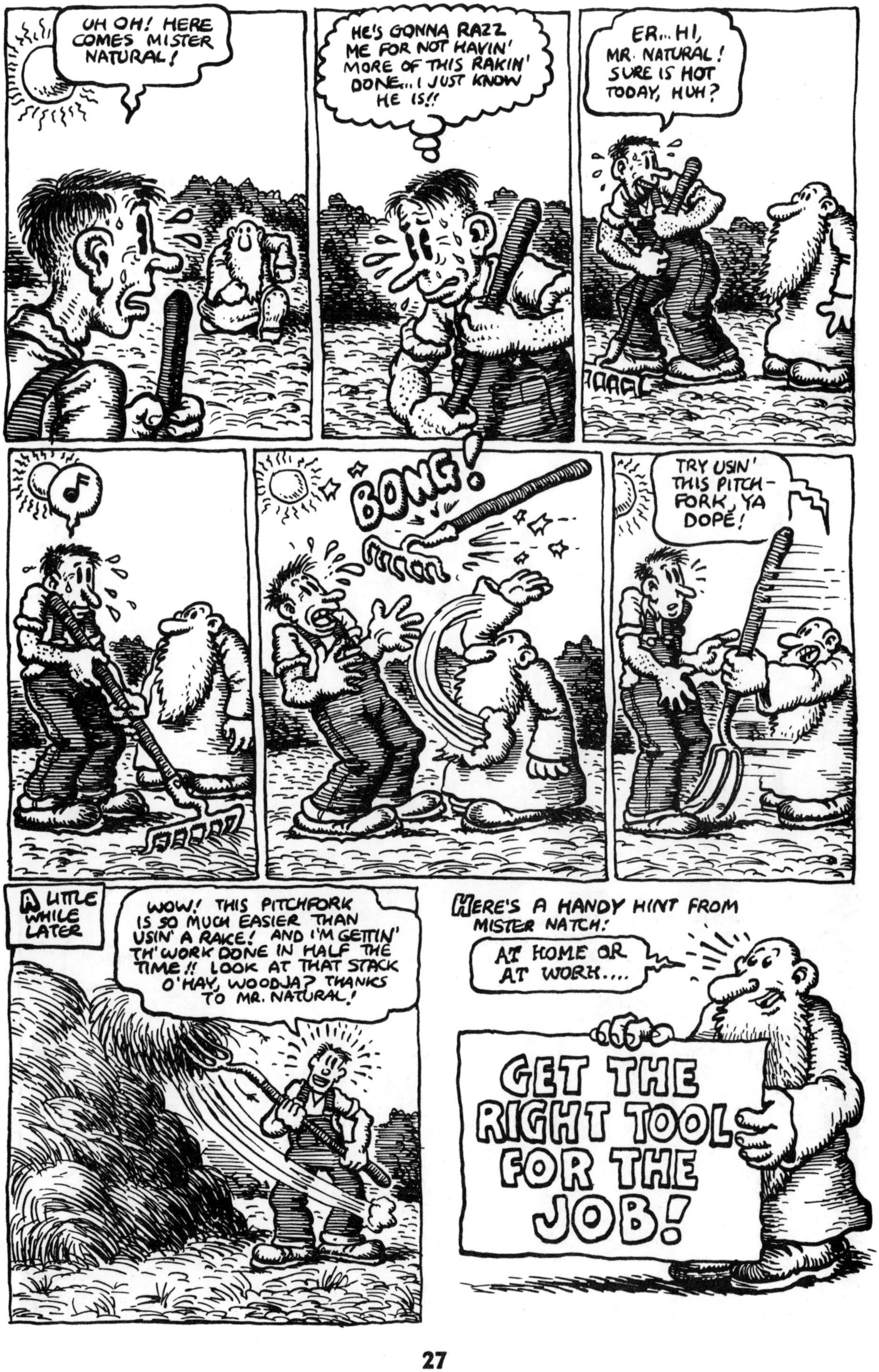

UH OH! HERE COMES MISTER NATURAL!
HE'S GONNA RAZZ ME FOR NOT HAVIN' MORE OF THIS RAKIN' DONE... I JUST KNOW HE IS!!
ER... HI, MR. NATURAL! SURE IS HOT TODAY, HUH?
BONG!
TRY USIN' THIS PITCH-FORK, YA DOPE!
A LITTLE WHILE LATER
WOW! THIS PITCHFORK IS SO MUCH EASIER THAN USIN' A RAKE! AND I'M GETTIN' TH' WORK DONE IN HALF THE TIME!! LOOK AT THAT STACK O' HAY, WOODJA? THANKS TO MR. NATURAL!
HERE'S A HANDY HINT FROM MISTER NATCH:
AT HOME OR AT WORK....
GET THE RIGHT TOOL FOR THE JOB!

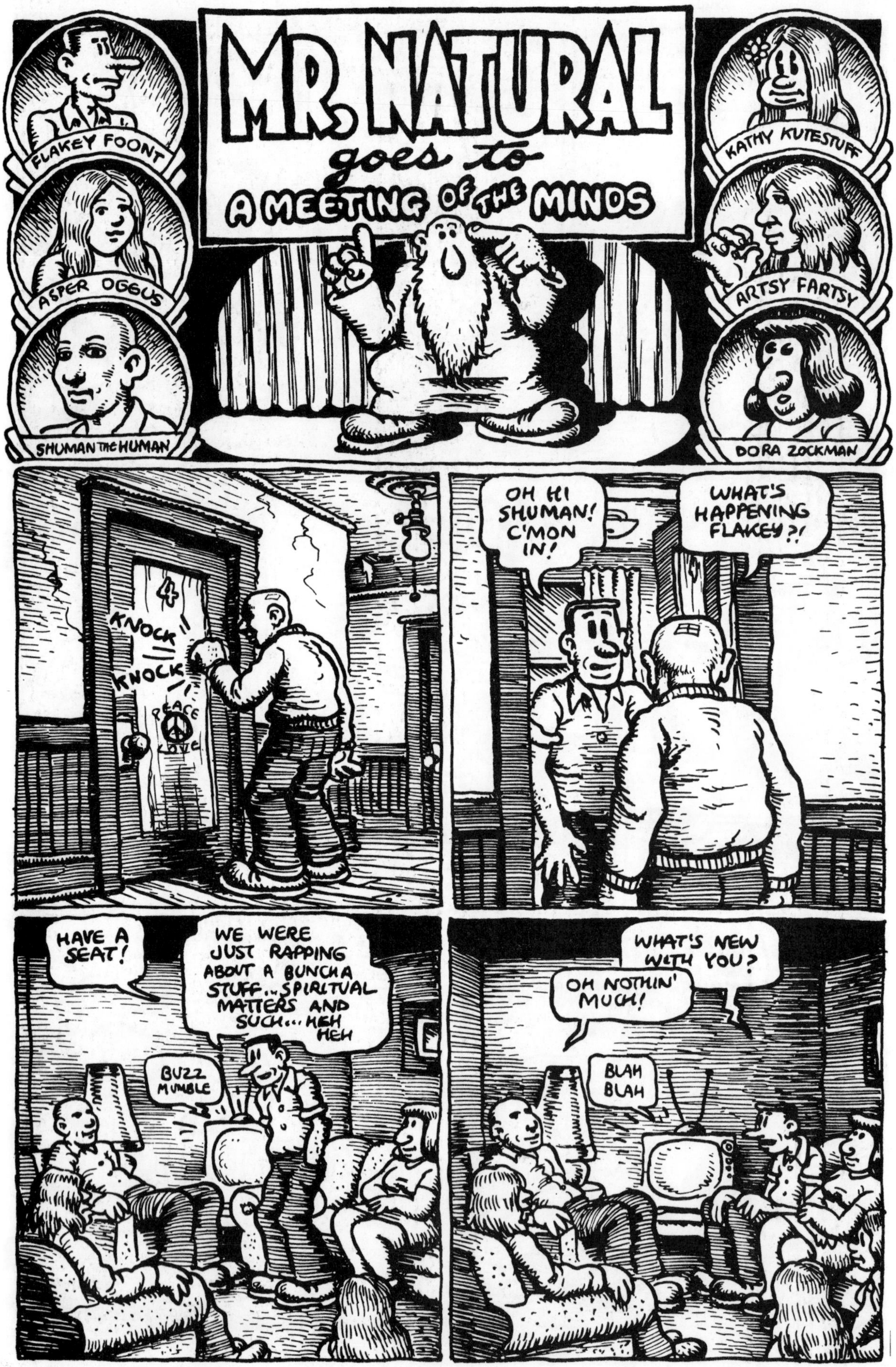

MR. NATURAL
goes to
A MEETING OF THE MINDS
FLAKEY FOONT
ASPER OGGUS
SHUMAN THE HUMAN
KATHY KUTESTUFF
ARTSY FARTSY
DORA ZOCKMAN
4
KNOCK
KNOCK
PEACE
LOVE
OH HI SHUMAN! C'MON IN!
WHAT'S HAPPENING FLAKEY?!
HAVE A SEAT!
WE WERE JUST RAPPING ABOUT A BUNCHA STUFF... SPIRITUAL MATTERS AND SUCH... HEH HEH
BUZZ MUMBLE
WHAT'S NEW WITH YOU?
OH NOTHIN' MUCH!
BLAH BLAH

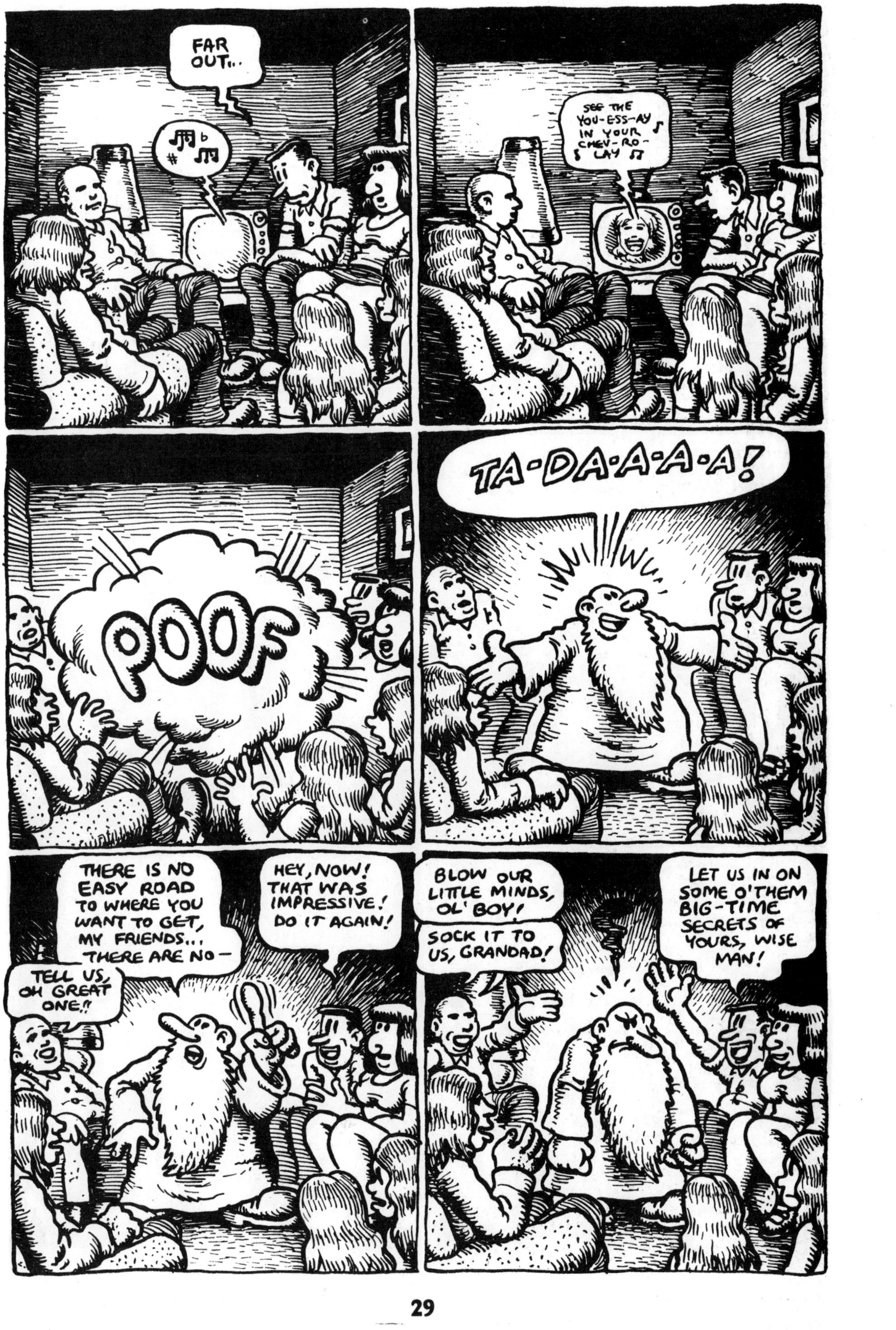

FAR OUT...
SEE THE YOU-ESS-AY IN YOUR CHEV-RO-LAY
POOF
TA-DA-A-A-A!
THERE IS NO EASY ROAD TO WHERE YOU WANT TO GET, MY FRIENDS... THERE ARE NO—
HEY, NOW! THAT WAS IMPRESSIVE! DO IT AGAIN!
TELL US, OH GREAT ONE!!
BLOW OUR LITTLE MINDS, OL' BOY!
SOCK IT TO US, GRANDAD!
LET US IN ON SOME O'THEM BIG-TIME SECRETS OF YOURS, WISE MAN!

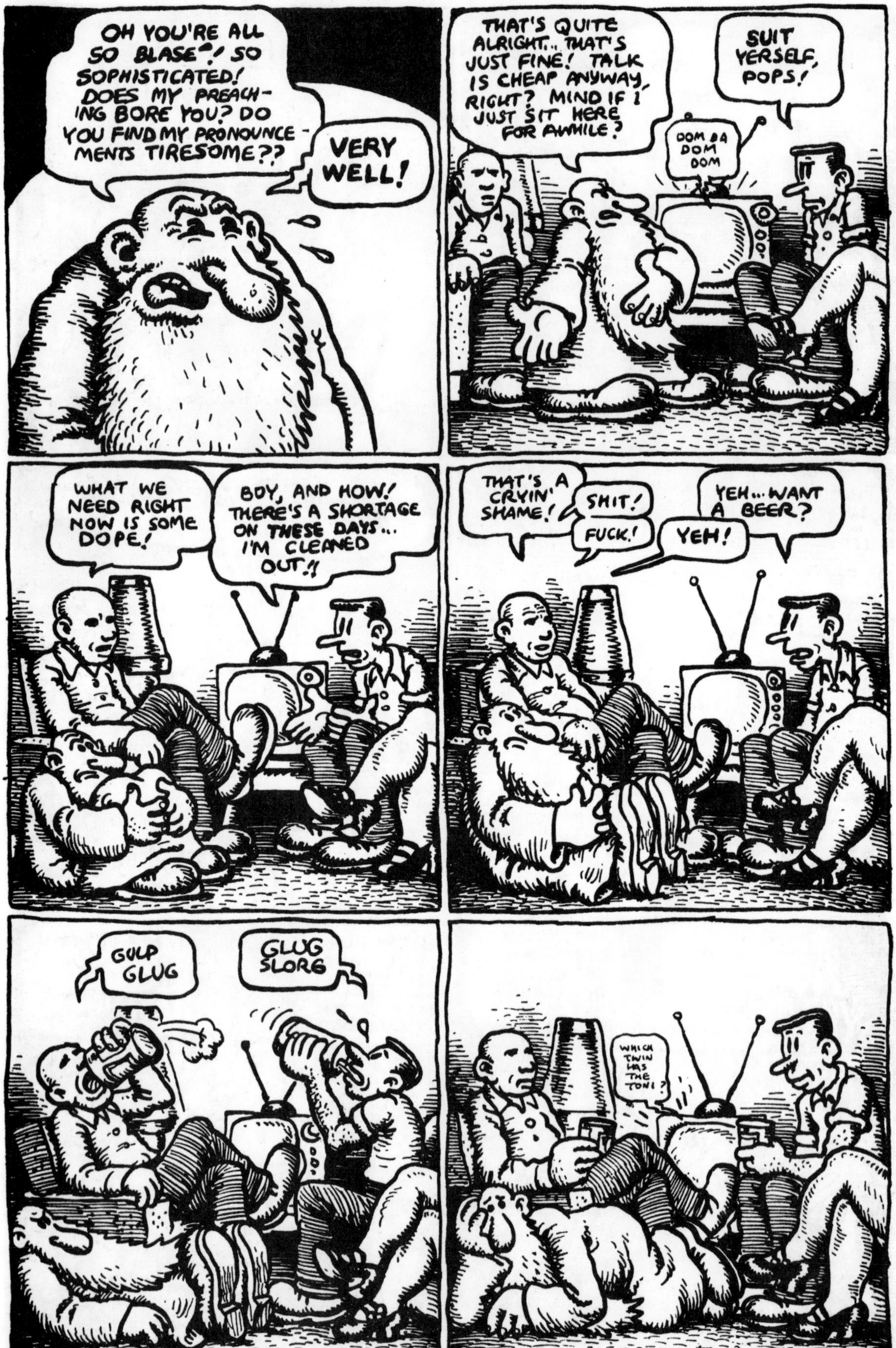
OH YOU'RE ALL SO BLASÉ! SO SOPHISTICATED! DOES MY PREACHING BORE YOU? DO YOU FIND MY PRONOUNCEMENTS TIRESOME??
VERY WELL!
THAT'S QUITE ALRIGHT... THAT'S JUST FINE! TALK IS CHEAP ANYWAY, RIGHT? MIND IF I JUST SIT HERE FOR AWHILE?
DOM DA DOM DOM
SUIT YERSELF, POPS!
WHAT WE NEED RIGHT NOW IS SOME DOPE!
BOY, AND HOW! THERE'S A SHORTAGE ON THESE DAYS... I'M CLEANED OUT!!
THAT'S A CRYIN' SHAME!
SHIT!
FUCK!
YEH... WANT A BEER?
YEH!
GULP GLUG
GLUG SLORG
WHICH TWIN HAS THE TONI?

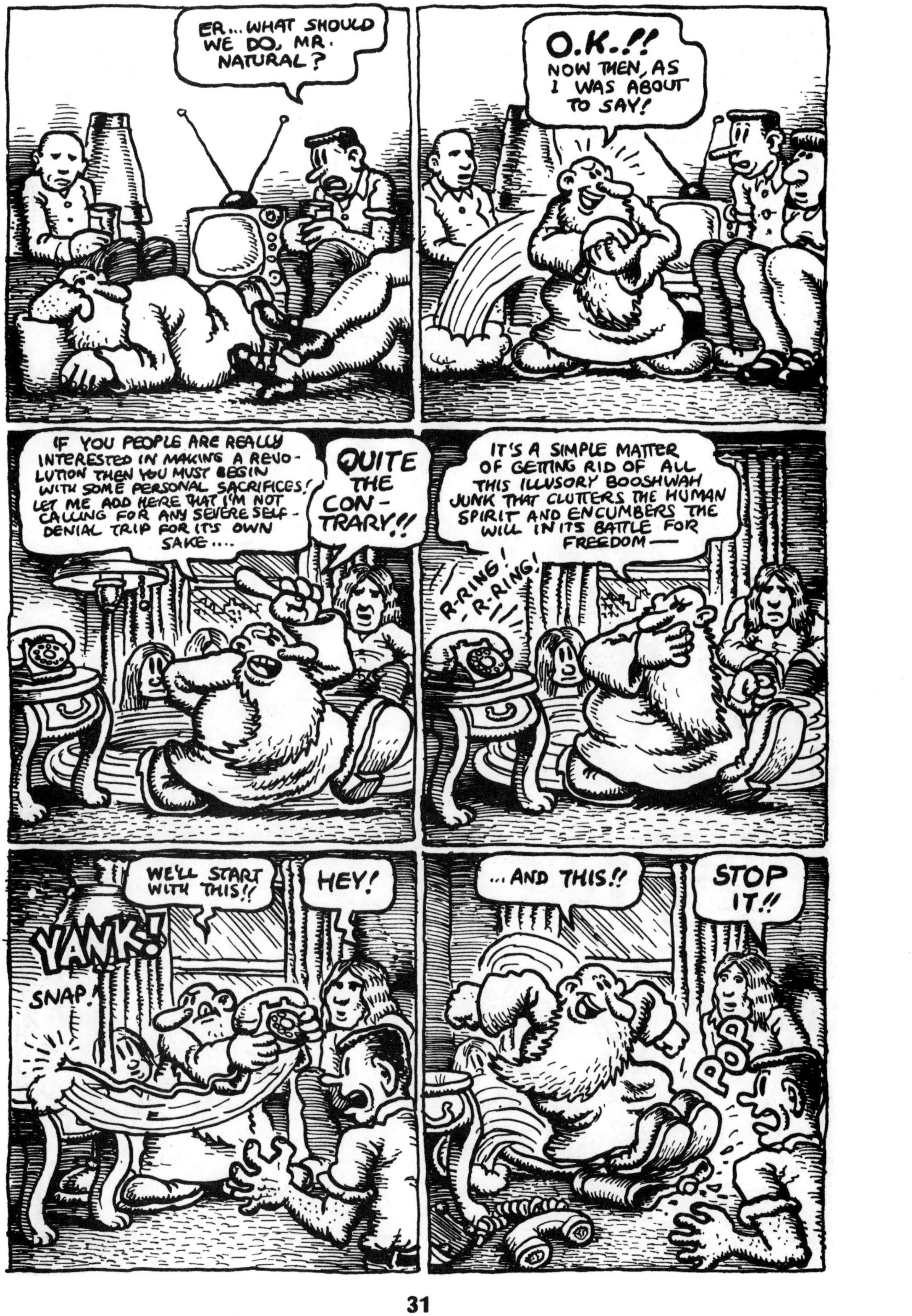
ER... WHAT SHOULD WE DO, MR. NATURAL?
O.K.!! NOW THEN, AS I WAS ABOUT TO SAY!
IF YOU PEOPLE ARE REALLY INTERESTED IN MAKING A REVOLUTION THEN YOU MUST BEGIN WITH SOME PERSONAL SACRIFICES! LET ME ADD HERE THAT I'M NOT CALLING FOR ANY SEVERE SELF-DENIAL TRIP FOR ITS OWN SAKE....
QUITE THE CONTRARY!!
IT'S A SIMPLE MATTER OF GETTING RID OF ALL THIS ILLUSORY BOOSHWAH JUNK THAT CLUTTERS THE HUMAN SPIRIT AND ENCUMBERS THE WILL IN ITS BATTLE FOR FREEDOM—
R-RING! R-RING!
YANK!
SNAP!
WE'LL START WITH THIS!!
HEY!
...AND THIS!!
STOP IT!!
POP

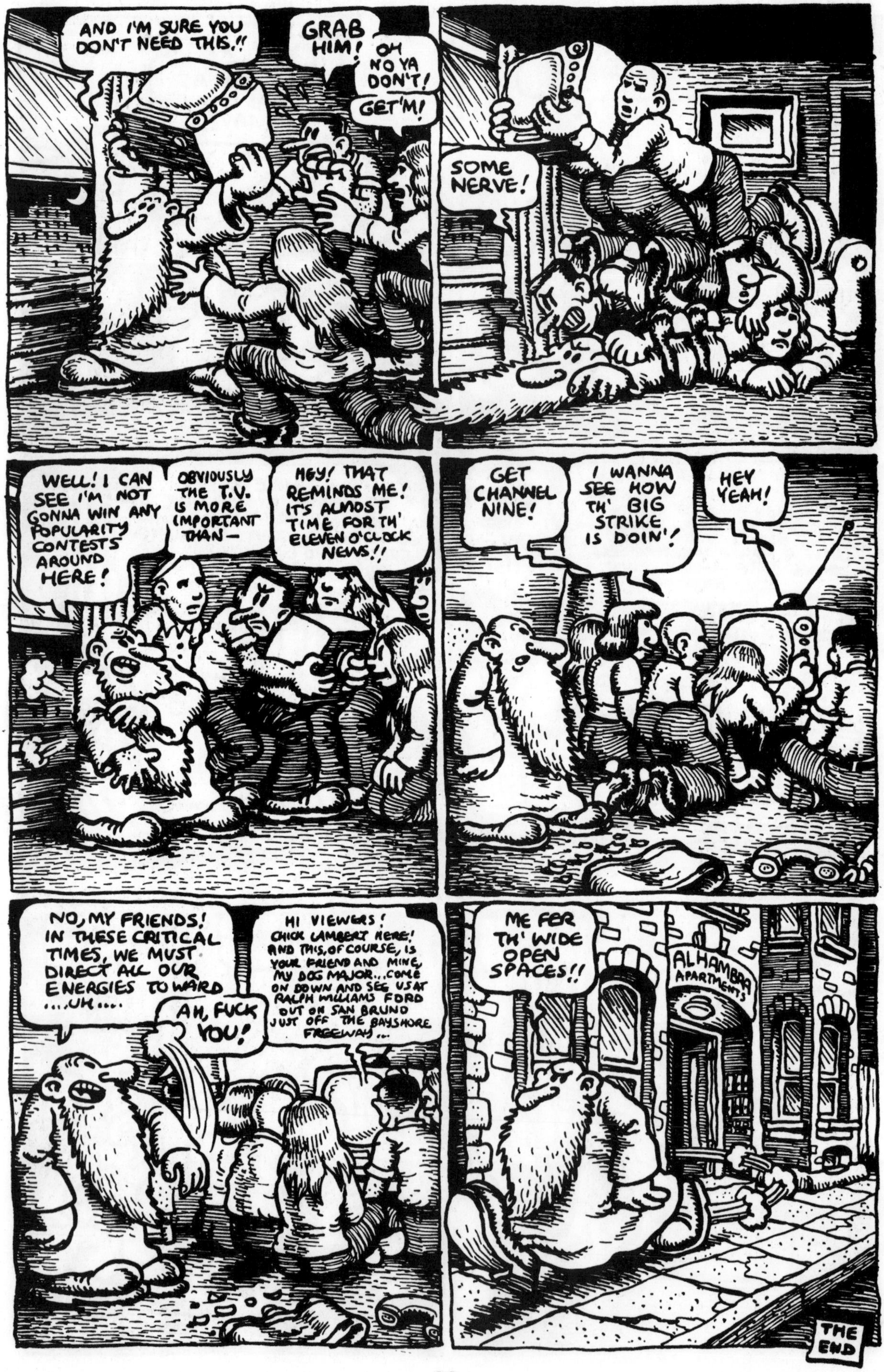
AND I'M SURE YOU DON'T NEED THIS.!!
GRAB HIM!
OH NO YA DON'T!
GET'M!
SOME NERVE!
WELL! I CAN SEE I'M NOT GONNA WIN ANY POPULARITY CONTESTS AROUND HERE!
OBVIOUSLY THE T.V. IS MORE IMPORTANT THAN—
HEY! THAT REMINDS ME! IT'S ALMOST TIME FOR TH' ELEVEN O'CLOCK NEWS!!
GET CHANNEL NINE!
I WANNA SEE HOW TH' BIG STRIKE IS DOIN'!
HEY YEAH!
NO, MY FRIENDS! IN THESE CRITICAL TIMES, WE MUST DIRECT ALL OUR ENERGIES TOWARD ....UH....
AH, FUCK YOU!
HI VIEWERS! CHICK LAMBERT HERE! AND THIS, OF COURSE, IS YOUR FRIEND AND MINE, MY DOG MAJOR... COME ON DOWN AND SEE US AT RALPH WILLIAMS FORD OUT ON SAN BRUNO JUST OFF THE BAYSHORE FREEWAY...
ME FER TH' WIDE OPEN SPACES!!
ALHAMBRA APARTMENTS
THE END

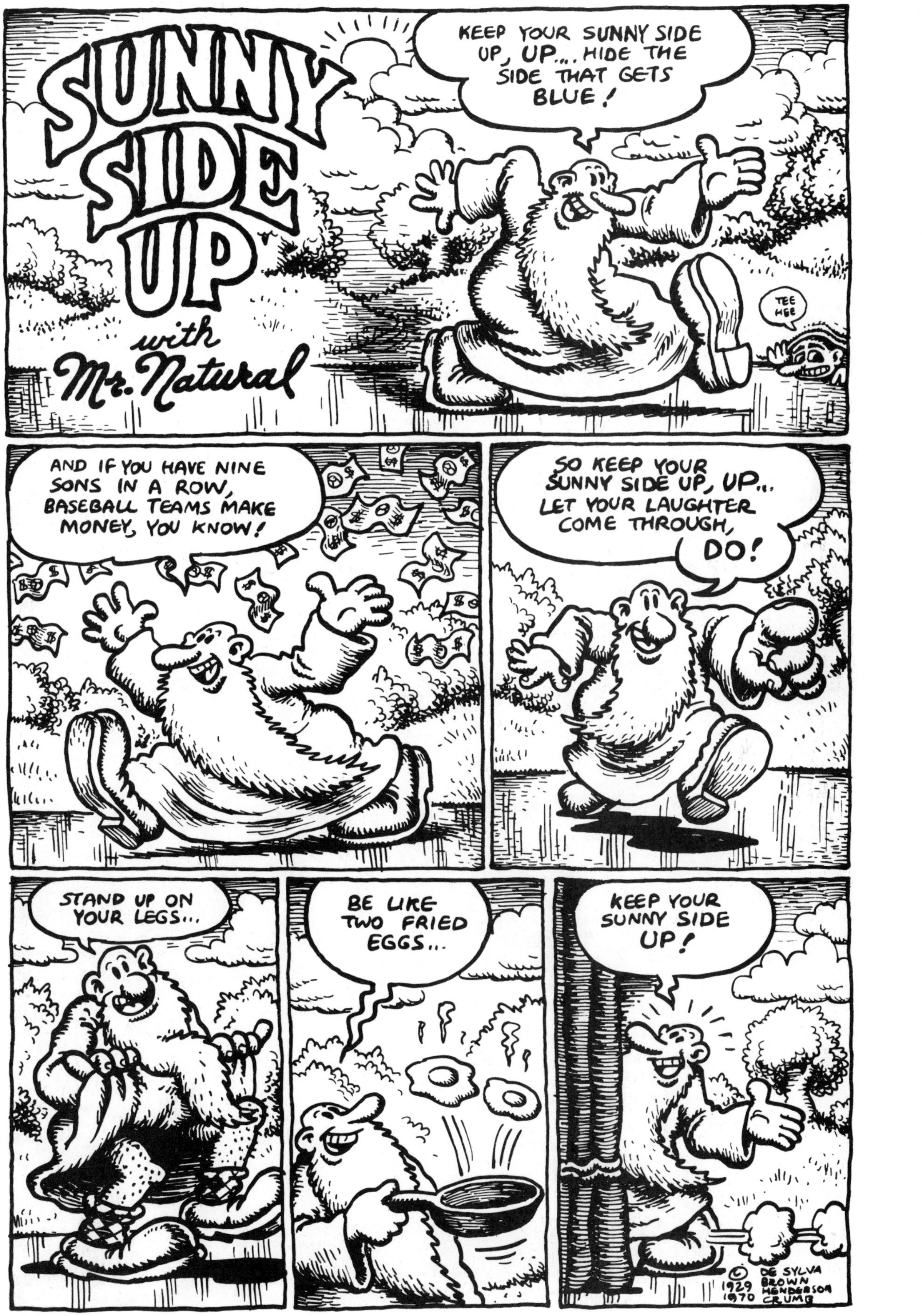
SUNNY SIDE UP
with Mr. Natural
KEEP YOUR SUNNY SIDE UP, UP.... HIDE THE SIDE THAT GETS BLUE!
TEE HEE
AND IF YOU HAVE NINE SONS IN A ROW, BASEBALL TEAMS MAKE MONEY, YOU KNOW!
SO KEEP YOUR SUNNY SIDE UP, UP... LET YOUR LAUGHTER COME THROUGH, DO!
STAND UP ON YOUR LEGS...
BE LIKE TWO FRIED EGGS...
KEEP YOUR SUNNY SIDE UP!
© 1929 1970 DE SYLVA BROWN HENDERSON CRUMB

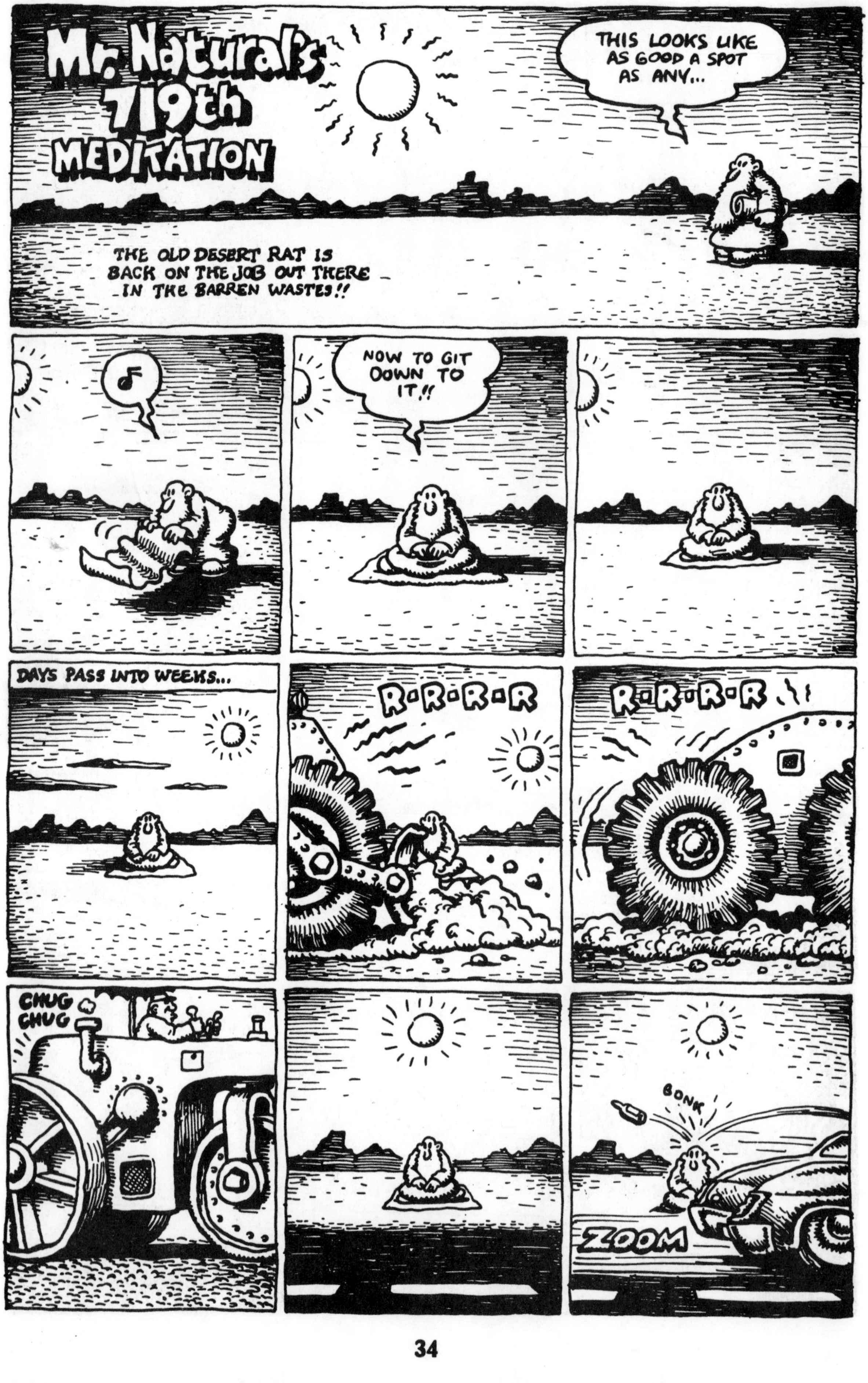
Mr. Natural's 719th MEDITATION
THIS LOOKS LIKE AS GOOD A SPOT AS ANY...
THE OLD DESERT RAT IS BACK ON THE JOB OUT THERE IN THE BARREN WASTES!!
NOW TO GIT DOWN TO IT!!
DAYS PASS INTO WEEKS...
R-R-R-R-R
R-R-R-R-R
CHUG CHUG
BONK
ZOOM

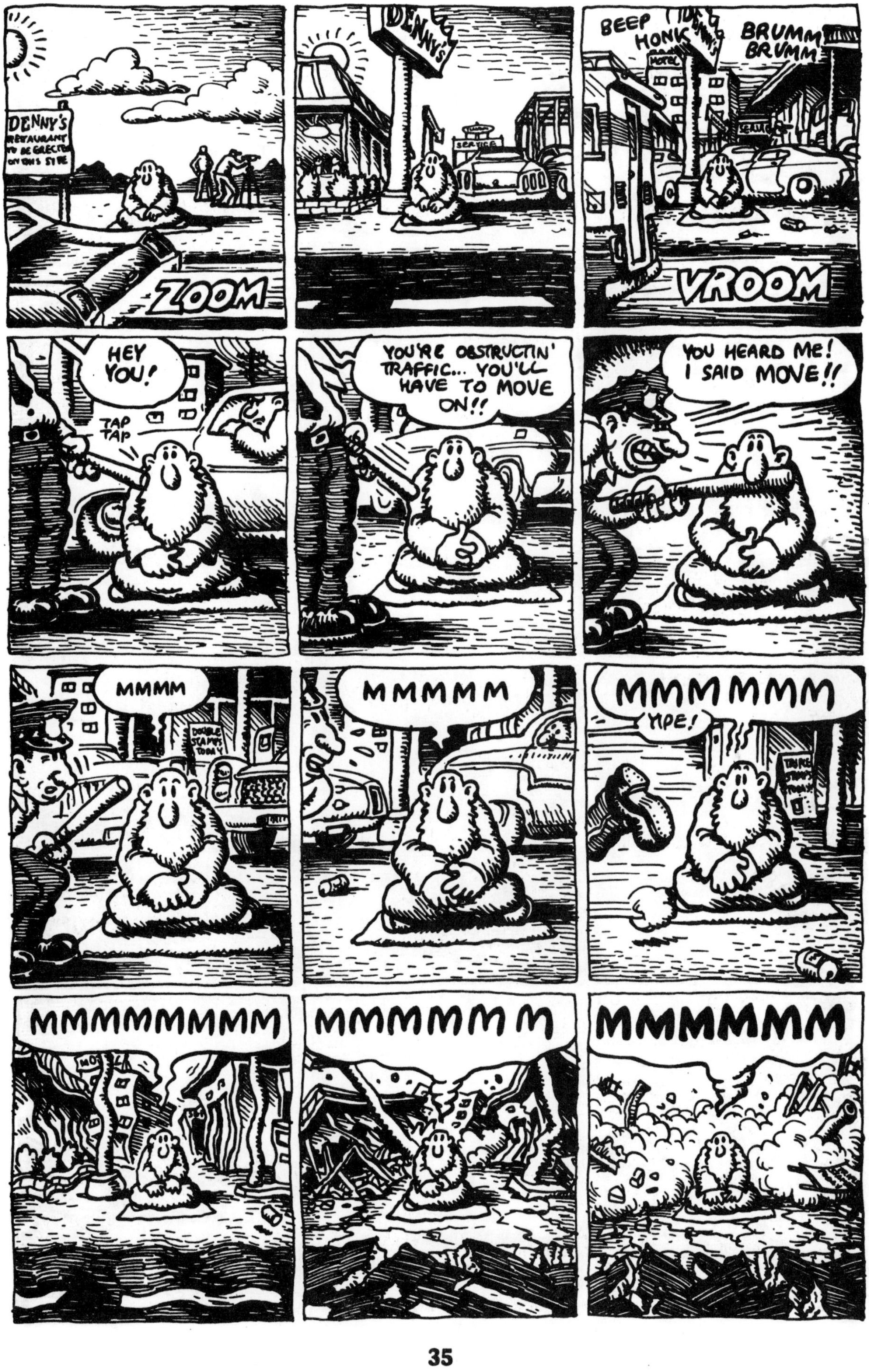
DENNY'S RESTAURANT TO BE ERECTED ON THIS SITE
ZOOM
DENNY'S
SERVICE
BEEP
HONK
BRUMM BRUMM
MOTEL
VROOM
HEY YOU!
TAP TAP
YOU'RE OBSTRUCTIN' TRAFFIC... YOU'LL HAVE TO MOVE ON!!
YOU HEARD ME! I SAID MOVE!!
MMMM
DOUBLE STAMPS TODAY
MMMMM
MMMMMM
YIPE!
MMMMMMMMM
MMMMMMM
MMMMMM

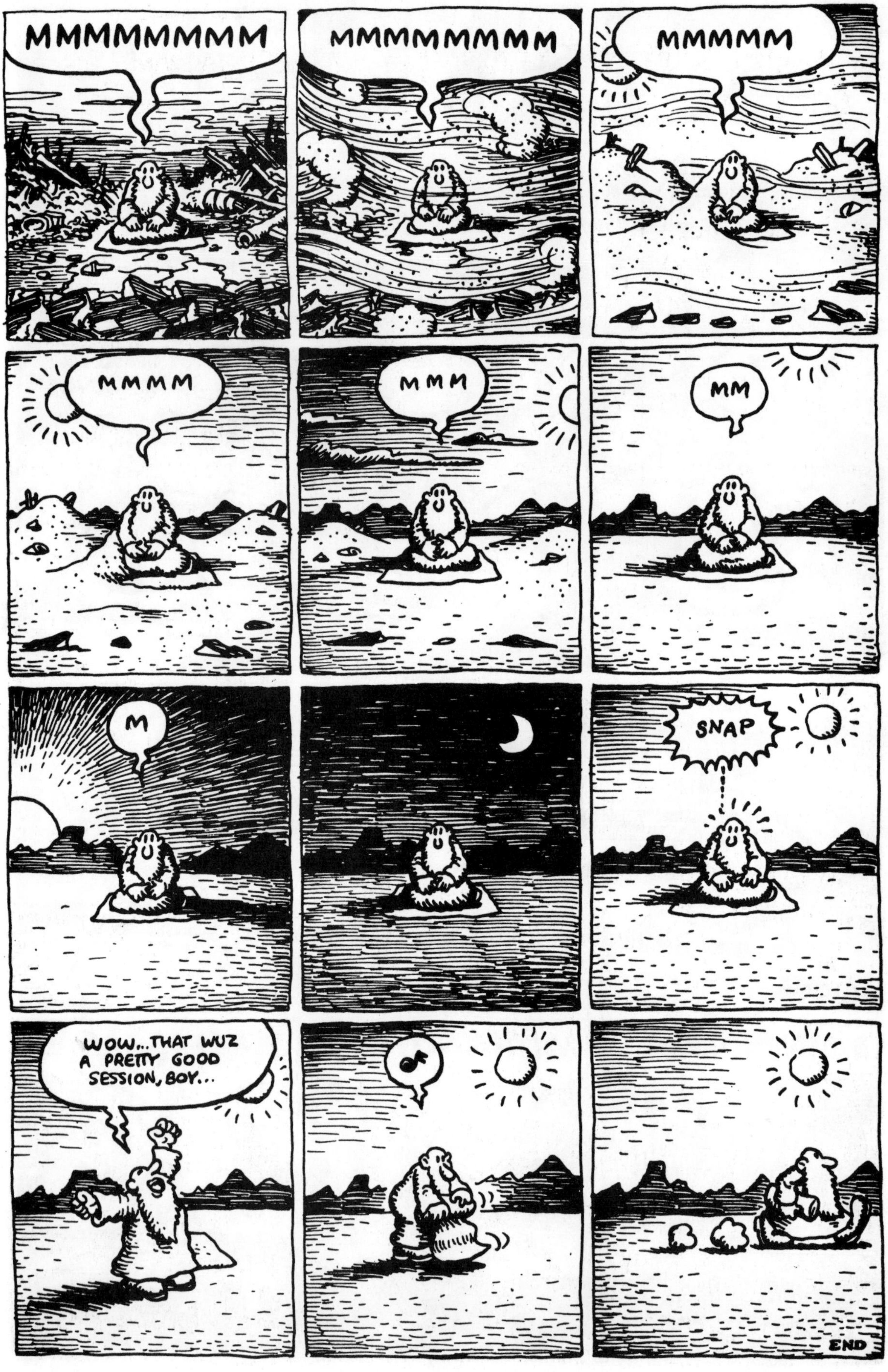
MMMMMMMM
MMMMMMMMM
MMMMM
MMMM
MMM
MM
M
SNAP
WOW...THAT WUZ A PRETTY GOOD SESSION, BOY...
END

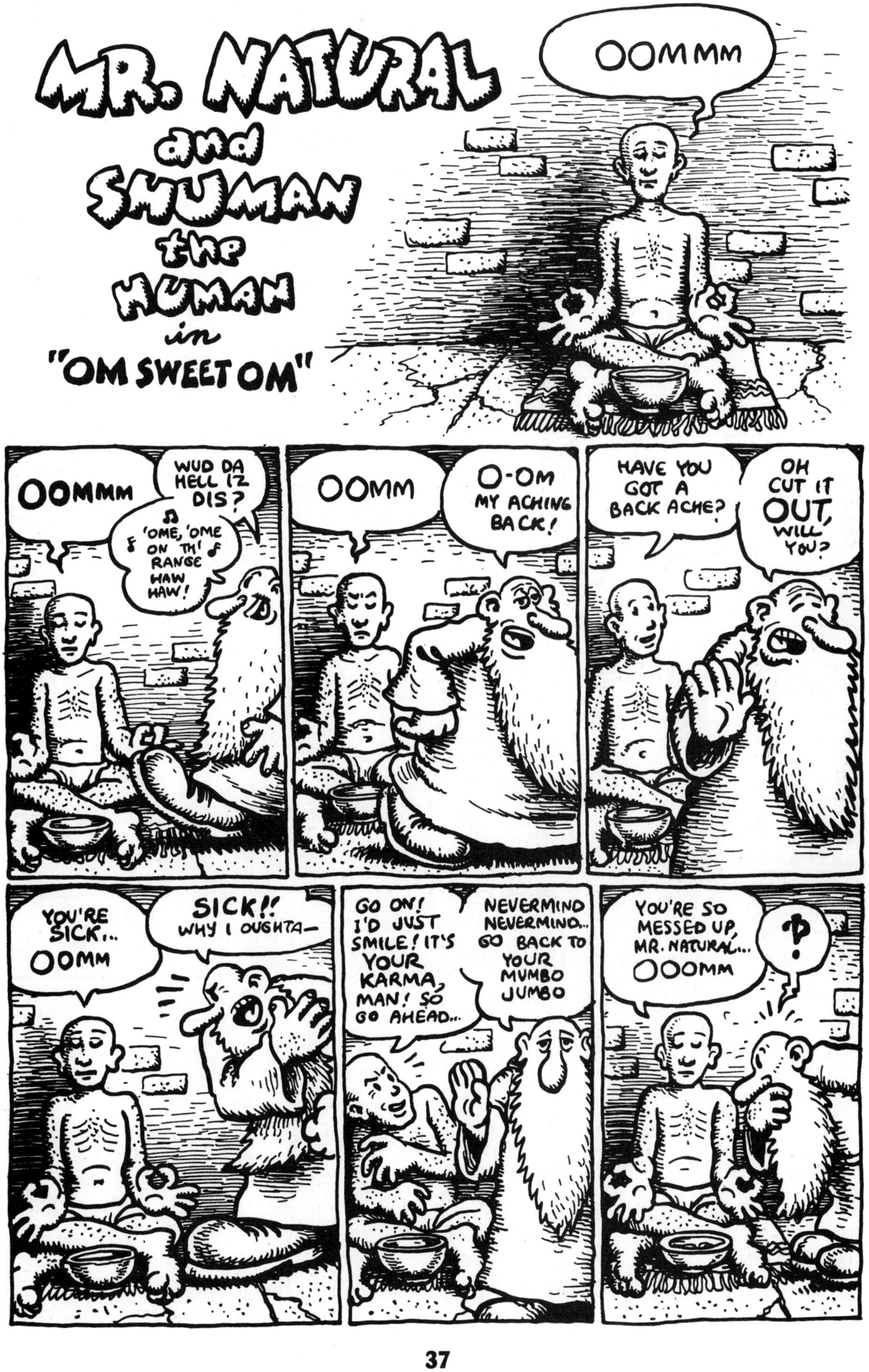
MR. NATURAL
and
SHUMAN
the
HUMAN
in
"OM SWEET OM"
OOMMM
OOMMM
WUD DA HELL IZ DIS?
'OME, 'OME ON TH' RANGE HAW HAW!
OOMM
O-OM MY ACHING BACK!
HAVE YOU GOT A BACK ACHE?
OH CUT IT OUT, WILL YOU?
YOU'RE SICK... OOMM
SICK!! WHY I OUGHTA—
GO ON! I'D JUST SMILE! IT'S YOUR KARMA, MAN! SO GO AHEAD...
NEVERMIND NEVERMIND... GO BACK TO YOUR MUMBO JUMBO
YOU'RE SO MESSED UP, MR. NATURAL... OOOMM
?

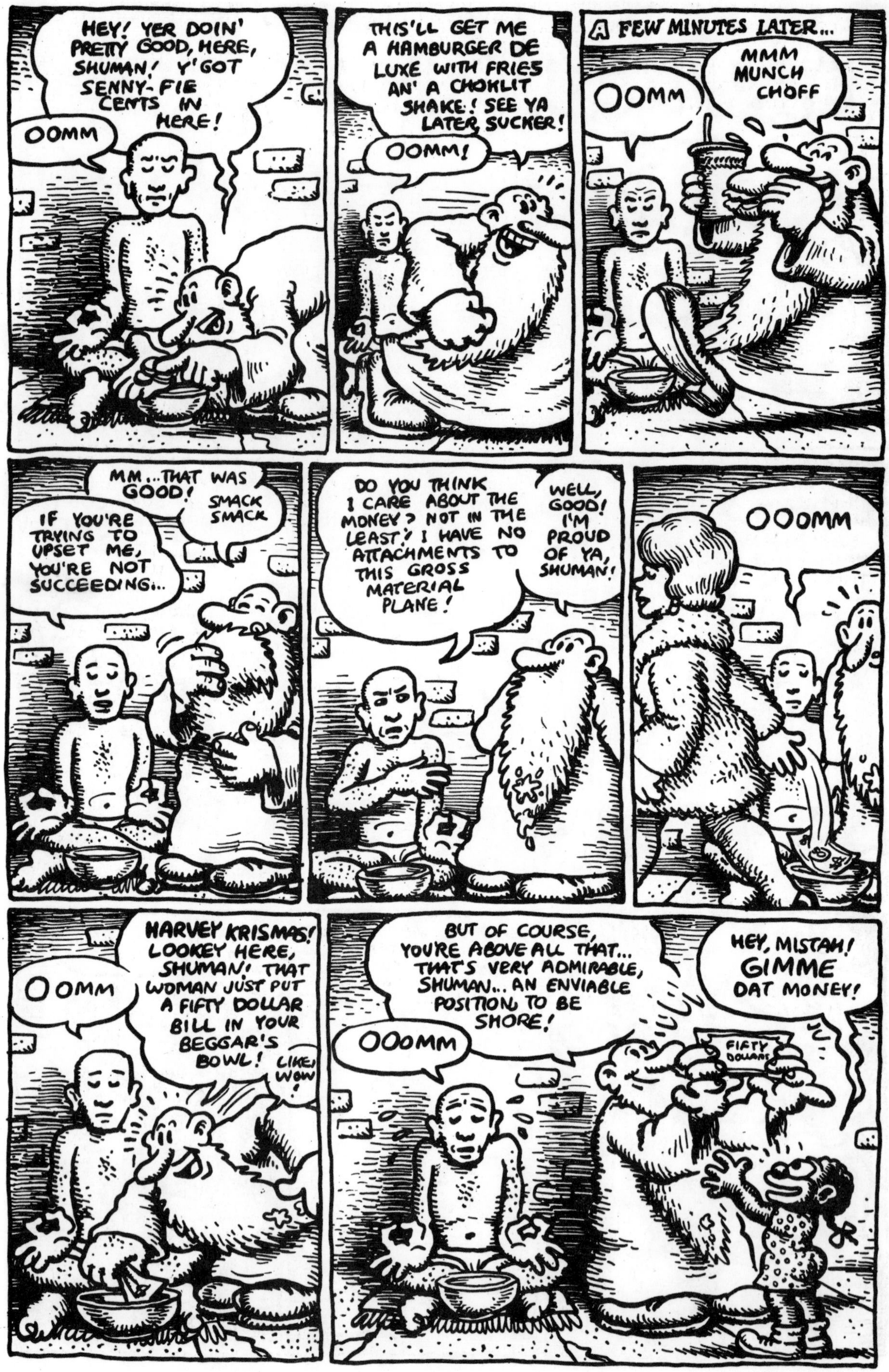
HEY! YER DOIN' PRETTY GOOD, HERE, SHUMAN! Y'GOT SENNY-FIE CENTS IN HERE!
OOMM
THIS'LL GET ME A HAMBURGER DE LUXE WITH FRIES AN' A CHOKLIT SHAKE! SEE YA LATER SUCKER!
OOMM!
A FEW MINUTES LATER...
OOMM
MMM MUNCH CHOFF
MM... THAT WAS GOOD!
SMACK SMACK
IF YOU'RE TRYING TO UPSET ME, YOU'RE NOT SUCCEEDING...
DO YOU THINK I CARE ABOUT THE MONEY? NOT IN THE LEAST! I HAVE NO ATTACHMENTS TO THIS GROSS MATERIAL PLANE!
WELL, GOOD! I'M PROUD OF YA, SHUMAN!
OOOMM
OOMM
HARVEY KRISMAS! LOOKEY HERE, SHUMAN! THAT WOMAN JUST PUT A FIFTY DOLLAR BILL IN YOUR BEGGAR'S BOWL!
LIKE! WOW!
BUT OF COURSE, YOU'RE ABOVE ALL THAT... THAT'S VERY ADMIRABLE, SHUMAN... AN ENVIABLE POSITION, TO BE SHORE!
OOOMM
HEY, MISTAH! GIMME DAT MONEY!
FIFTY DOLLARS

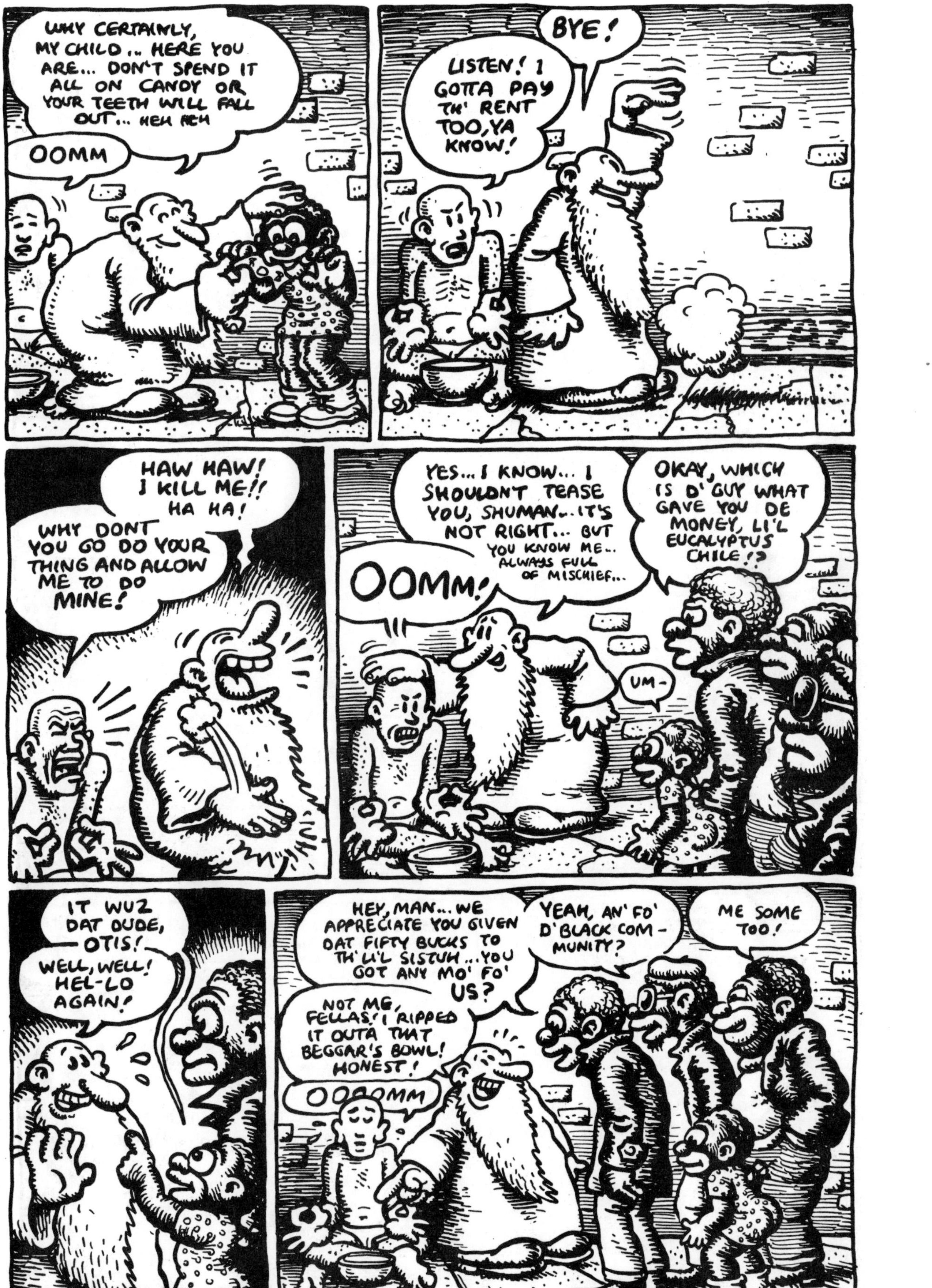
WHY CERTAINLY, MY CHILD.. HERE YOU ARE... DON'T SPEND IT ALL ON CANDY OR YOUR TEETH WILL FALL OUT... HEH HEH
OOMM
LISTEN! I GOTTA PAY TH' RENT TOO, YA KNOW!
BYE!
HAW HAW! I KILL ME!! HA HA!
WHY DONT YOU GO DO YOUR THING AND ALLOW ME TO DO MINE!
YES...I KNOW... I SHOULDN'T TEASE YOU, SHUMAN.. IT'S NOT RIGHT... BUT YOU KNOW ME.. ALWAYS FULL OF MISCHIEF...
OOMM!
OKAY, WHICH IS D' GUY WHAT GAVE YOU DE MONEY, LI'L EUCALYPTUS CHILE!?
UM-
IT WUZ DAT DUDE, OTIS!
WELL, WELL! HEL-LO AGAIN!
HEY, MAN... WE APPRECIATE YOU GIVEN DAT FIFTY BUCKS TO TH' LI'L SISTUH... YOU GOT ANY MO' FO' US?
YEAH, AN' FO' D' BLACK COM-MUNITY?
ME SOME TOO!
NOT ME, FELLAS! I RIPPED IT OUTA THAT BEGGAR'S BOWL! HONEST!
OOOOMM

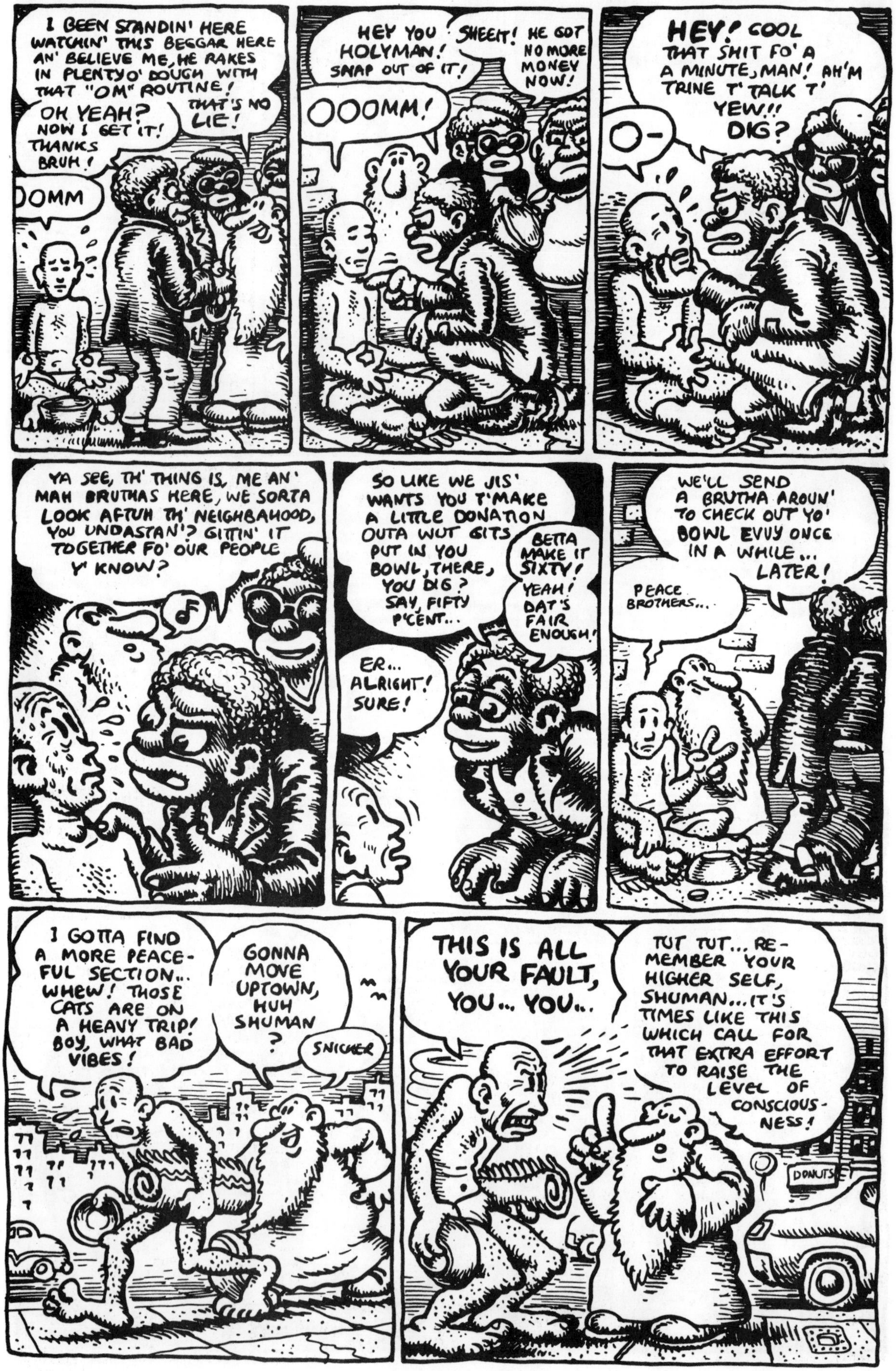
I BEEN STANDIN' HERE WATCHIN' THIS BEGGAR HERE AN' BELIEVE ME, HE RAKES IN PLENTY O' DOUGH WITH THAT "OM" ROUTINE!
OH YEAH? NOW I GET IT! THANKS BRUH!
THAT'S NO LIE!
OMM
HEY YOU HOLYMAN! SNAP OUT OF IT!
SHEEIT! HE GOT NO MORE MONEY NOW!
OOOMM!
HEY! COOL THAT SHIT FO' A A MINUTE, MAN! AH'M TRINE T' TALK T' YEW!! DIG?
O-
YA SEE, TH' THING IS, ME AN' MAH BRUTHAS HERE, WE SORTA LOOK AFTUH TH' NEIGHBAHOOD, YOU UNDASTAN'? GITTIN' IT TOGETHER FO' OUR PEOPLE Y' KNOW?
SO LIKE WE JIS' WANTS YOU T'MAKE A LITTLE DONATION OUTA WUT GITS PUT IN YOU BOWL, THERE, YOU DIG? SAY, FIFTY P'CENT...
BETTA MAKE IT SIXTY!
YEAH! DAT'S FAIR ENOUGH!
ER... ALRIGHT! SURE!
WE'LL SEND A BRUTHA AROUN' TO CHECK OUT YO' BOWL EVUY ONCE IN A WHILE... LATER!
PEACE BROTHERS...
I GOTTA FIND A MORE PEACE-FUL SECTION... WHEW! THOSE CATS ARE ON A HEAVY TRIP! BOY, WHAT BAD VIBES!
GONNA MOVE UPTOWN, HUH SHUMAN?
SNICKER
THIS IS ALL YOUR FAULT, YOU... YOU...
TUT TUT... RE-MEMBER YOUR HIGHER SELF, SHUMAN... IT'S TIMES LIKE THIS WHICH CALL FOR THAT EXTRA EFFORT TO RAISE THE LEVEL OF CONSCIOUS-NESS!
DONUTS

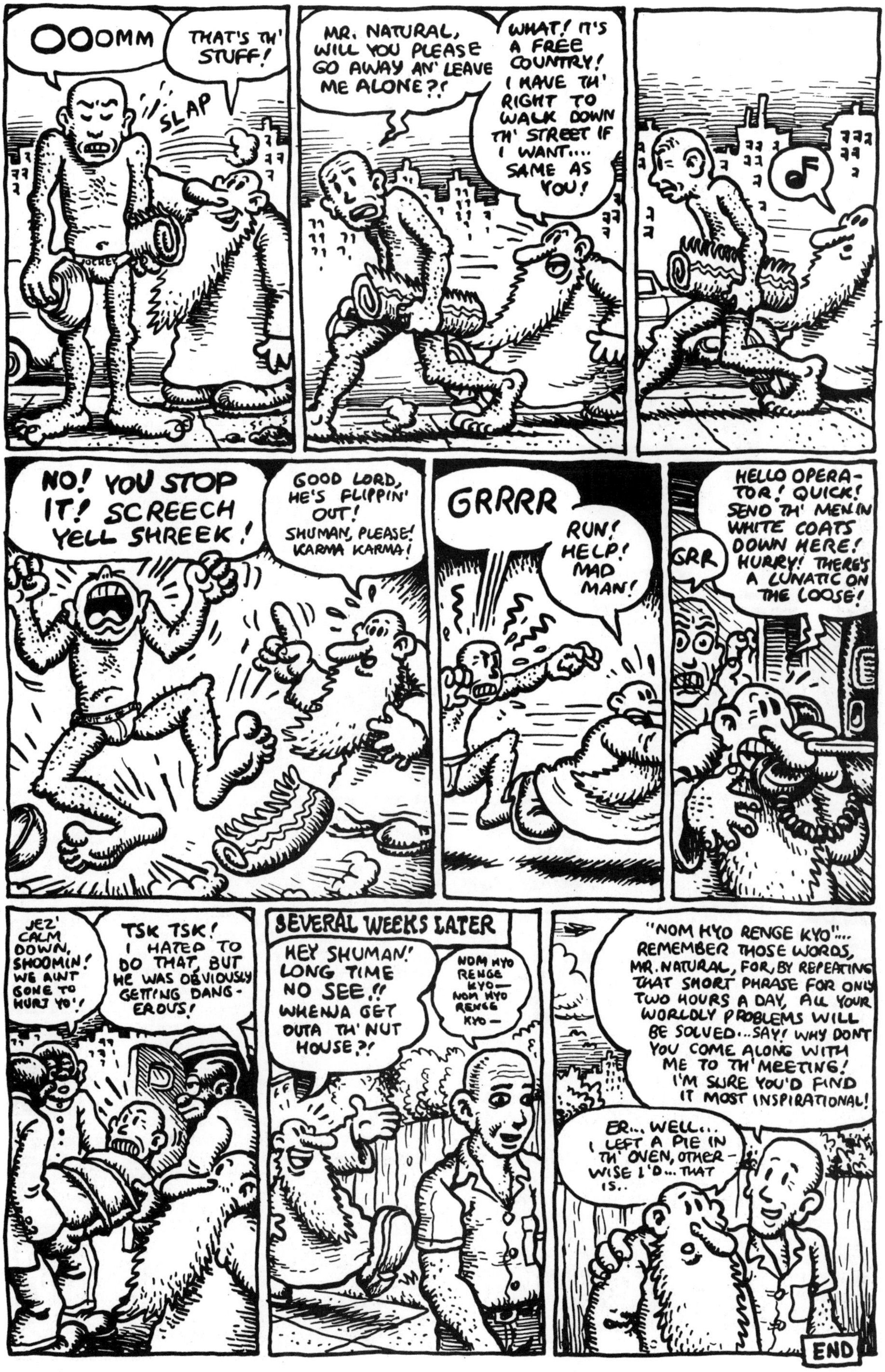
OOOMM
THAT'S TH' STUFF!
SLAP
MR. NATURAL, WILL YOU PLEASE GO AWAY AN' LEAVE ME ALONE?!
WHAT! IT'S A FREE COUNTRY! I HAVE TH' RIGHT TO WALK DOWN TH' STREET IF I WANT.... SAME AS YOU!
NO! YOU STOP IT! SCREECH YELL SHREEK!
GOOD LORD, HE'S FLIPPIN' OUT! SHUMAN, PLEASE! KARMA KARMA!
GRRRR
RUN! HELP! MAD MAN!
GRR
HELLO OPERATOR! QUICK! SEND TH' MEN IN WHITE COATS DOWN HERE! HURRY! THERE'S A LUNATIC ON THE LOOSE!
JEZ' CALM DOWN, SHOOMIN! WE AINT GONE TO HURT YO'!
TSK TSK! I HATED TO DO THAT, BUT HE WAS OBVIOUSLY GETTING DANGEROUS!
SEVERAL WEEKS LATER
HEY SHUMAN! LONG TIME NO SEE!! WHENJA GET OUTA TH' NUT HOUSE?!
NOM HYO RENGE KYO— NOM HYO RENGE KYO—
"NOM HYO RENGE KYO"... REMEMBER THOSE WORDS, MR. NATURAL, FOR, BY REPEATING THAT SHORT PHRASE FOR ONLY TWO HOURS A DAY, ALL YOUR WORLDLY PROBLEMS WILL BE SOLVED...SAY! WHY DON'T YOU COME ALONG WITH ME TO TH' MEETING! I'M SURE YOU'D FIND IT MOST INSPIRATIONAL!
ER... WELL... I LEFT A PIE IN TH' OVEN, OTHERWISE I'D... THAT IS..
END

The Origins of MR. NATURAL

THIS TINY BATTERED PHOTOGRAPH MAY BE THE FIRST ONE EVER TAKEN OF MR. NATURAL, BUT THE EXPERTS HAVE DIFFERENT OPINIONS. BACK OF PHOTO IS INSCRIBED WITH THE NAME "FRED" BUT IS NOT MR. NATURAL'S HANDWRITING.

EARLIST KNOWN PHOTOGRAPH THAT IS DEFINITELY THE VENERABLE ONE IS THIS PORTRAIT SIGNED "F. NATURAL, WESSINGTON SPRINGS, S.D., 1908." HANDWRITING EXPERTS HAVE VERIFIED THE SIGNATURE, AND AN OLD-TIMER STILL LIVING IN ALCESTER, SOUTH DAKOTA, RECALLS A MAN NAMED FRED NATURAL WHO JOBBED AROUND THAT AREA IN THOSE DAYS. HE REMEMBERS HIM AS A "NICE QUIET FELLOW."

MANY OF YOU Mr. Natural fans have asked that we run an article on the man's past life and early background. Certainly a life history on Mr. Natural is a fascinating idea, and so, with a certain amount of skepticism, we set about investigating. Our doubts were confirmed as we ran into one blind alley after another, and finally were forced to abandon trying to fill in several large gaps in his past. Whole decades, in fact, are entirely missing. A frustrating experience for the conscientious historian and Mr. Natural enthusiast.

His childhood is completey clouded in obscurity. His birthplace and birthdate are entirely unknown. No records have been found, and no relatives, and, of course, no one has been able to squeeze an ounce of information out of the Old Man Himself (except, according to him, that his father is still alive and well, but he won't tell us where). All knowledge of his life has been gathered without his help or support, and the whole

project leaves him "Cold", as he puts it.

The 1908 photograph is the earliest proof we have of his existence. The photo was sent to us by Mrs. Ada Cooper, a Mr. Natural fan, who found the old picture in a trunk full of her mother's belongings. Mrs. Cooper says she can never remember her mother, now deceased, ever mentioning that she knew Mr. Natural.

As for his age at the time the photograph was taken, he appears to have been between thirty-five and forty, which would make him close to one-hundred years old today!!

Not a clue exists as to his whereabouts between 1908 and 1921, the year our wild young wiseman moved to Chicago, where he stayed up to 1929. Here we lose track of the elusive sage for another seven years. But we managed to hunt down several people who knew him in "that toddlin' town" in the twenties, and so have gathered a fairly complete picture of Mr. Natural's adventures through that lurid decade.

In the fall of 1921 Mr. Natural got a job in a drugstore as an errand runner on the near north side. (Some believe the drugstore was a front for a speak-easy and that it was Natch's job to deliver

42

the illegal booze to thirsty customers, but this is mere here-say). It may have been while in the employ of this pharmacy that he became interested in the drug field, for two years later, in 1923, he was promoting a "Wonder Drug" that he claimed could cure all "mental and spiritual ills" and had a small but enthusiastic cult of followers, mostly women, who endorsed this claim vigorously.. Going under the name of "Dr. Von Natürlich," he travelled through the midwest for a short time, selling the "wonder elixir" and "healing" the sick, until he was arrested in Peoria, Illinois, convicted of Fraud and spent six months in the county jail. There are still those who applaud Dr. Von Naturlich's Wonder-Drug, and curse the day his entire stock was confiscated by the police. Mrs. Vicki Hodgetts, now of Los Angeles, said to me when I talked with her, "Well, yes! It certainly was a wonder drug! I know it was, because I was absolutely neurotic! I was miserable, believe me! Then along comes this Dr. Von Naturlich... and.. well, I've been a very happy person ever since!!"

The police file on the case, which was still in the Peoria Courthouse, states, "Although purported to possess potent powers over the mind and spirit, a close scrutiny of this so-called "Wonder Drug" under a microscope has proven without a shadow of a doubt that it is nothing more than plain ordinary tap-water."

A Great New Message of
HEALTH
"A HEALTHY MIND MEANS A HEALTHY BODY" says Dr. Von Natürlich, the Internationally Acclaimed Expert on the Human Mind, Body & Spirit
Hear the Man who has rebuilt thousands of broken lives by his scientifically proved NEW METHOD!
7 FREE LECTURES
TRINITY AUDITORIUM
AUGUST 8 THRU 15
8:00 P.M.

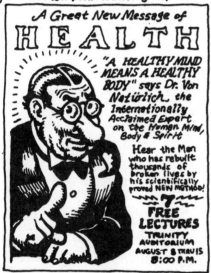

HANDBILL SHOWING "DR. VON NATÜRLICH" IN THE YEAR 1924

After his release from jail, he turned his talents to magic, and for a few months performed his feats of mystic hoodoo in Vaudeville houses around Chicago. He was billed as "Mr. Natural the Magnificent". This career, too, met with opposition from the conservatives of that primitive time, and his show was cut short one night by a panic-stricken theatre manager who ordered the curtain brought down on Mr. Natural's "Unnatural Act" which he was about to perform on an hypnotized lady participant. He was blacklisted and never performed as a magician again.

Evidently, he was undaunted by past defeats, and in the spring of 1926 he somehow managed to get together a small dance band and began a successful career in the music business as a band-leader.

This band was known as "Mr. Natural and his Seven Lyrical Lechers" at first and later the group was enlarged to thirteen members under the name of "Mr. Natural's Lyrical Lechers and their Orchestra". They were a popular group around Chicago for almost two years, playing in roadhouses and Cafes, and an occasional College Prom or Hotel Ballroom. Mr. Natural himself wrote many of the songs in their repertoire and even played an assortment of unlikely instruments. Their arrangements had a strangely unique sound as evidenced by a few surviving records.

RADIEX
BOSTON U.S.A.
FOX TROT
VOCAL & SPOONS BY MR. NATURAL
ALL THE MEAT YOU CAN EAT
(MR. NATURAL)
Natural's Lyrical Lechers
1983
R

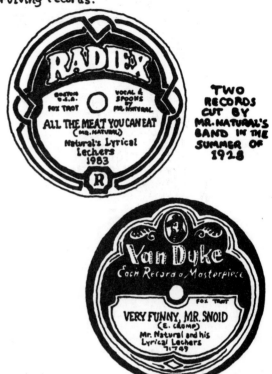

TWO RECORDS CUT BY MR. NATURAL'S BAND IN THE SUMMER OF 1928

Van Dyke
Each Record a Masterpiece
FOX TROT
VERY FUNNY, MR. SNOID
(E. CROMP)
Mr. Natural and his Lyrical Lechers
71749

It was an era of easy money and within a year, Mr. Natural had accumulated a small fortune. In 1928 he was living in a large plush home in a Chicago suburb, owned two Packard limousines, employed the services of a maid, butler and chauffeur and threw huge wild parties.

Then, suddenly, and unexpectedly, he gave it all away to some bum he'd picked up on the street, typical of the restless, unfathomable nature of his perfect being. His friends were totally baffled by this sudden change, and when he moved to a cheap skid-row hotel, he gradually lost contact with his former well-to-do whoopee-making friends.

Harry Baines, the drummer in the band, says "We had some good times back then. I'll never understand why Natchy threw it all away. Everybody thought he was nuts! Of course, two years later, the rest of us went down the tubes along with him!"

"It looked to me liked he just flipped his noodle!" —Joey Norton, banjo player in the group.

"I still can't figure it! I used to think he was a smart operator 'til he pulled that stunt! And he even had it put in writing! Crackers!" —Doris Hall, wife of Cafe owner Monte Hall.

From the winter of '28-'29, when Mr. Natural moved to skid-row, until a full seven years later, nothing is known of him.

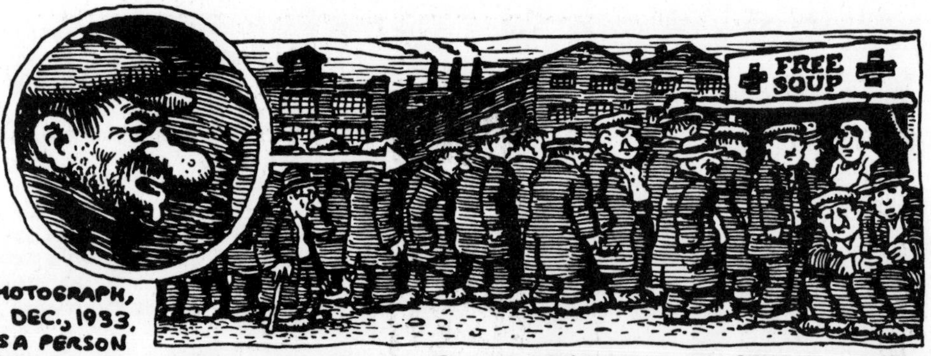
FREE SOUP

THIS PHOTOGRAPH, MADE IN DEC., 1933, CONTAINS A PERSON WHO MIGHT BE MR. NATURAL, ACCORDING TO THE SAN MATEO CHAPTER OF THE MR. NATURAL SOCIETY, WHO FOUND THE PICTURE. "WHO ELSE COULD IT BE?" SAYS THE GROUP'S PRESIDENT. INDEED, THERE IS A STRONG RESEMBLANCE IN THE FEATURES OF THE DOWN-AND-OUT CHAP ABOVE TO THOSE OF THE LIVING SAINT. PHOTO WAS TAKEN IN CHICAGO, BUT NO ONE HAS TURNED UP WHO KNEW HIM THERE AFTER 1929.

In 1936 he popped up again on the west coast, where he met another great American folk hero and all-around geek, the "Old Pooperoo". The Old Poop was working as a fruit picker in Central California in the late thirties, and he and Mr. Natural crossed paths in a working-man's bar in Modesto one night in October, 1936. They became close friends and traveled together, picking up a few dollars now and then working in the fields or on construction jobs, getting drunk and whoring and hopping freight cars all over the United States.

"Natural was a good ol' boy, yep... we went through plenty of troubles together, you bet! Why, we musta been in every calaboose in this land of Liberty, from Maine to California and back again! We fought about women and cried on each other's shoulder over lost romances,.. we talked about old times back home for hours, an' when we had a few bucks we lived like royal Turks! But they was generally tough times, so I got in with some sharpies in Philly and for awhile there I was rakin' it in. This was around '39 or '40. I didn't see Natural much after that. I guess I got too Booshwah fer him. He wuz uneasy around my business associates. I s'pose we did put on some airs.. haw haw... strictly high-hat! So he got bored and headed back west an' I didn't see him again, liked I said. But I started hearing stories about him gettin' in with small-time crooks an' dope fiends, so I sent him some cash to come east an' get in the business with me, but of course he just spent the money and wrote askin' me for more and more 'til I got fed up and wouldn't send him any. I figured he was Hell-bent on a dead-end course. Last I heard, he wuz runnin' around with a tough twerp from Tulsa name of Judy Holiday... not th' same one as th' movie star, but a nice lookin' dish from what I heard." No one seems to know what became of this Tulsa sweetheart.

When the War broke out Mr. Natural once again vanished from the scene. He has talked vaguely of this period of his life, but will not give us any specific details (He claims he can't remember). By his own admission, if we can trust him, he was in the Middle and Far East through the war years and after. He says he was in India, traveled to China, the Himalayas, Tibet and Afghanistan, where he got work as a Taxi driver, and, in his own words "learned many strange and wonderful things" in those distant lands.

He returned to America in 1953, "for some stupid reason" and loafed around for a year "getting very depressed about the world situation," he tells us, and so, renouncing all worldly pursuits and pleasures, he retreated to Death Valley in 1955 to "start anew."

In June, 1960, a small group of ardent devotees formed the first chapter of the Mr. Natural Fan Clubs of America in Southern California. They kept close ties with his spiritual development in the desert, as well as looking after his financial matters. In 1965 he began making speaking tours, visiting Colleges and Universities, and by 1966 he was already coming into his own as a recognized powerful spiritual force on this planet, a great religious leader, and a living model of Godlike perfection for all of Humanity to emulate. His moving words of wisdom have been translated into German, French, Spanish, Italian, Norwegian, Dutch and Japanese, and his presence on this globe has changed it for the better, as we all know!!

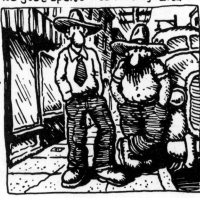

THE OLD POOPEROO AND MR. NATURAL IN CHEYENNE WYOMING, 1938

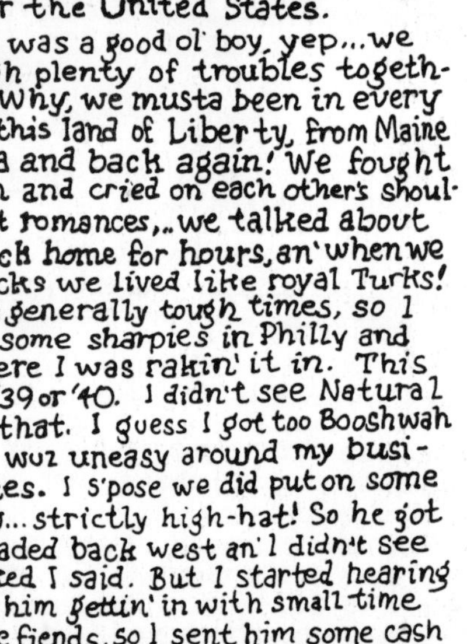

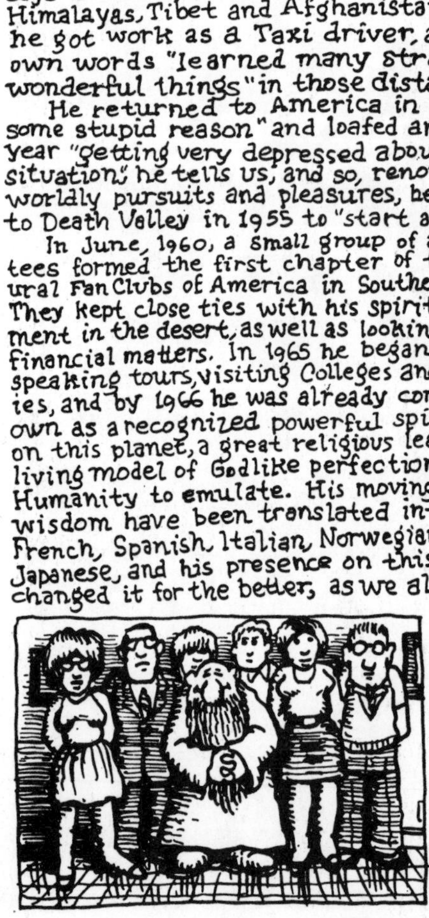

MR. NATURAL WITH A GROUP OF EARLY DISCIPLES IN LOS ANGELES CALIFORNIA, MARCH 1962

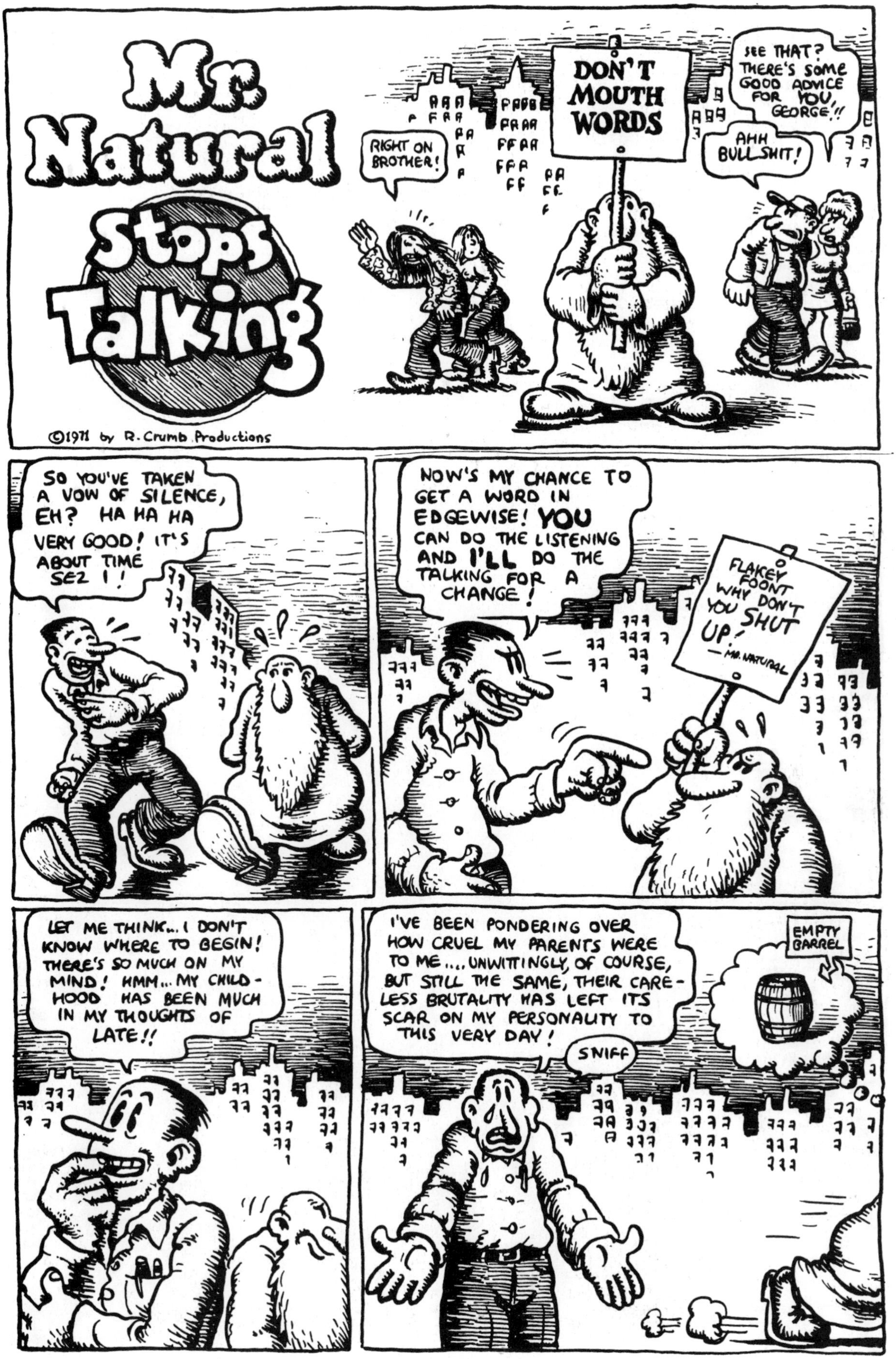
Mr. Natural
Stops Talking
RIGHT ON BROTHER!
DON'T MOUTH WORDS
SEE THAT? THERE'S SOME GOOD ADVICE FOR YOU, GEORGE!!
AHH BULLSHIT!
©1971 by R. Crumb Productions
SO YOU'VE TAKEN A VOW OF SILENCE, EH? HA HA HA VERY GOOD! IT'S ABOUT TIME SEZ I!
NOW'S MY CHANCE TO GET A WORD IN EDGEWISE! YOU CAN DO THE LISTENING AND I'LL DO THE TALKING FOR A CHANGE!
FLAKEY FOONT WHY DON'T YOU SHUT UP! —MR. NATURAL
LET ME THINK... I DON'T KNOW WHERE TO BEGIN! THERE'S SO MUCH ON MY MIND! HMM... MY CHILD-HOOD HAS BEEN MUCH IN MY THOUGHTS OF LATE!!
I'VE BEEN PONDERING OVER HOW CRUEL MY PARENTS WERE TO ME.... UNWITTINGLY, OF COURSE, BUT STILL THE SAME, THEIR CARE-LESS BRUTALITY HAS LEFT ITS SCAR ON MY PERSONALITY TO THIS VERY DAY!
SNIFF
EMPTY BARREL

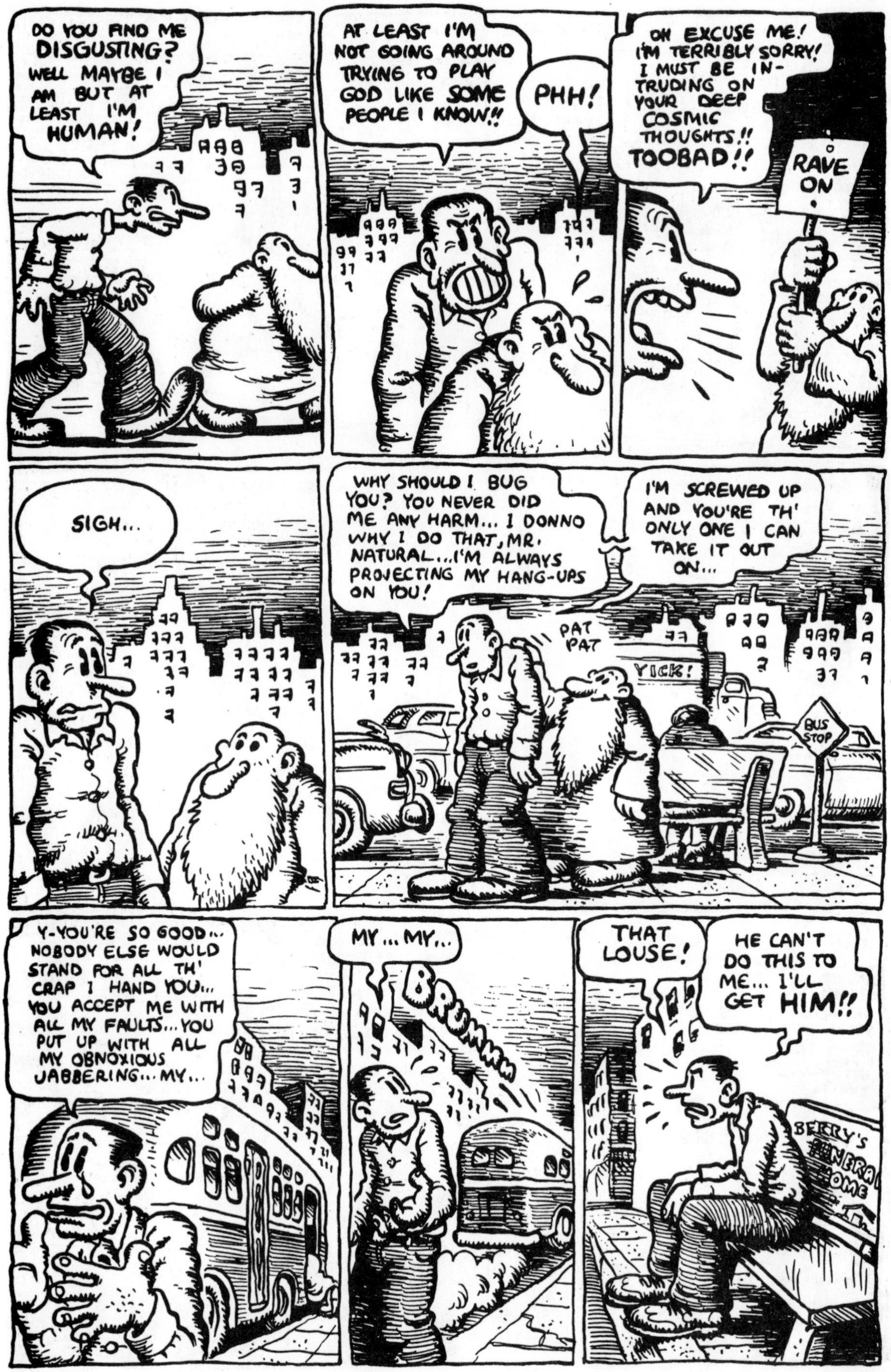
DO YOU FIND ME DISGUSTING? WELL MAYBE I AM BUT AT LEAST I'M HUMAN!
AT LEAST I'M NOT GOING AROUND TRYING TO PLAY GOD LIKE SOME PEOPLE I KNOW!!
PHH!
OH EXCUSE ME! I'M TERRIBLY SORRY! I MUST BE IN-TRUDING ON YOUR DEEP COSMIC THOUGHTS!! TOOBAD!!
RAVE ON
SIGH...
WHY SHOULD I BUG YOU? YOU NEVER DID ME ANY HARM... I DONNO WHY I DO THAT, MR. NATURAL...I'M ALWAYS PROJECTING MY HANG-UPS ON YOU!
I'M SCREWED UP AND YOU'RE TH' ONLY ONE I CAN TAKE IT OUT ON...
PAT PAT
YICK!
BUS STOP
Y-YOU'RE SO GOOD... NOBODY ELSE WOULD STAND FOR ALL TH' CRAP I HAND YOU... YOU ACCEPT ME WITH ALL MY FAULTS... YOU PUT UP WITH ALL MY OBNOXIOUS JABBERING... MY...
MY... MY...
BRUMMM
THAT LOUSE!
HE CAN'T DO THIS TO ME... I'LL GET HIM!!
BERRY'S FUNERAL HOME

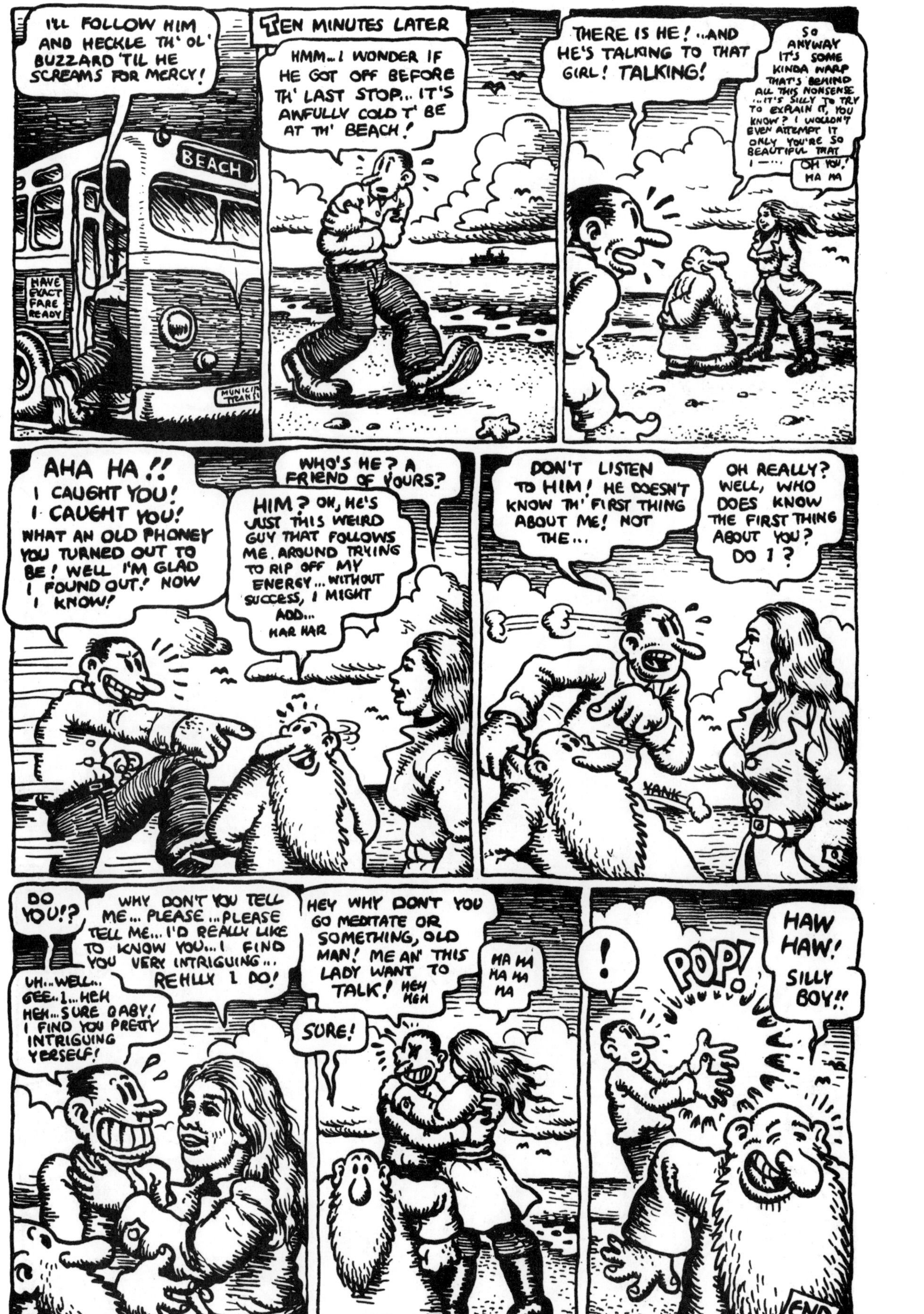

I'LL FOLLOW HIM AND HECKLE TH' OL' BUZZARD 'TIL HE SCREAMS FOR MERCY!
BEACH
HAVE EXACT FARE READY
TEN MINUTES LATER
HMM... I WONDER IF HE GOT OFF BEFORE TH' LAST STOP... IT'S AWFULLY COLD T' BE AT TH' BEACH!
THERE IS HE! ...AND HE'S TALKING TO THAT GIRL! TALKING!
SO ANYWAY IT'S SOME KINDA WARP THAT'S BEHIND ALL THIS NONSENSE ...IT'S SILLY TO TRY TO EXPLAIN IT, YOU KNOW? I WOULDN'T EVEN ATTEMPT IT ONLY YOU'RE SO BEAUTIFUL THAT I.....
OH YOU! HA HA
AHA HA!! I CAUGHT YOU! I CAUGHT YOU! WHAT AN OLD PHONEY YOU TURNED OUT TO BE! WELL I'M GLAD I FOUND OUT! NOW I KNOW!
WHO'S HE? A FRIEND OF YOURS?
HIM? OH, HE'S JUST THIS WEIRD GUY THAT FOLLOWS ME AROUND TRYING TO RIP OFF MY ENERGY... WITHOUT SUCCESS, I MIGHT ADD... HAR HAR
DON'T LISTEN TO HIM! HE DOESN'T KNOW TH' FIRST THING ABOUT ME! NOT THE...
OH REALLY? WELL, WHO DOES KNOW THE FIRST THING ABOUT YOU? DO I?
YANK
DO YOU!?
WHY DON'T YOU TELL ME... PLEASE... PLEASE TELL ME... I'D REALLY LIKE TO KNOW YOU... I FIND YOU VERY INTRIGUING... REHLLY I DO!
UH... WELL.. GEE.. I... HEH HEH... SURE BABY! I FIND YOU PRETTY INTRIGUING YERSELF!
HEY WHY DON'T YOU GO MEDITATE OR SOMETHING, OLD MAN! ME AN' THIS LADY WANT TO TALK! HEH HEH
HA HA HA HA HA
SURE!
!
POP!
HAW HAW! SILLY BOY!!
END

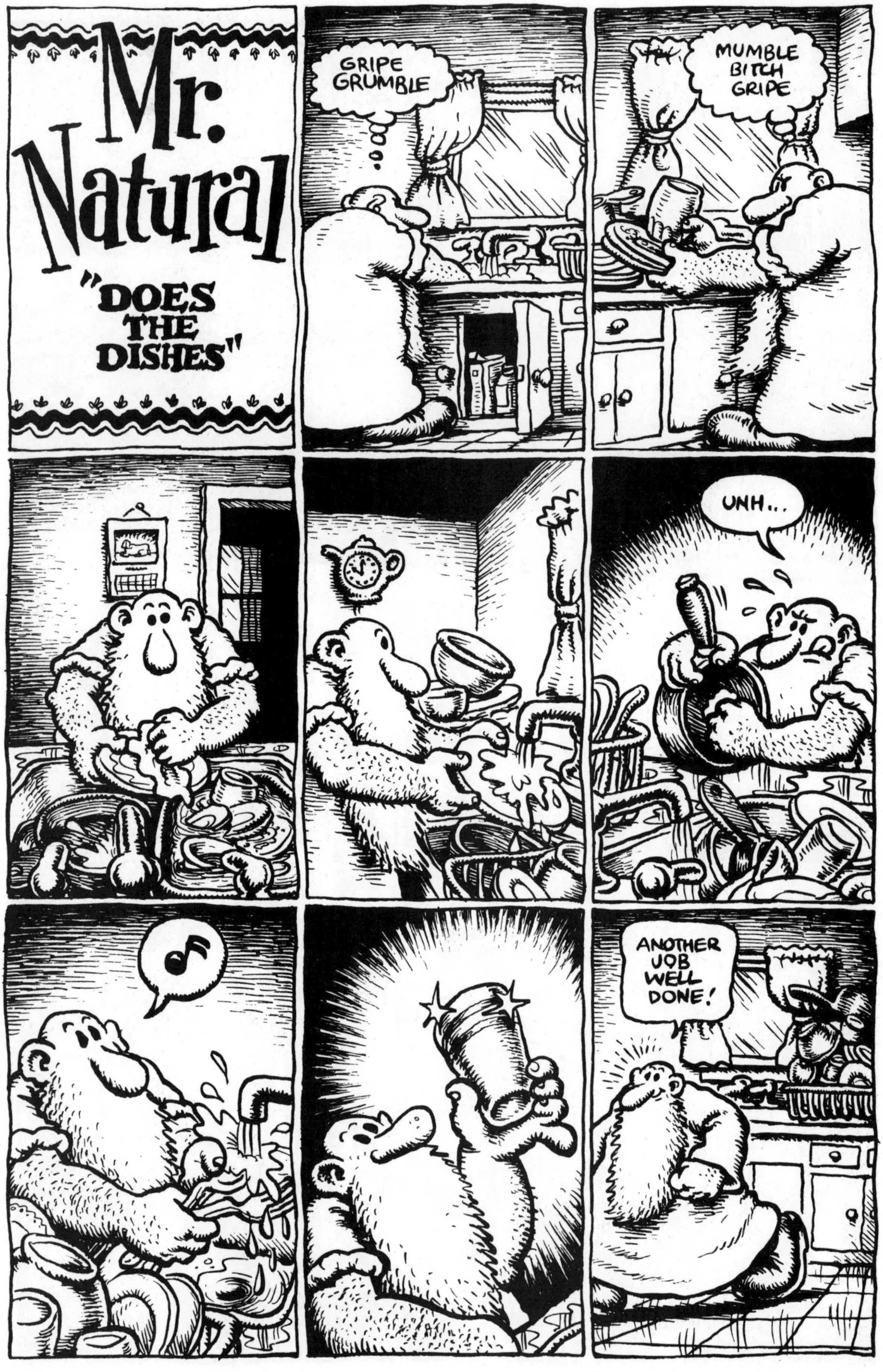

Mr. Natural
"DOES THE DISHES"
GRIPE GRUMBLE
MUMBLE BITCH GRIPE
UNH...
ANOTHER JOB WELL DONE!

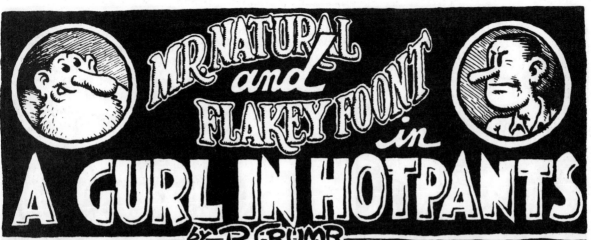

MR. NATURAL and FLAKEY FOONT in
A GURL IN HOTPANTS
by R. CRUMB

WHERE WILL IT ALL END?

IN THE GRAVE, MY BOY IN THE GRAVE!

WOULDJA LOOK AT THAT LI'L UNIT IN TH' HOTPANTS, THOUGH!

WELL, THEN, IS SEX THE ANSWER?

NO, I WOULDNT SAY THAT!

SEX, MY BOY, IS THE QUESTION!

OW!

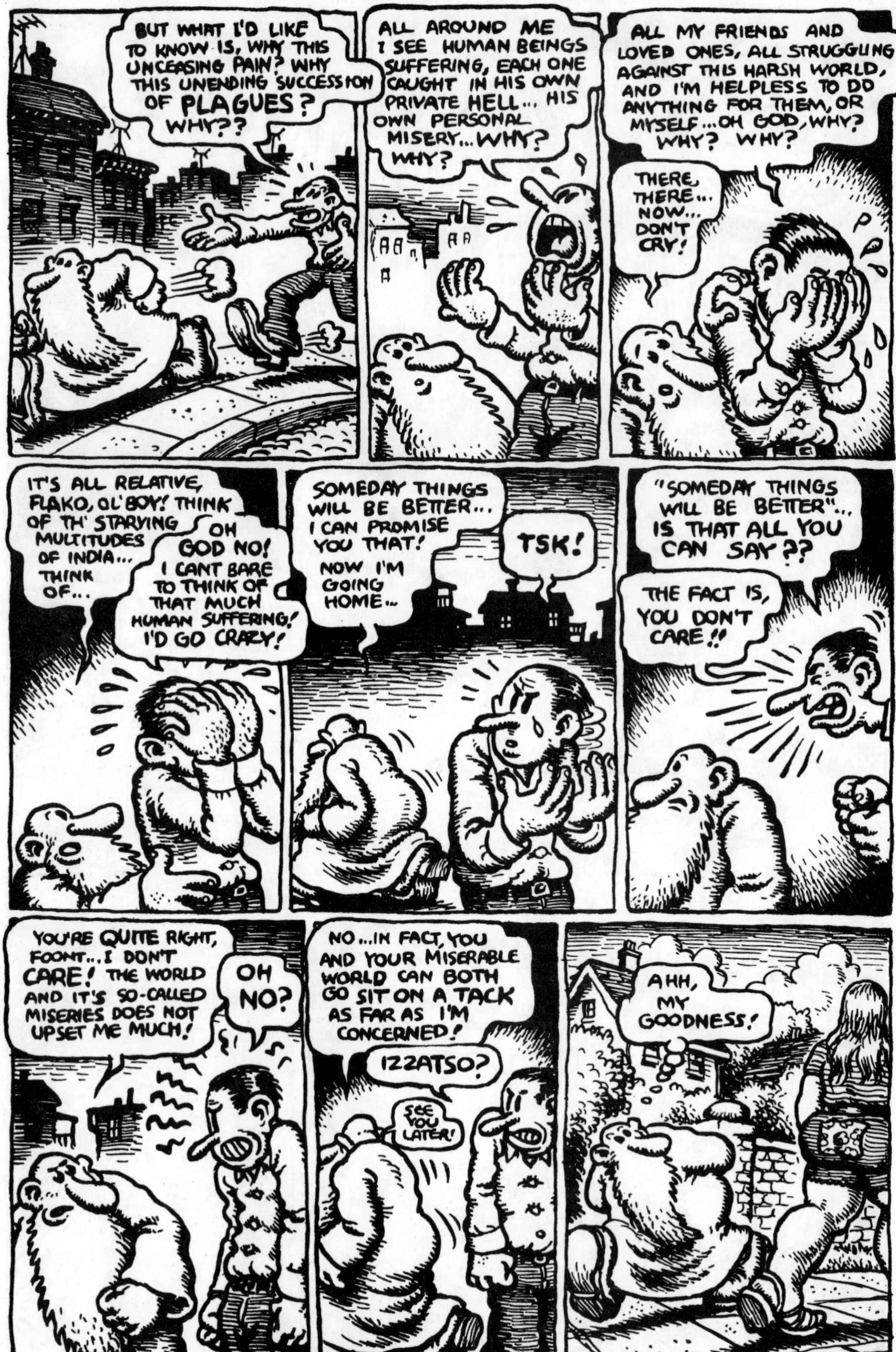
BUT WHAT I'D LIKE TO KNOW IS, WHY THIS UNCEASING PAIN? WHY THIS UNENDING SUCCESSION OF PLAGUES? WHY??
ALL AROUND ME I SEE HUMAN BEINGS SUFFERING, EACH ONE CAUGHT IN HIS OWN PRIVATE HELL... HIS OWN PERSONAL MISERY... WHY? WHY?
ALL MY FRIENDS AND LOVED ONES, ALL STRUGGLING AGAINST THIS HARSH WORLD, AND I'M HELPLESS TO DO ANYTHING FOR THEM, OR MYSELF... OH GOD, WHY? WHY? WHY?
THERE, THERE... NOW... DON'T CRY!
IT'S ALL RELATIVE, FLAKO, OL' BOY! THINK OF TH' STARVING MULTITUDES OF INDIA... THINK OF...
OH GOD NO! I CANT BARE TO THINK OF THAT MUCH HUMAN SUFFERING! I'D GO CRAZY!
SOMEDAY THINGS WILL BE BETTER... I CAN PROMISE YOU THAT! NOW I'M GOING HOME...
TSK!
"SOMEDAY THINGS WILL BE BETTER"... IS THAT ALL YOU CAN SAY??
THE FACT IS, YOU DON'T CARE!!
YOU'RE QUITE RIGHT, FOONT... I DON'T CARE! THE WORLD AND IT'S SO-CALLED MISERIES DOES NOT UPSET ME MUCH!
OH NO?
NO... IN FACT, YOU AND YOUR MISERABLE WORLD CAN BOTH GO SIT ON A TACK AS FAR AS I'M CONCERNED!
IZZATSO?
SEE YOU LATER!
AHH, MY GOODNESS!

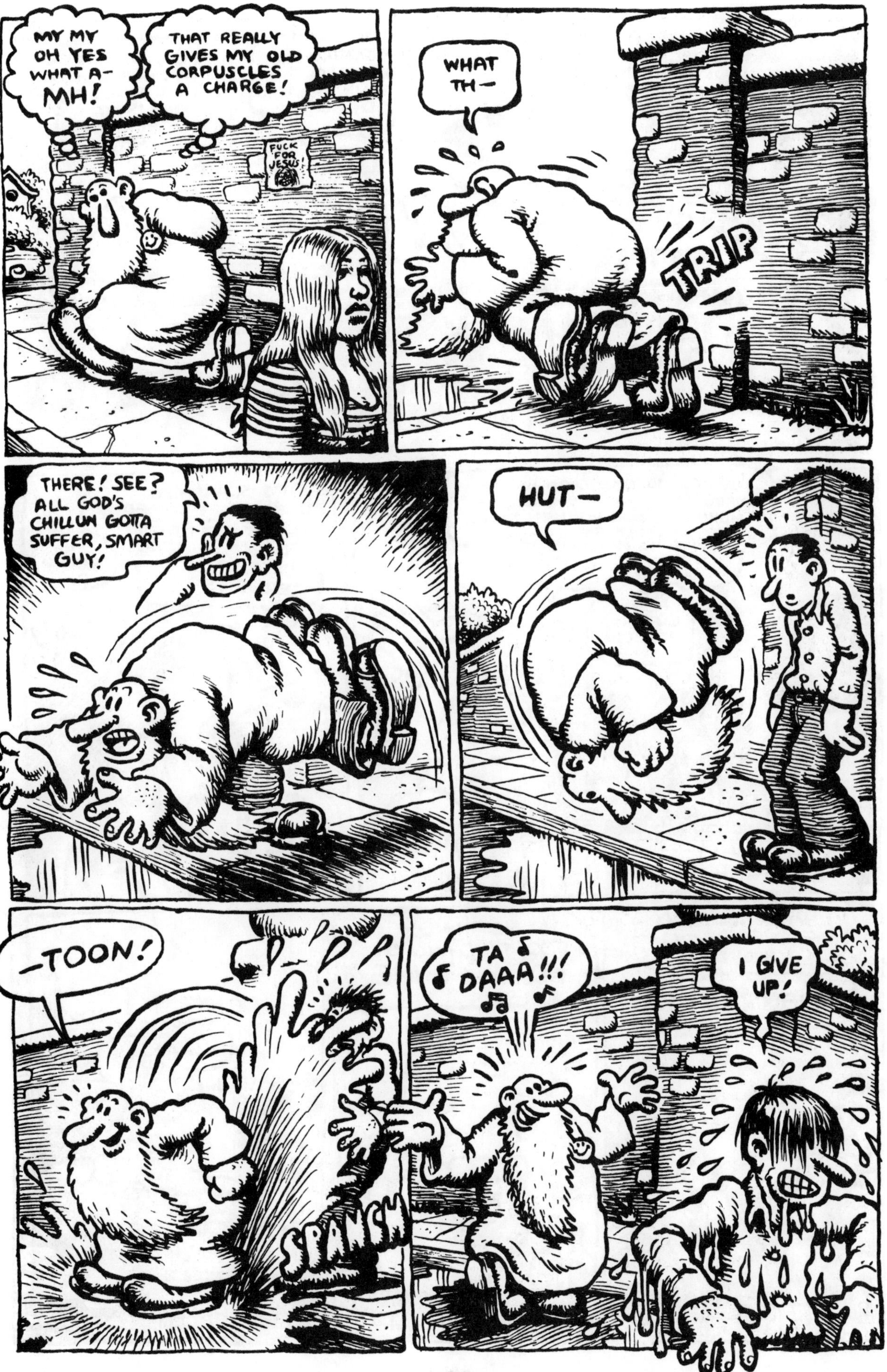
MY MY OH YES WHAT A-MH!
THAT REALLY GIVES MY OLD CORPUSCLES A CHARGE!
FUCK FOR JESUS!
WHAT TH-
TRIP
THERE! SEE? ALL GOD'S CHILLUN GOTTA SUFFER, SMART GUY!
HUT-
-TOON!
SPANCH
TA DAAA!!!
I GIVE UP!

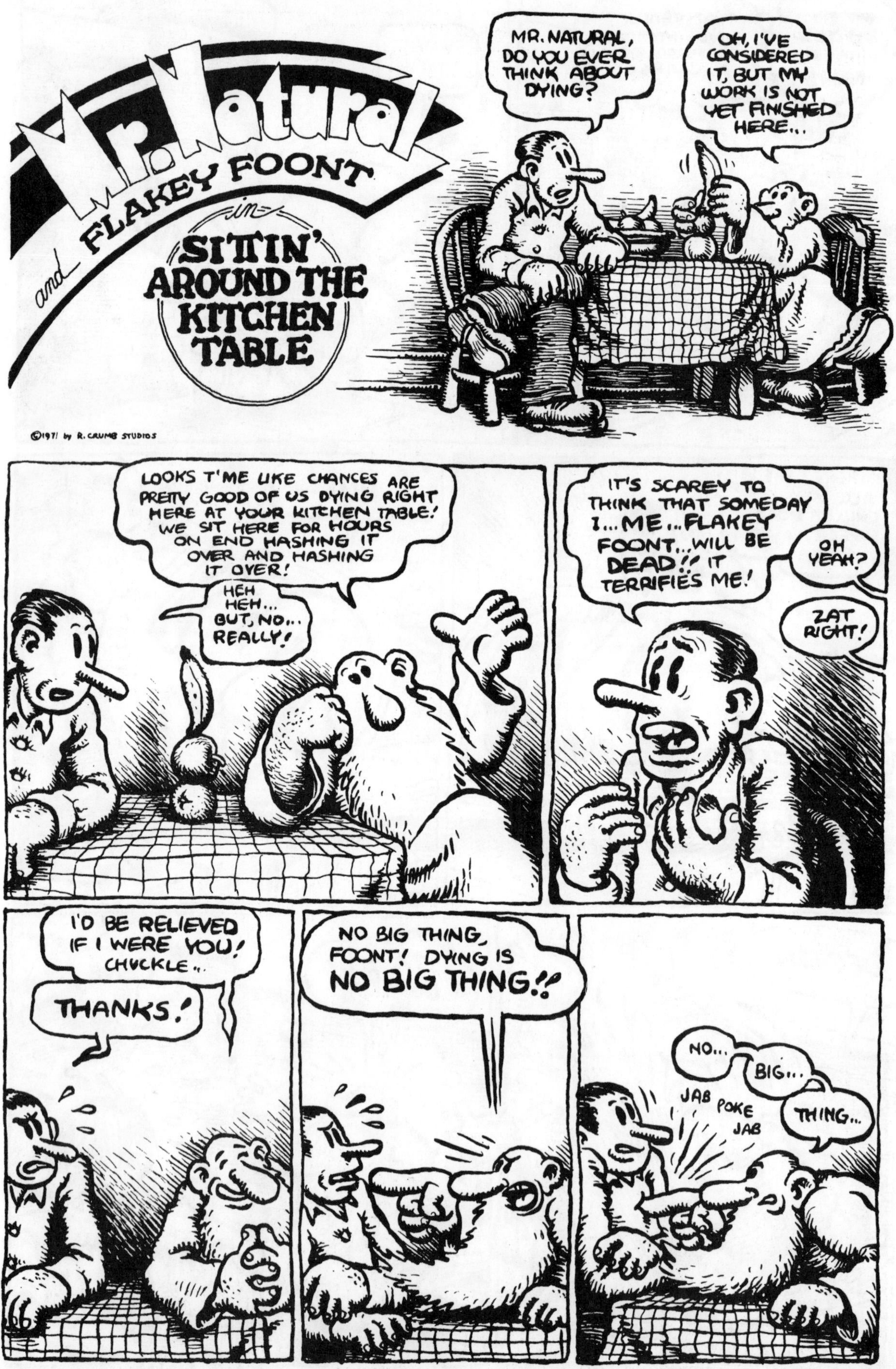

Mr. Natural
and FLAKEY FOONT
in
SITTIN' AROUND THE KITCHEN TABLE
MR. NATURAL, DO YOU EVER THINK ABOUT DYING?
OH, I'VE CONSIDERED IT, BUT MY WORK IS NOT YET FINISHED HERE...
©1971 by R. CRUMB STUDIOS
LOOKS T'ME LIKE CHANCES ARE PRETTY GOOD OF US DYING RIGHT HERE AT YOUR KITCHEN TABLE! WE SIT HERE FOR HOURS ON END HASHING IT OVER AND HASHING IT OVER!
HEH HEH... BUT, NO... REALLY!
IT'S SCAREY TO THINK THAT SOMEDAY I... ME... FLAKEY FOONT... WILL BE DEAD!! IT TERRIFIES ME!
OH YEAH?
ZAT RIGHT!
I'D BE RELIEVED IF I WERE YOU! CHUCKLE..
THANKS!
NO BIG THING, FOONT! DYING IS NO BIG THING!!
NO...
BIG...
THING...
JAB POKE JAB

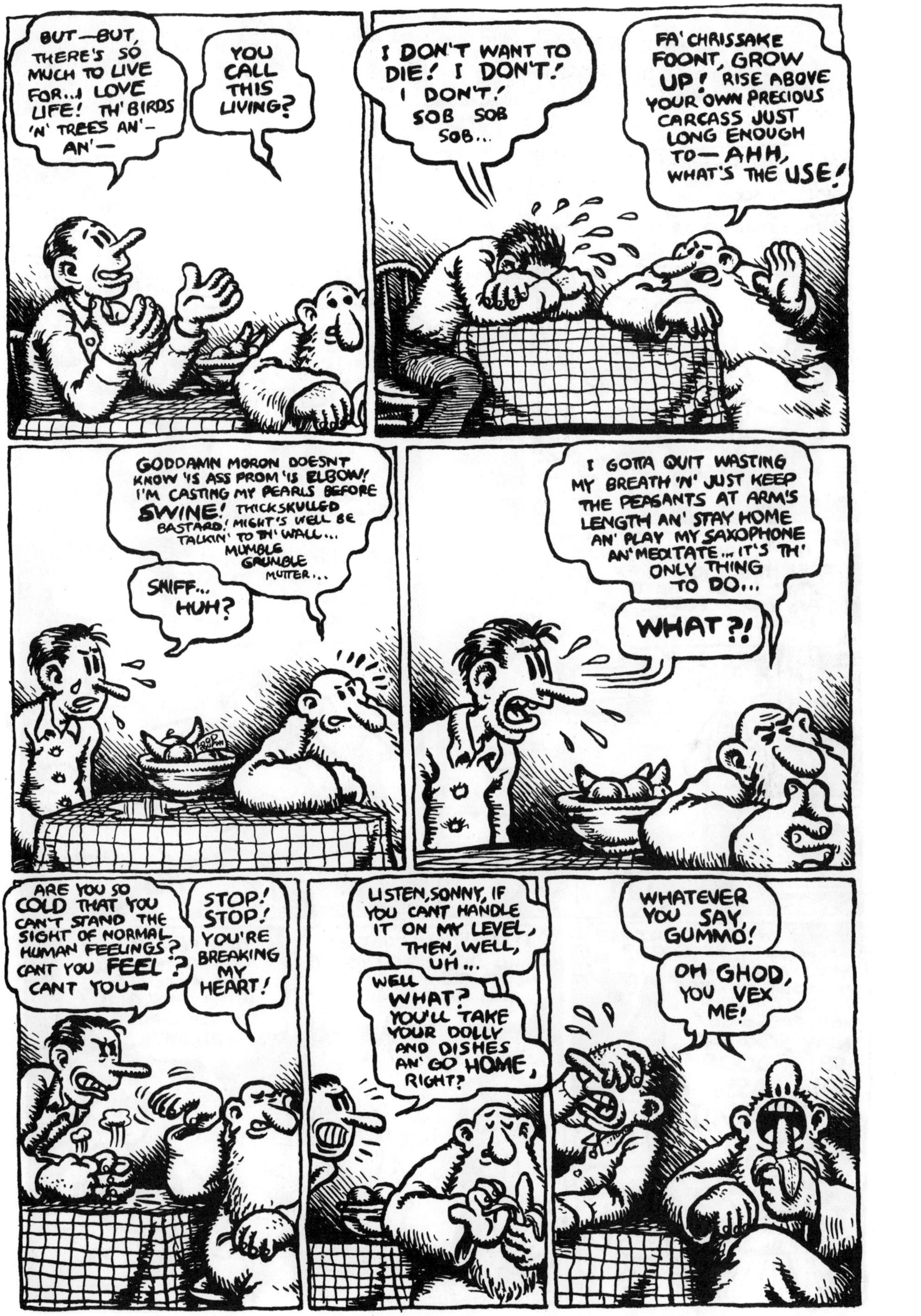
BUT—BUT, THERE'S SO MUCH TO LIVE FOR...I LOVE LIFE! TH' BIRDS 'N' TREES AN'— AN'—
YOU CALL THIS LIVING?
I DON'T WANT TO DIE! I DON'T! I DON'T! SOB SOB SOB...
FA' CHRISSAKE FOONT, GROW UP! RISE ABOVE YOUR OWN PRECIOUS CARCASS JUST LONG ENOUGH TO— AHH, WHAT'S THE USE!
GODDAMN MORON DOESNT KNOW 'IS ASS FROM 'IS ELBOW! I'M CASTING MY PEARLS BEFORE SWINE! THICKSKULLED BASTARD! MIGHT'S WELL BE TALKIN' TO TH' WALL... MUMBLE GRUMBLE MUTTER...
SNIFF... HUH?
I GOTTA QUIT WASTING MY BREATH 'N' JUST KEEP THE PEASANTS AT ARM'S LENGTH AN' STAY HOME AN' PLAY MY SAXOPHONE AN' MEDITATE... IT'S TH' ONLY THING TO DO...
WHAT?!
ARE YOU SO COLD THAT YOU CAN'T STAND THE SIGHT OF NORMAL HUMAN FEELINGS? CANT YOU FEEL? CANT YOU—
STOP! STOP! YOU'RE BREAKING MY HEART!
LISTEN, SONNY, IF YOU CANT HANDLE IT ON MY LEVEL, THEN, WELL, UH...
WELL WHAT? YOU'LL TAKE YOUR DOLLY AND DISHES AN' GO HOME, RIGHT?
WHATEVER YOU SAY, GUMMO!
OH GHOD, YOU VEX ME!

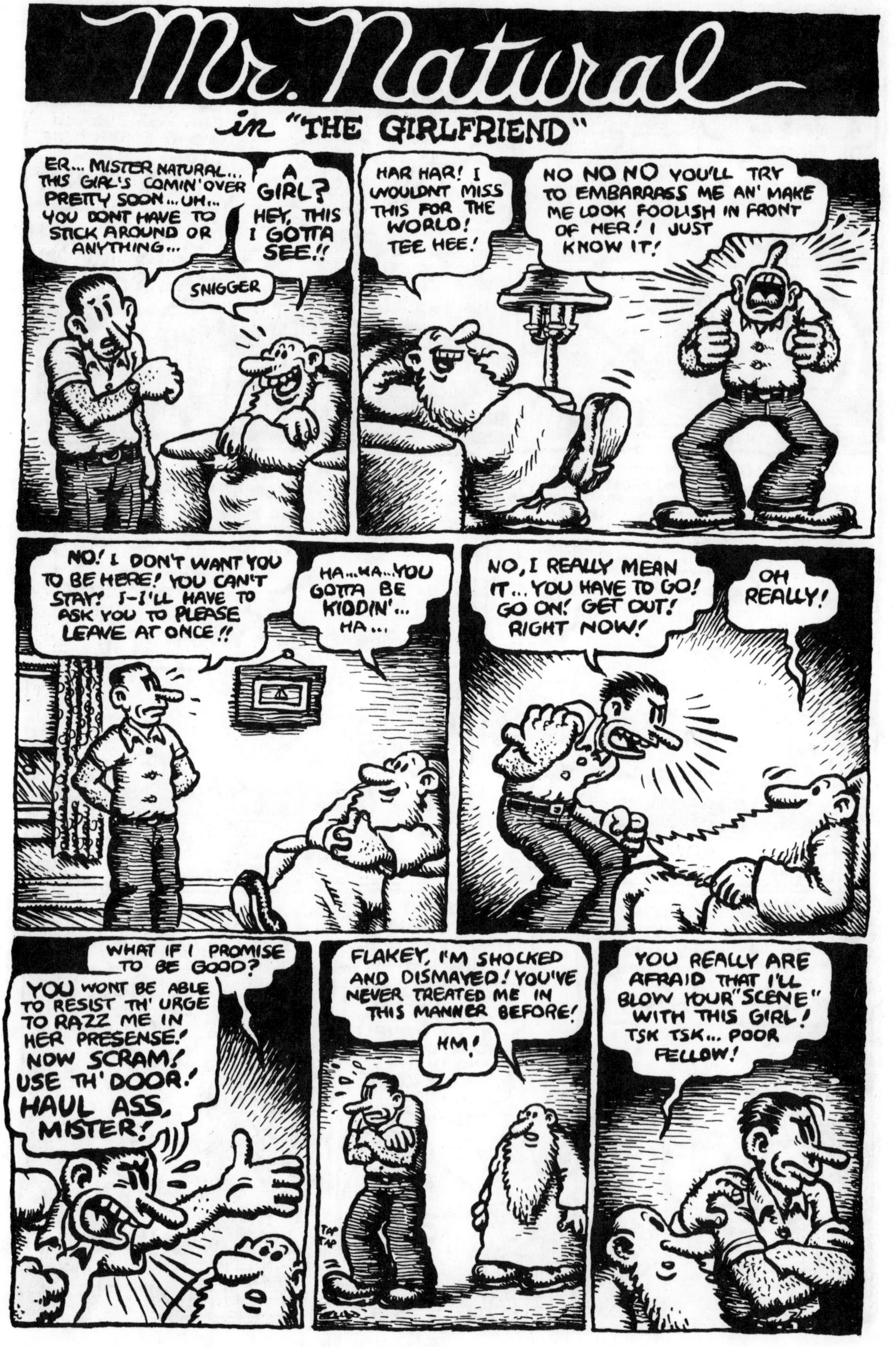
Mr. Natural
in "THE GIRLFRIEND"
ER... MISTER NATURAL... THIS GIRL'S COMIN' OVER PRETTY SOON... UH... YOU DONT HAVE TO STICK AROUND OR ANYTHING...
A GIRL? HEY, THIS I GOTTA SEE!!
SNIGGER
HAR HAR! I WOULDNT MISS THIS FOR THE WORLD! TEE HEE!
NO NO NO YOU'LL TRY TO EMBARRASS ME AN' MAKE ME LOOK FOOLISH IN FRONT OF HER! I JUST KNOW IT!
NO! I DON'T WANT YOU TO BE HERE! YOU CAN'T STAY! I-I'LL HAVE TO ASK YOU TO PLEASE LEAVE AT ONCE!!
HA...HA...YOU GOTTA BE KIDDIN'... HA...
NO, I REALLY MEAN IT... YOU HAVE TO GO! GO ON! GET OUT! RIGHT NOW!
OH REALLY!
WHAT IF I PROMISE TO BE GOOD?
YOU WONT BE ABLE TO RESIST TH' URGE TO RAZZ ME IN HER PRESENSE! NOW SCRAM! USE TH' DOOR! HAUL ASS, MISTER!
FLAKEY, I'M SHOCKED AND DISMAYED! YOU'VE NEVER TREATED ME IN THIS MANNER BEFORE!
HM!
TAP TAP
YOU REALLY ARE AFRAID THAT I'LL BLOW YOUR "SCENE" WITH THIS GIRL! TSK TSK... POOR FELLOW!

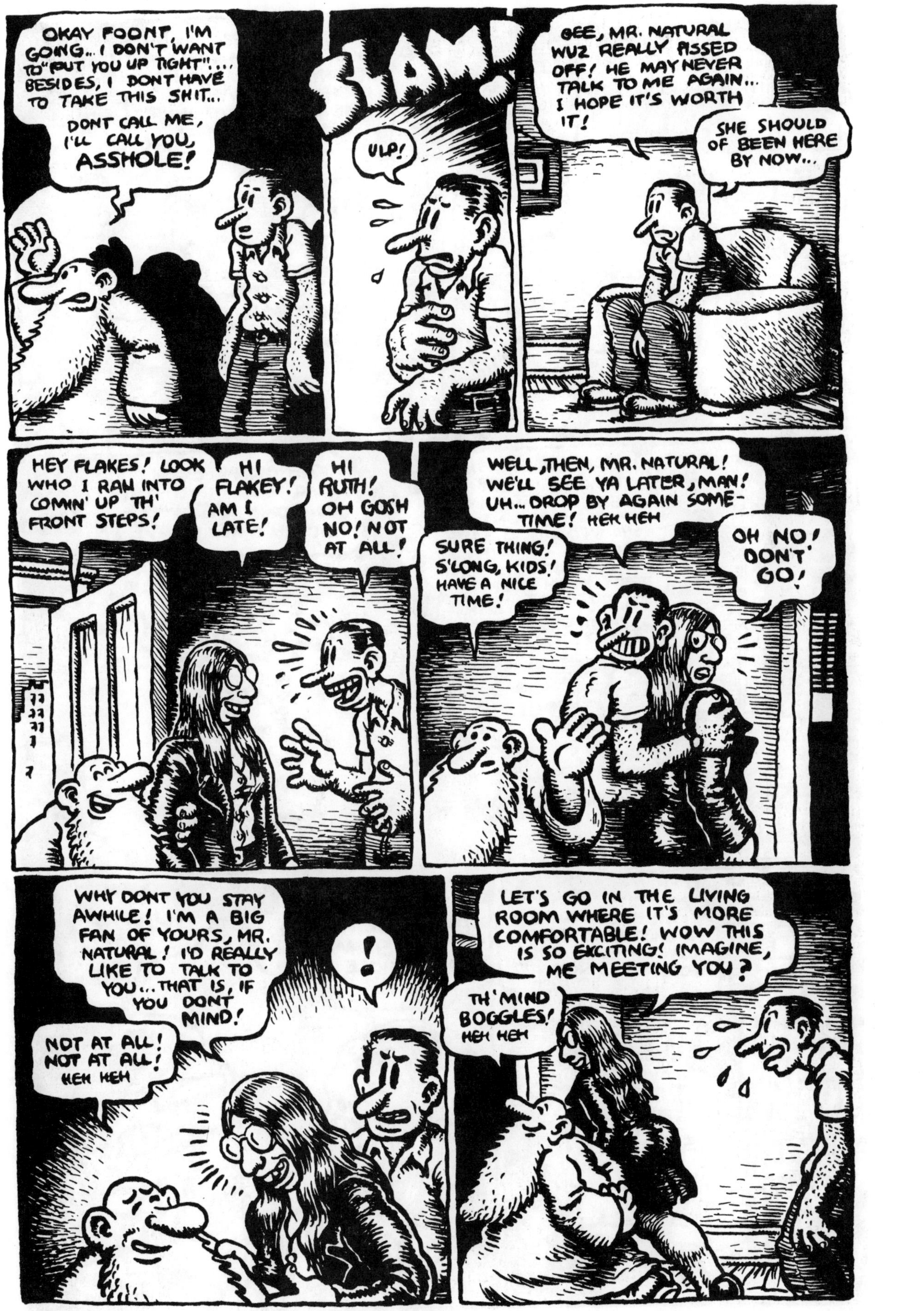
OKAY FOONT, I'M GOING... I DON'T WANT TO "PUT YOU UP TIGHT"!... BESIDES, I DONT HAVE TO TAKE THIS SHIT...
DONT CALL ME, I'LL CALL YOU, ASSHOLE!
SLAM!
ULP!
GEE, MR. NATURAL WUZ REALLY PISSED OFF! HE MAY NEVER TALK TO ME AGAIN... I HOPE IT'S WORTH IT!
SHE SHOULD OF BEEN HERE BY NOW...
HEY FLAKES! LOOK WHO I RAN INTO COMIN' UP TH' FRONT STEPS!
HI FLAKEY! AM I LATE!
HI RUTH! OH GOSH NO! NOT AT ALL!
WELL, THEN, MR. NATURAL! WE'LL SEE YA LATER, MAN! UH... DROP BY AGAIN SOME-TIME! HEH HEH
SURE THING! S'LONG, KIDS! HAVE A NICE TIME!
OH NO! DON'T GO!
WHY DONT YOU STAY AWHILE! I'M A BIG FAN OF YOURS, MR. NATURAL! I'D REALLY LIKE TO TALK TO YOU... THAT IS, IF YOU DONT MIND!
!
NOT AT ALL! NOT AT ALL! HEH HEH
LET'S GO IN THE LIVING ROOM WHERE IT'S MORE COMFORTABLE! WOW THIS IS SO EXCITING! IMAGINE, ME MEETING YOU?
TH' MIND BOGGLES! HEH HEH

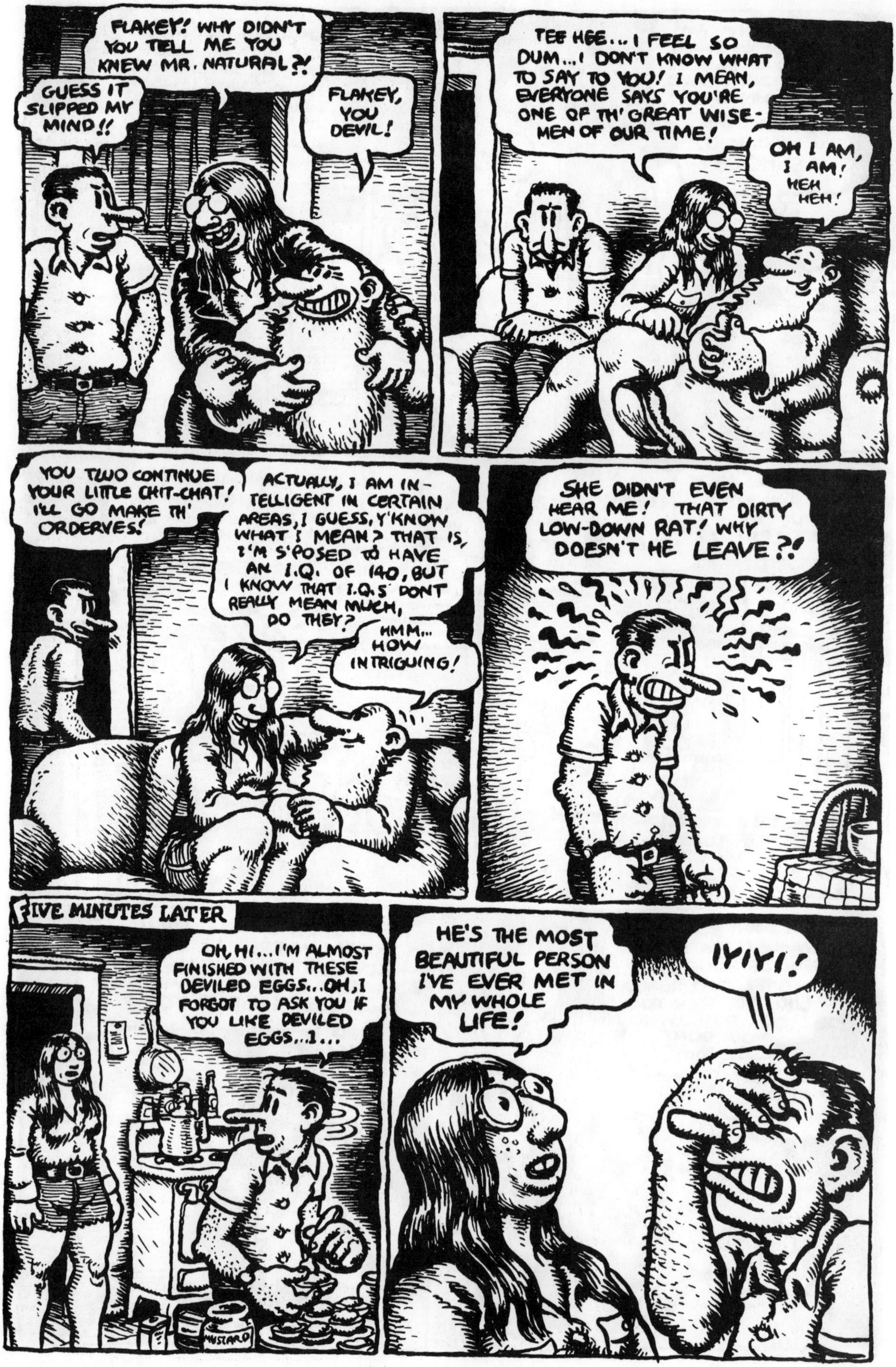
FLAKEY! WHY DIDN'T YOU TELL ME YOU KNEW MR. NATURAL?!
GUESS IT SLIPPED MY MIND!!
FLAKEY, YOU DEVIL!
TEE HEE... I FEEL SO DUM... I DON'T KNOW WHAT TO SAY TO YOU! I MEAN, EVERYONE SAYS YOU'RE ONE OF TH' GREAT WISE-MEN OF OUR TIME!
OH I AM, I AM! HEH HEH!
YOU TWO CONTINUE YOUR LITTLE CHIT-CHAT! I'LL GO MAKE TH' ORDERVES!
ACTUALLY, I AM IN-TELLIGENT IN CERTAIN AREAS, I GUESS, Y'KNOW WHAT I MEAN? THAT IS, I'M S'POSED TO HAVE AN I.Q. OF 140, BUT I KNOW THAT I.Q.S DONT REALLY MEAN MUCH, DO THEY?
HMM... HOW INTRIGUING!
SHE DIDN'T EVEN HEAR ME! THAT DIRTY LOW-DOWN RAT! WHY DOESN'T HE LEAVE?!
FIVE MINUTES LATER
OH, HI... I'M ALMOST FINISHED WITH THESE DEVILED EGGS... OH, I FORGOT TO ASK YOU IF YOU LIKE DEVILED EGGS... I...
MUSTARD
HE'S THE MOST BEAUTIFUL PERSON I'VE EVER MET IN MY WHOLE LIFE!
IYIYI!

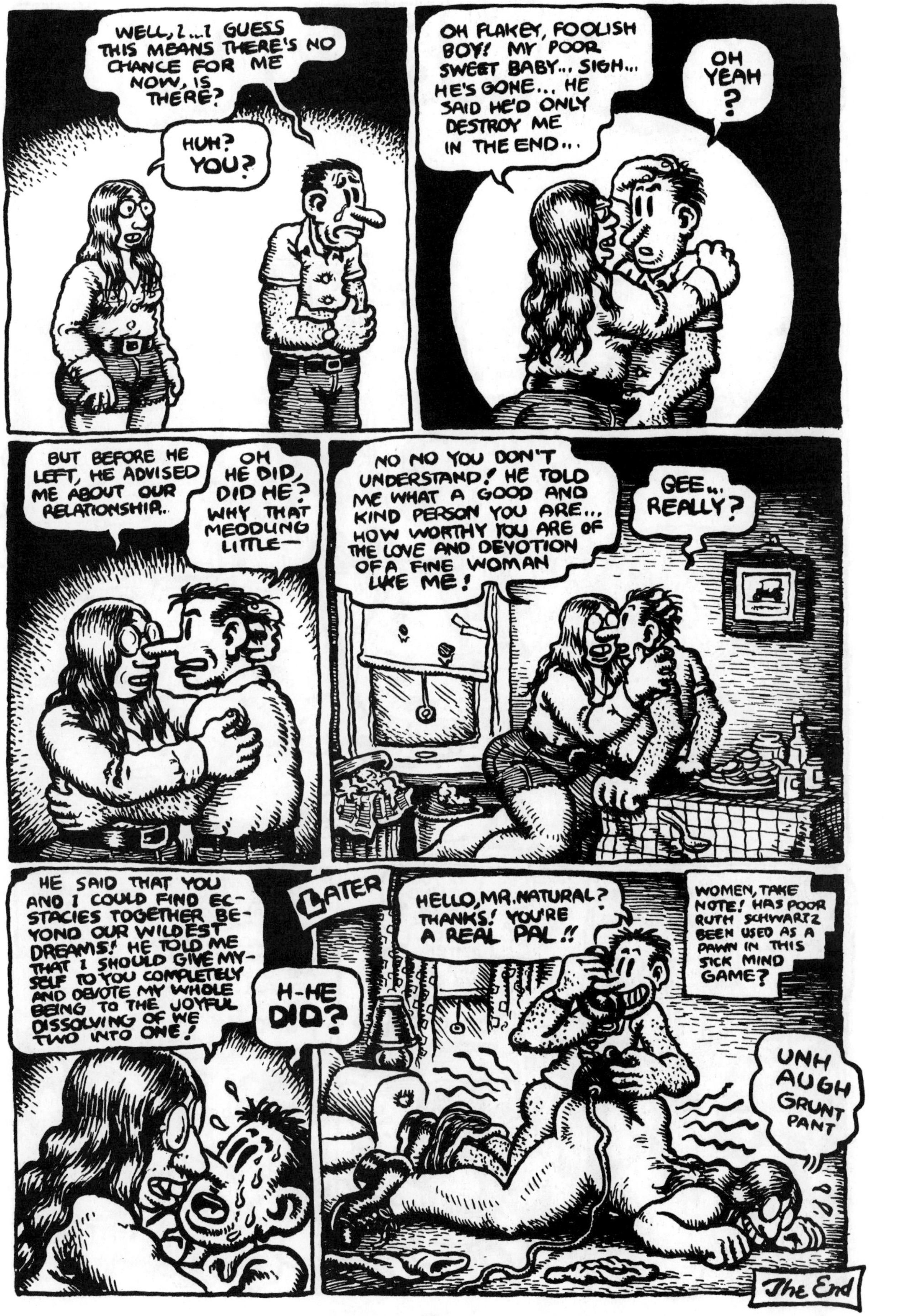
WELL, I...I GUESS THIS MEANS THERE'S NO CHANCE FOR ME NOW, IS THERE?
HUH? YOU?
OH FLAKEY, FOOLISH BOY! MY POOR SWEET BABY... SIGH... HE'S GONE... HE SAID HE'D ONLY DESTROY ME IN THE END...
OH YEAH ?
BUT BEFORE HE LEFT, HE ADVISED ME ABOUT OUR RELATIONSHIP..
OH HE DID, DID HE? WHY THAT MEODUNG LITTLE—
NO NO YOU DON'T UNDERSTAND! HE TOLD ME WHAT A GOOD AND KIND PERSON YOU ARE... HOW WORTHY YOU ARE OF THE LOVE AND DEVOTION OF A FINE WOMAN LIKE ME!
GEE... REALLY?
HE SAID THAT YOU AND I COULD FIND ECSTACIES TOGETHER BEYOND OUR WILDEST DREAMS! HE TOLD ME THAT I SHOULD GIVE MYSELF TO YOU COMPLETELY AND DEVOTE MY WHOLE BEING TO THE JOYFUL DISSOLVING OF WE TWO INTO ONE!
H-HE DID?
LATER
HELLO, MR. NATURAL? THANKS! YOU'RE A REAL PAL!!
WOMEN, TAKE NOTE! HAS POOR RUTH SCHWARTZ BEEN USED AS A PAWN IN THIS SICK MIND GAME?
UNH AUGH GRUNT PANT
The End

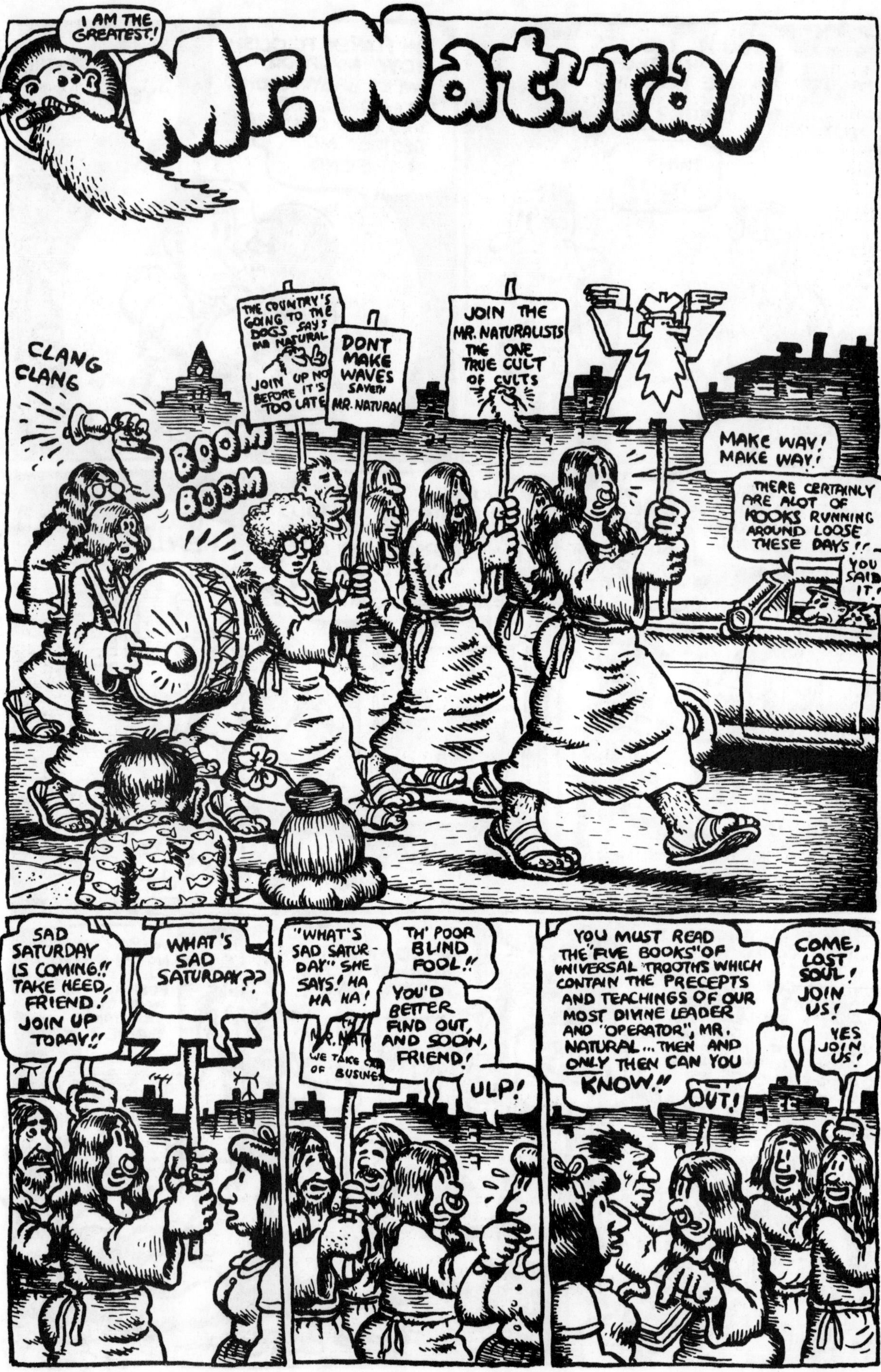
I AM THE GREATEST!
Mr. Natural
THE COUNTRY'S GOING TO THE DOGS SAYS MR NATURAL JOIN UP NOW BEFORE IT'S TOO LATE
DONT MAKE WAVES SAYETH MR. NATURAL
JOIN THE MR. NATURALISTS THE ONE TRUE CULT OF CULTS
CLANG CLANG
BOOM BOOM
MAKE WAY! MAKE WAY!
THERE CERTAINLY ARE ALOT OF KOOKS RUNNING AROUND LOOSE THESE DAYS!!
YOU SAID IT!
SAD SATURDAY IS COMING!! TAKE HEED, FRIEND! JOIN UP TODAY!!
WHAT'S SAD SATURDAY??
"WHAT'S SAD SATURDAY" SHE SAYS! HA HA HA!
TH' POOR BLIND FOOL!!
YOU'D BETTER FIND OUT, AND SOON, FRIEND!
ULP!
YOU MUST READ THE "FIVE BOOKS" OF UNIVERSAL TROOTHS WHICH CONTAIN THE PRECEPTS AND TEACHINGS OF OUR MOST DIVINE LEADER AND "OPERATOR", MR. NATURAL... THEN AND ONLY THEN CAN YOU KNOW!!
OUT!
COME, LOST SOUL! JOIN US!
YES JOIN US!

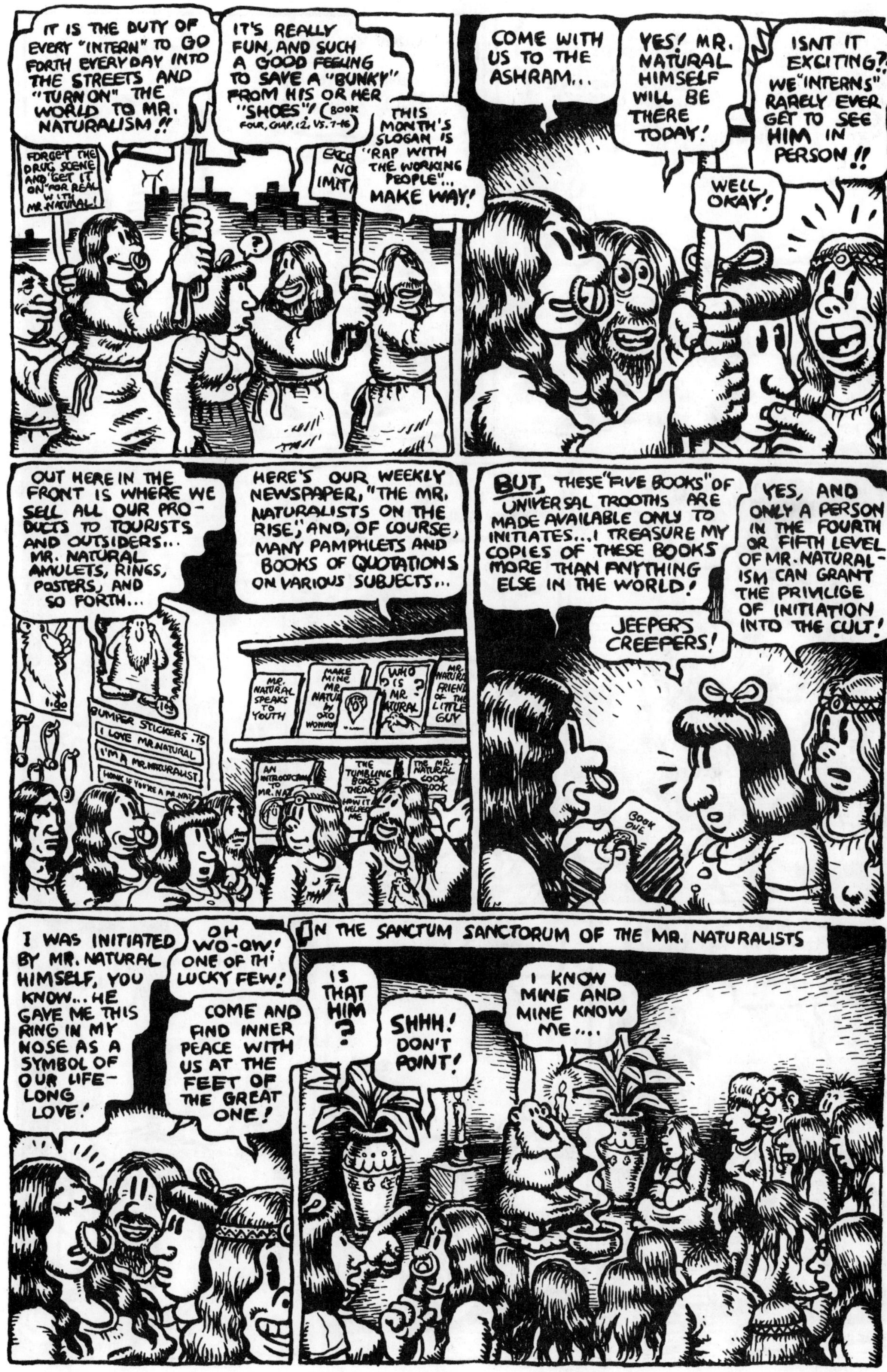
IT IS THE DUTY OF EVERY "INTERN" TO GO FORTH EVERYDAY INTO THE STREETS AND "TURN ON" THE WORLD TO MR. NATURALISM!!
IT'S REALLY FUN, AND SUCH A GOOD FEELING TO SAVE A "BUNKY" FROM HIS OR HER "SHOES"! (BOOK FOUR, CHAP. 12, VS. 7-16)
THIS MONTH'S SLOGAN IS "RAP WITH THE WORKING PEOPLE"... MAKE WAY!
FORGET THE DRUG SCENE AND "GET IT ON" FOR REAL WITH MR. NATURAL!
COME WITH US TO THE ASHRAM...
YES! MR. NATURAL HIMSELF WILL BE THERE TODAY!
ISNT IT EXCITING?! WE "INTERNS" RARELY EVER GET TO SEE HIM IN PERSON!!
WELL, OKAY!
OUT HERE IN THE FRONT IS WHERE WE SELL ALL OUR PRODUCTS TO TOURISTS AND OUTSIDERS... MR. NATURAL AMULETS, RINGS, POSTERS, AND SO FORTH...
HERE'S OUR WEEKLY NEWSPAPER, "THE MR. NATURALISTS ON THE RISE," AND, OF COURSE, MANY PAMPHLETS AND BOOKS OF QUOTATIONS ON VARIOUS SUBJECTS...
BUMPER STICKERS .75
I LOVE MR. NATURAL
I'M A MR. NATURALIST
MR. NATURAL SPEAKS TO YOUTH
MAKE MINE MR. NATURAL
WHO IS MR. NATURAL?
MR. NATURAL FRIEND OF THE LITTLE GUY
THE TUMBLING BOXES THEORY
THE MR. NATURAL COOK BOOK
HOW IT HELPED ME
BUT, THESE "FIVE BOOKS" OF UNIVERSAL TROOTHS ARE MADE AVAILABLE ONLY TO INITIATES... I TREASURE MY COPIES OF THESE BOOKS MORE THAN ANYTHING ELSE IN THE WORLD!
YES, AND ONLY A PERSON IN THE FOURTH OR FIFTH LEVEL OF MR. NATURALISM CAN GRANT THE PRIVILIGE OF INITIATION INTO THE CULT!
JEEPERS CREEPERS!
BOOK ONE
I WAS INITIATED BY MR. NATURAL HIMSELF, YOU KNOW... HE GAVE ME THIS RING IN MY NOSE AS A SYMBOL OF OUR LIFE-LONG LOVE!
OH WO-OW! ONE OF TH' LUCKY FEW!
COME AND FIND INNER PEACE WITH US AT THE FEET OF THE GREAT ONE!
IN THE SANCTUM SANCTORUM OF THE MR. NATURALISTS
IS THAT HIM?
SHHH! DON'T POINT!
I KNOW MINE AND MINE KNOW ME....

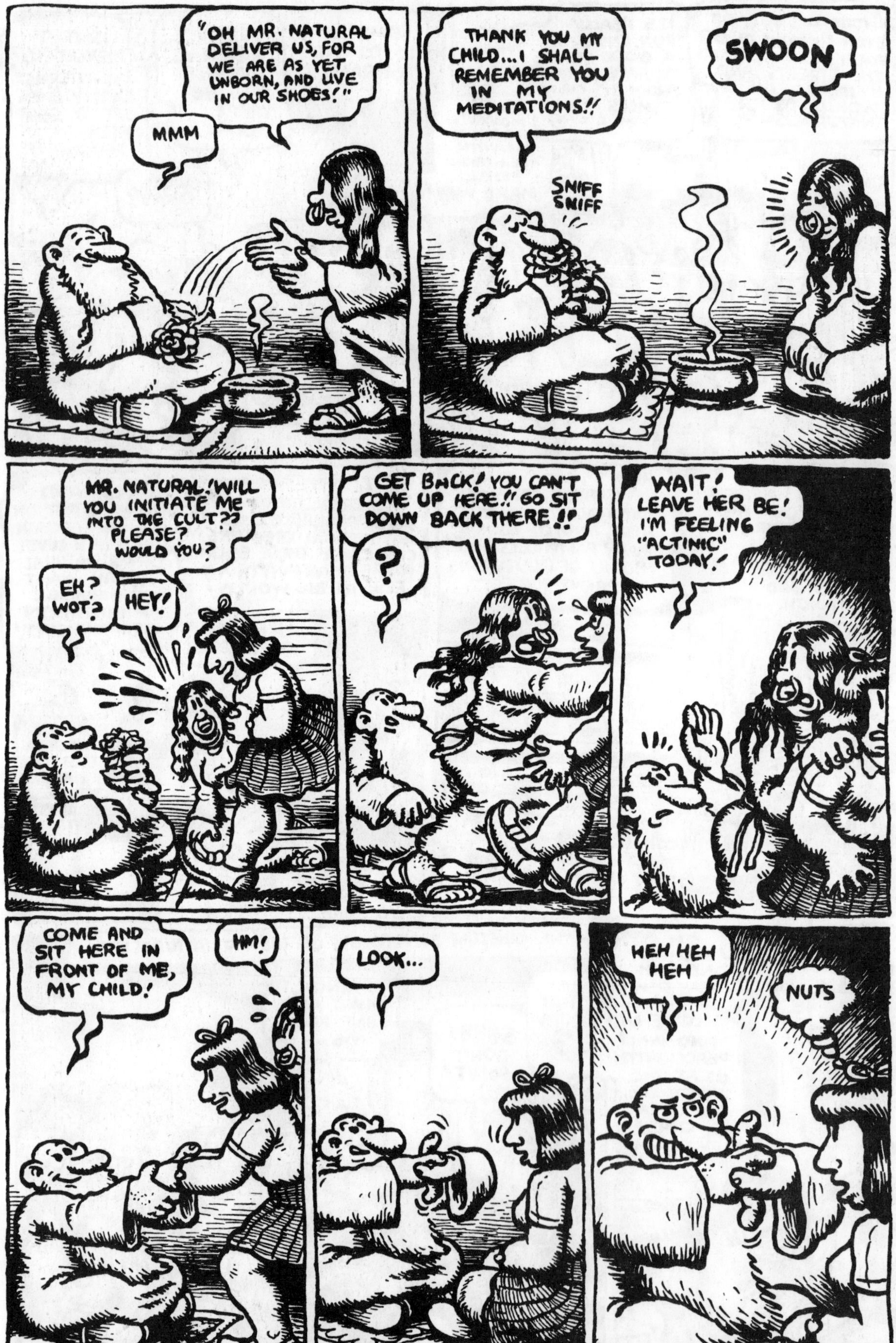
"OH MR. NATURAL DELIVER US, FOR WE ARE AS YET UNBORN, AND LIVE IN OUR SHOES!"
MMM
THANK YOU MY CHILD...I SHALL REMEMBER YOU IN MY MEDITATIONS!!
SNIFF SNIFF
SWOON
MR. NATURAL! WILL YOU INITIATE ME INTO THE CULT?? PLEASE? WOULD YOU?
EH? WOT?
HEY!
GET BACK! YOU CAN'T COME UP HERE!! GO SIT DOWN BACK THERE!!
?
WAIT! LEAVE HER BE! I'M FEELING "ACTINIC" TODAY!
COME AND SIT HERE IN FRONT OF ME, MY CHILD!
HM!
LOOK...
HEH HEH HEH
NUTS

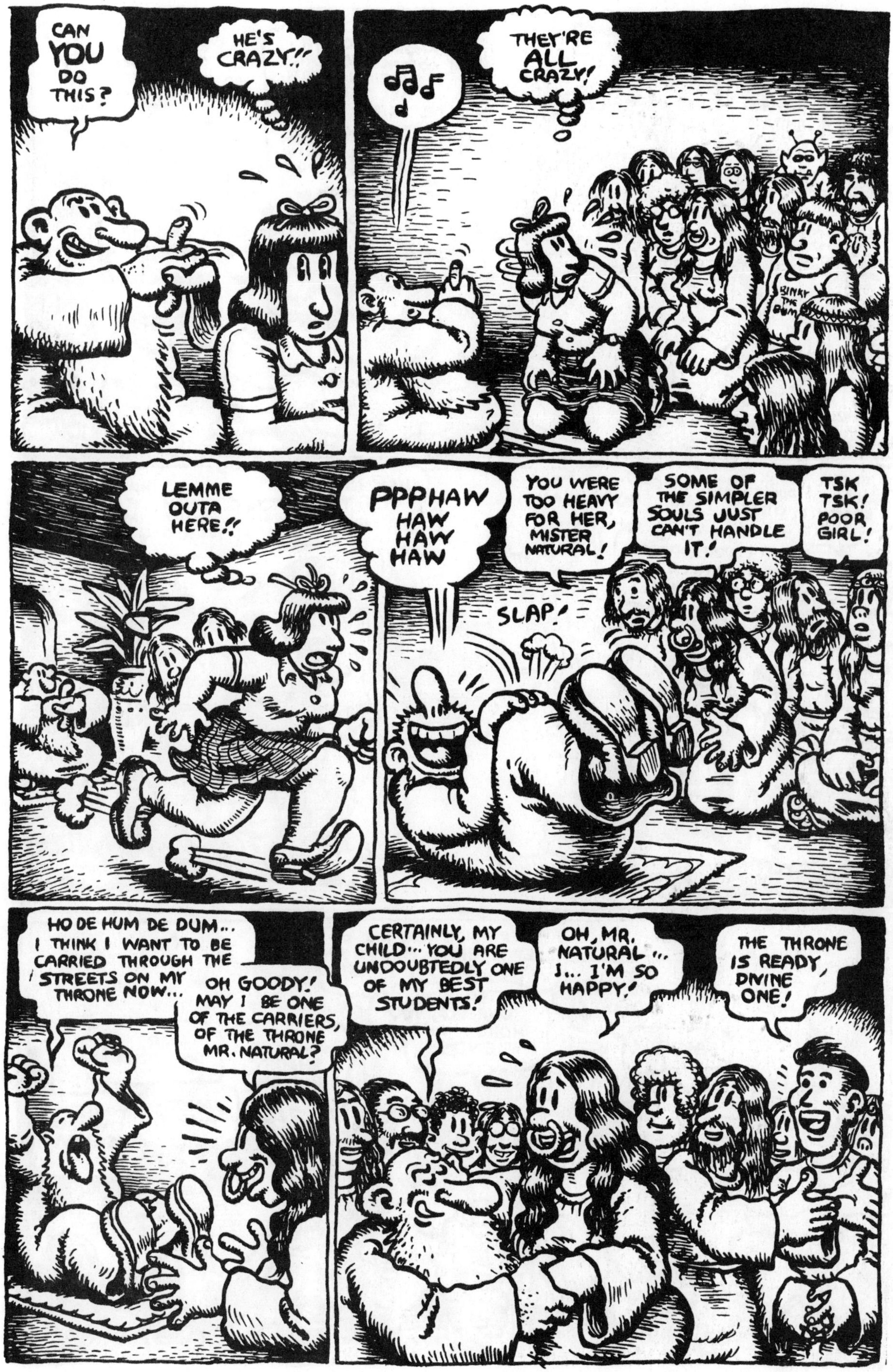

CAN YOU DO THIS?
HE'S CRAZY!!
THEY'RE ALL CRAZY!
LEMME OUTA HERE!!
PPPHAW HAW HAW HAW
YOU WERE TOO HEAVY FOR HER, MISTER NATURAL!
SOME OF THE SIMPLER SOULS JUST CAN'T HANDLE IT!
TSK TSK! POOR GIRL!
SLAP!
HO DE HUM DE DUM... I THINK I WANT TO BE CARRIED THROUGH THE STREETS ON MY THRONE NOW...
OH GOODY! MAY I BE ONE OF THE CARRIERS, OF THE THRONE MR. NATURAL?
CERTAINLY, MY CHILD... YOU ARE UNDOUBTEDLY ONE OF MY BEST STUDENTS!
OH, MR. NATURAL... I... I'M SO HAPPY!
THE THRONE IS READY, DIVINE ONE!

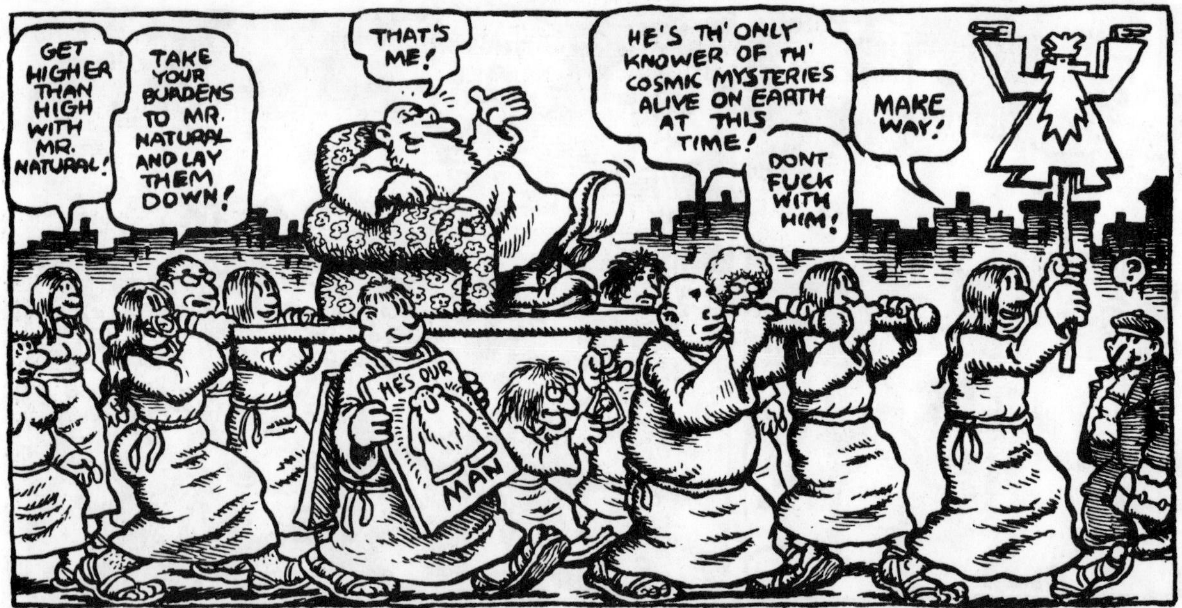
GET HIGHER THAN HIGH WITH MR. NATURAL!
TAKE YOUR BURDENS TO MR. NATURAL AND LAY THEM DOWN!
THAT'S ME!
HE'S TH' ONLY KNOWER OF TH' COSMIC MYSTERIES ALIVE ON EARTH AT THIS TIME!
DONT FUCK WITH HIM!
MAKE WAY!
HE'S OUR MAN
?

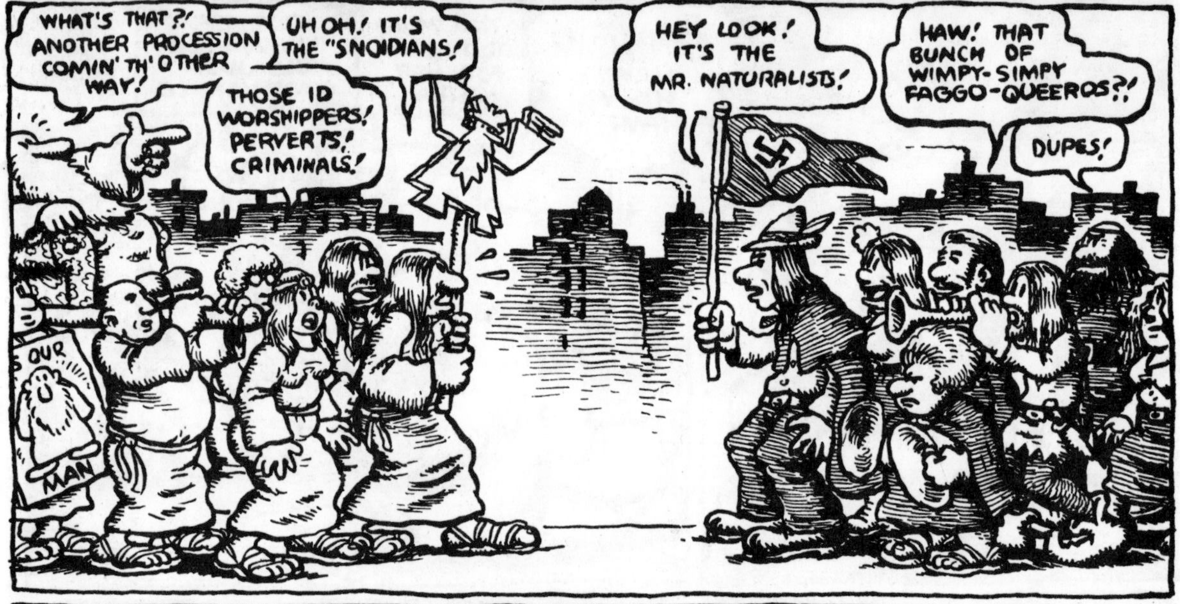
WHAT'S THAT?! ANOTHER PROCESSION COMIN' TH' OTHER WAY!
UH OH! IT'S THE "SNOIDIANS"!
THOSE ID WORSHIPPERS! PERVERTS! CRIMINALS!
HEY LOOK! IT'S THE MR. NATURALISTS!
HAW! THAT BUNCH OF WIMPY-SIMPY FAGGO-QUEEROS?!
DUPES!
OUR MAN

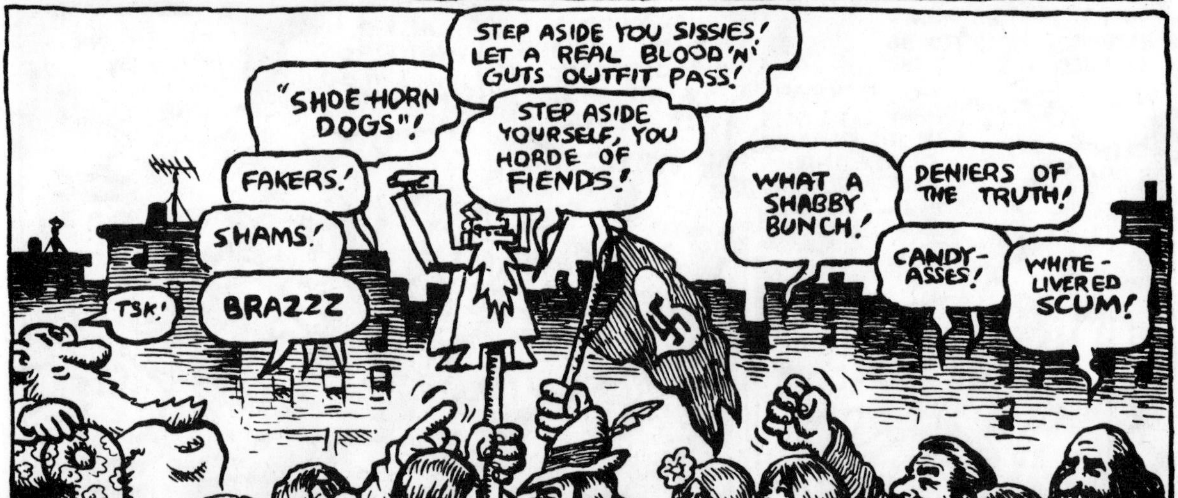
STEP ASIDE YOU SISSIES! LET A REAL BLOOD 'N' GUTS OUTFIT PASS!
"SHOE-HORN DOGS"!
STEP ASIDE YOURSELF, YOU HORDE OF FIENDS!
FAKERS!
SHAMS!
TSK!
BRAZZZ
WHAT A SHABBY BUNCH!
DENIERS OF THE TRUTH!
CANDY-ASSES!
WHITE-LIVERED SCUM!
OUR

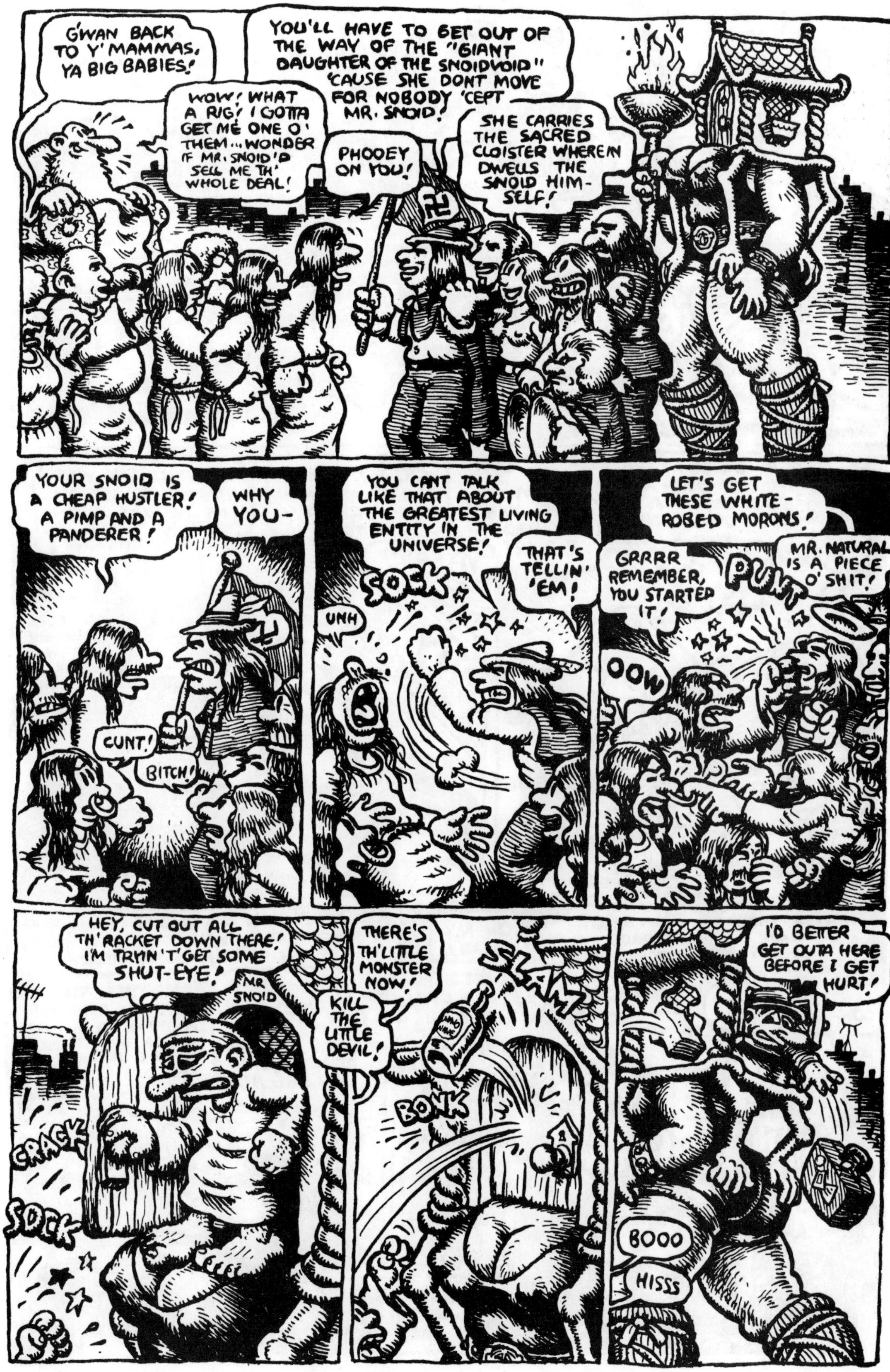

G'WAN BACK TO Y' MAMMAS, YA BIG BABIES!
YOU'LL HAVE TO GET OUT OF THE WAY OF THE "GIANT DAUGHTER OF THE SNOIDVOID" 'CAUSE SHE DONT MOVE FOR NOBODY 'CEPT MR. SNOID!
WOW! WHAT A RIG! I GOTTA GET ME ONE O' THEM... WONDER IF MR. SNOID'D SELL ME TH' WHOLE DEAL!
PHOOEY ON YOU!
SHE CARRIES THE SACRED CLOISTER WHEREIN DWELLS THE SNOID HIM-SELF!
YOUR SNOID IS A CHEAP HUSTLER! A PIMP AND A PANDERER!
WHY YOU-
CUNT!
BITCH!
YOU CANT TALK LIKE THAT ABOUT THE GREATEST LIVING ENTITY IN THE UNIVERSE!
THAT'S TELLIN' 'EM!
SOCK
UNH
LET'S GET THESE WHITE-ROBED MORONS!
GRRRR REMEMBER, YOU STARTED IT!
MR. NATURAL IS A PIECE O' SHIT!
PUNT
OOW
HEY, CUT OUT ALL TH' RACKET DOWN THERE! I'M TRYIN' T' GET SOME SHUT-EYE!
MR. SNOID
CRACK
SOCK
THERE'S TH' LITTLE MONSTER NOW!
KILL THE LITTLE DEVIL!
SLAM
BONK
I'D BETTER GET OUTA HERE BEFORE I GET HURT!
BOOO
HISSS

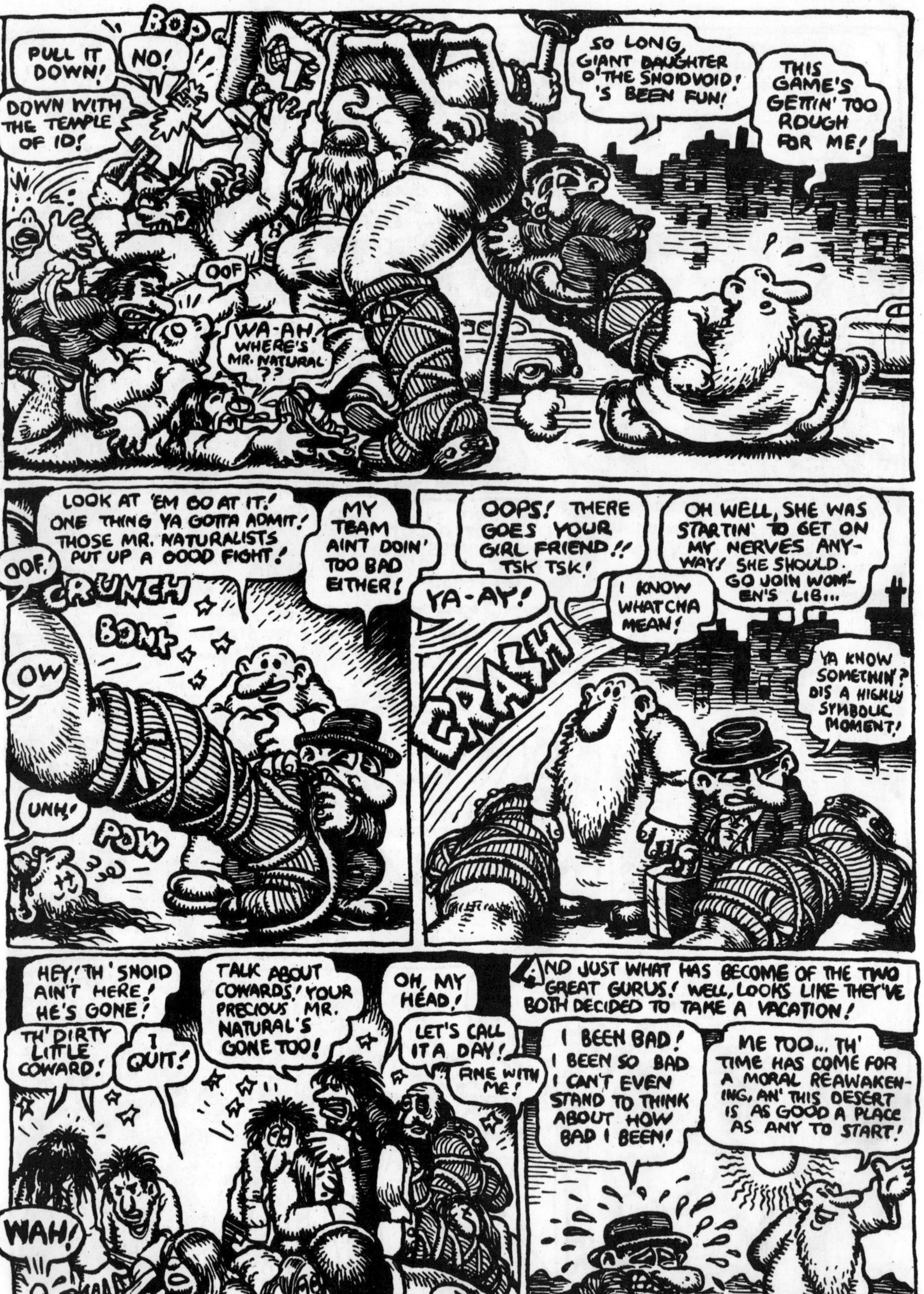
BOP
PULL IT DOWN!
NO!
DOWN WITH THE TEMPLE OF ID!
OOF
WA-AH! WHERE'S MR. NATURAL ??
SO LONG, GIANT DAUGHTER O' THE SNOIDVOID! 'S BEEN FUN!
THIS GAME'S GETTIN' TOO ROUGH FOR ME!
LOOK AT 'EM GO AT IT! ONE THING YA GOTTA ADMIT! THOSE MR. NATURALISTS PUT UP A GOOD FIGHT!
MY TEAM AINT DOIN' TOO BAD EITHER!
OOF
CRUNCH
BONK
OW
UNH!
POW
OOPS! THERE GOES YOUR GIRL FRIEND!! TSK TSK!
OH WELL, SHE WAS STARTIN' TO GET ON MY NERVES ANY-WAY! SHE SHOULD GO JOIN WOMEN'S LIB...
YA-AY!
I KNOW WHATCHA MEAN!
CRASH
YA KNOW SOMETHIN'? DIS A HIGHLY SYMBOLIC MOMENT!
HEY! TH' SNOID AIN'T HERE! HE'S GONE!
TH' DIRTY LITTLE COWARD!
I QUIT!
TALK ABOUT COWARDS! YOUR PRECIOUS MR. NATURAL'S GONE TOO!
OH, MY HEAD!
LET'S CALL IT A DAY!
FINE WITH ME!
WAH!
AND JUST WHAT HAS BECOME OF THE TWO GREAT GURUS! WELL, LOOKS LIKE THEY'VE BOTH DECIDED TO TAKE A VACATION!
I BEEN BAD! I BEEN SO BAD I CAN'T EVEN STAND TO THINK ABOUT HOW BAD I BEEN!
ME TOO... TH' TIME HAS COME FOR A MORAL REAWAKENING, AN' THIS DESERT IS AS GOOD A PLACE AS ANY TO START!
THE END

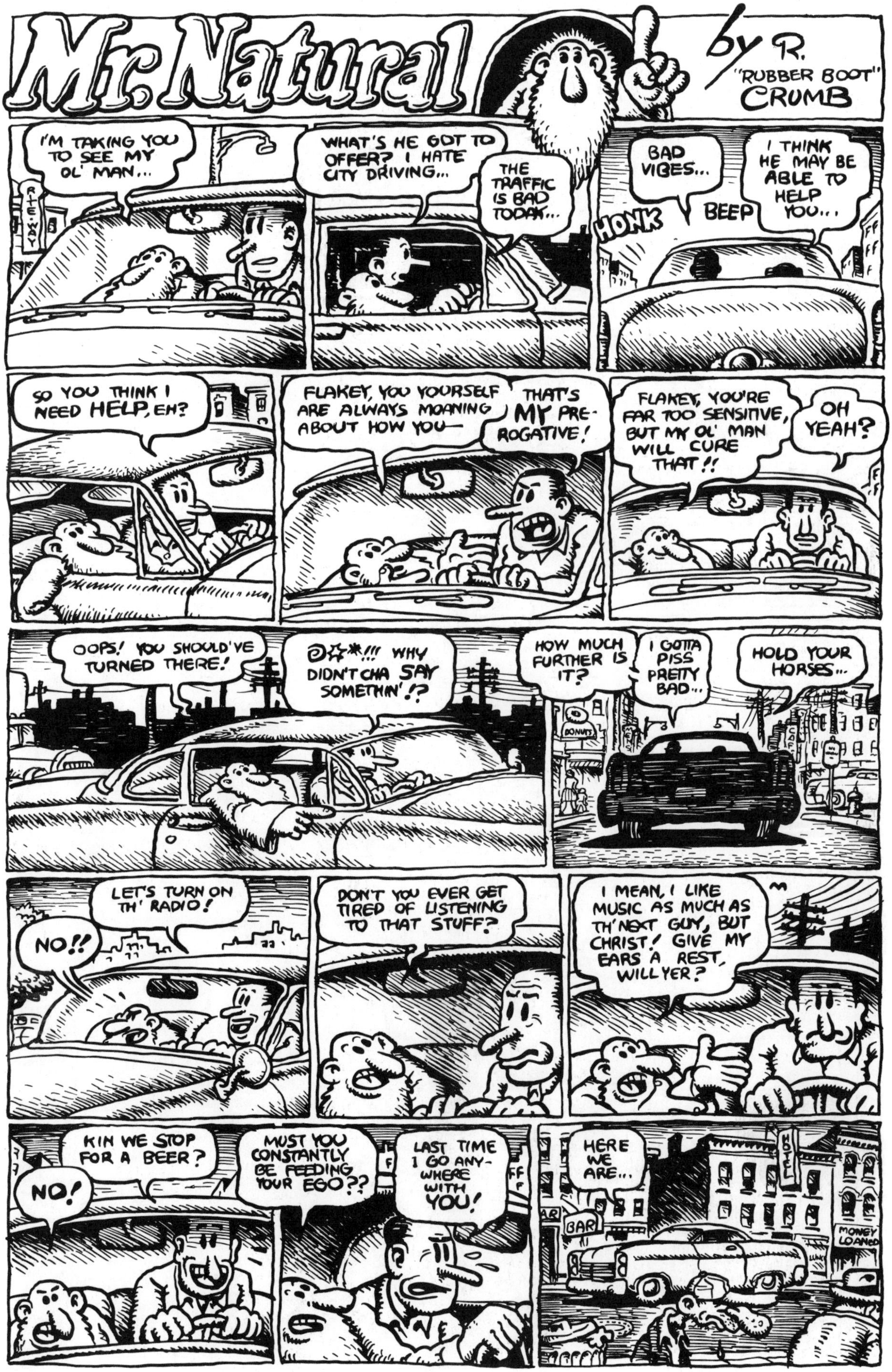
Mr. Natural
by R. "RUBBER BOOT" CRUMB
RITE-WAY
I'M TAKING YOU TO SEE MY OL' MAN...
WHAT'S HE GOT TO OFFER? I HATE CITY DRIVING...
THE TRAFFIC IS BAD TODAY...
BAD VIBES...
HONK
BEEP
I THINK HE MAY BE ABLE TO HELP YOU...
SO YOU THINK I NEED HELP, EH?
FLAKEY, YOU YOURSELF ARE ALWAYS MOANING ABOUT HOW YOU—
THAT'S MY PRE-ROGATIVE!
FLAKEY, YOU'RE FAR TOO SENSITIVE, BUT MY OL' MAN WILL CURE THAT!!
OH YEAH?
OOPS! YOU SHOULD'VE TURNED THERE!
@☆*!!! WHY DIDN'TCHA SAY SOMETHIN'!?
HOW MUCH FURTHER IS IT?
I GOTTA PISS PRETTY BAD...
HOLD YOUR HORSES...
BONUS
LET'S TURN ON TH' RADIO!
NO!!
DON'T YOU EVER GET TIRED OF LISTENING TO THAT STUFF?
I MEAN, I LIKE MUSIC AS MUCH AS TH' NEXT GUY, BUT CHRIST! GIVE MY EARS A REST, WILL YER?
KIN WE STOP FOR A BEER?
NO!
MUST YOU CONSTANTLY BE FEEDING YOUR EGO??
LAST TIME I GO ANY-WHERE WITH YOU!
HERE WE ARE...
HOTEL
BAR
MONEY LOANED

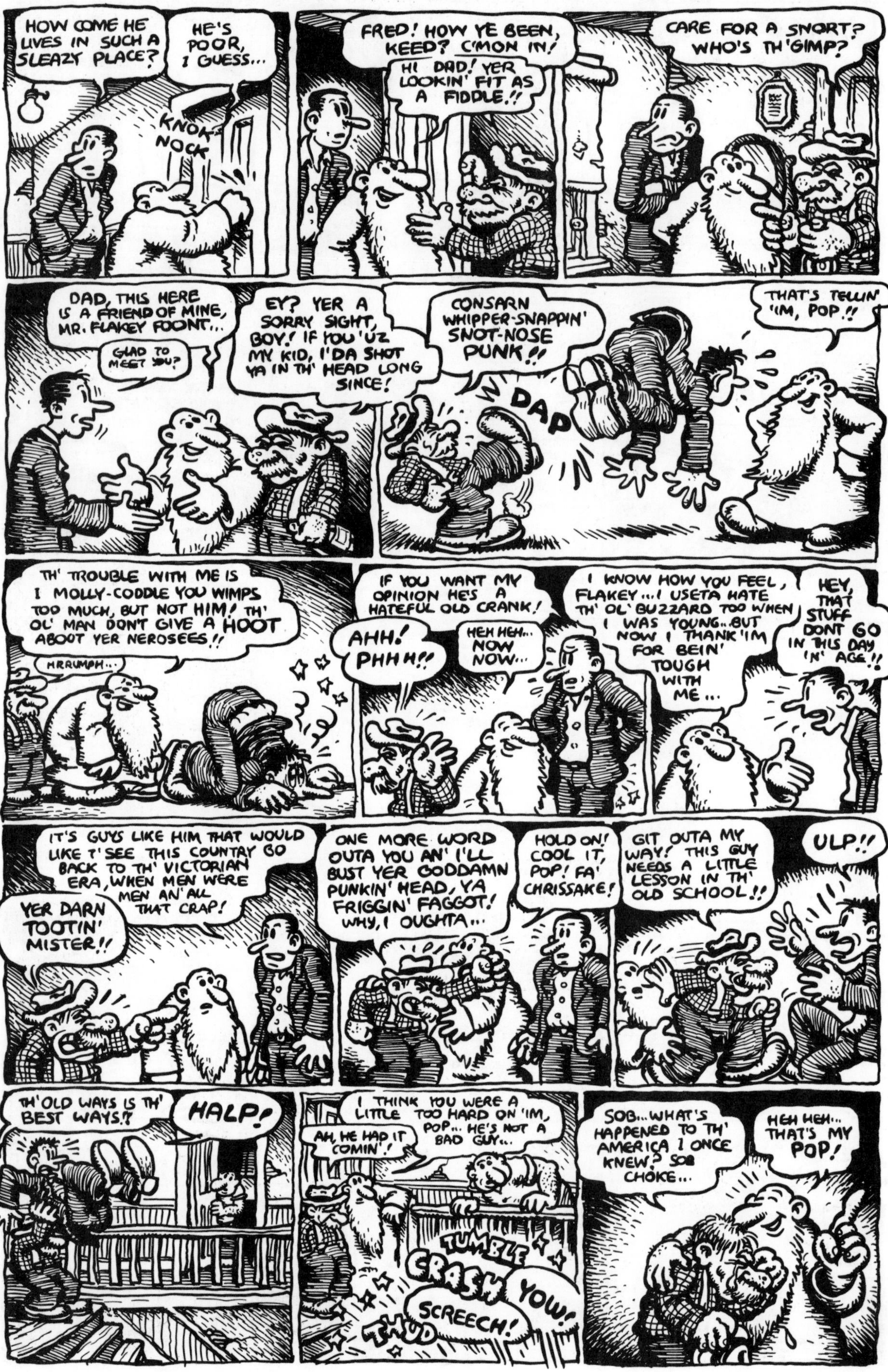

HOW COME HE LIVES IN SUCH A SLEAZY PLACE?
HE'S POOR, I GUESS...
KNOK KNOCK
FRED! HOW YE BEEN, KEED? C'MON IN!
HI DAD! YER LOOKIN' FIT AS A FIDDLE!!
CARE FOR A SNORT? WHO'S TH'GIMP?
DAD, THIS HERE IS A FRIEND OF MINE, MR. FLAKEY FOONT...
GLAD TO MEET YOU?
EY? YER A SORRY SIGHT, BOY! IF YOU'UZ MY KID, I'DA SHOT YA IN TH' HEAD LONG SINCE!
CONSARN WHIPPER-SNAPPIN' SNOT-NOSE PUNK!!
DAP
THAT'S TELLIN' 'IM, POP!!
TH' TROUBLE WITH ME IS I MOLLY-CODDLE YOU WIMPS TOO MUCH, BUT NOT HIM! TH' OL' MAN DON'T GIVE A HOOT ABOUT YER NEROSEES!!
HRRUMPH...
IF YOU WANT MY OPINION HE'S A HATEFUL OLD CRANK!
AHH! PHHH!!
HEH HEH... NOW NOW...
I KNOW HOW YOU FEEL, FLAKEY...I USETA HATE TH' OL' BUZZARD TOO WHEN I WAS YOUNG...BUT NOW I THANK 'IM FOR BEIN' TOUGH WITH ME...
HEY, THAT STUFF DONT GO IN THIS DAY 'N' AGE!!
IT'S GUYS LIKE HIM THAT WOULD LIKE T' SEE THIS COUNTRY GO BACK TO TH' VICTORIAN ERA, WHEN MEN WERE MEN AN' ALL THAT CRAP!
YER DARN TOOTIN' MISTER!!
ONE MORE WORD OUTA YOU AN' I'LL BUST YER GODDAMN PUNKIN' HEAD, YA FRIGGIN' FAGGOT! WHY, I OUGHTA...
HOLD ON! COOL IT, POP! FA' CHRISSAKE!
GIT OUTA MY WAY! THIS GUY NEEDS A LITTLE LESSON IN TH' OLD SCHOOL!!
ULP!!
TH'OLD WAYS IS TH' BEST WAYS!?
HALP!
I THINK YOU WERE A LITTLE TOO HARD ON 'IM, POP... HE'S NOT A BAD GUY...
AH, HE HAD IT COMIN'!
TUMBLE
CRASH
YOW!
SCREECH!
THUD
SOB...WHAT'S HAPPENED TO TH' AMERICA I ONCE KNEW? SOB CHOKE...
HEH HEH... THAT'S MY POP!

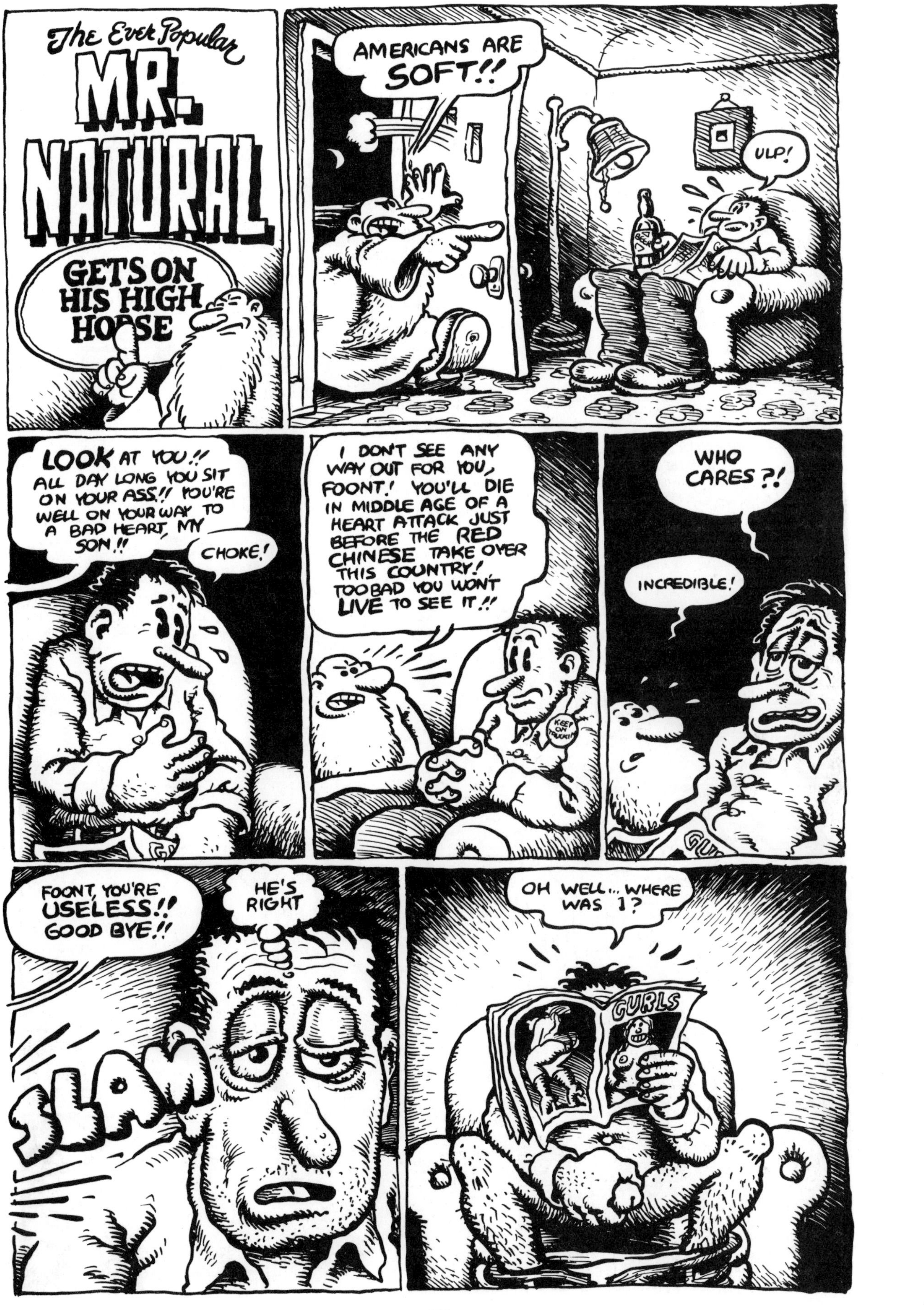

The Ever Popular
MR. NATURAL
GETS ON HIS HIGH HORSE
AMERICANS ARE SOFT!!
ULP!
BEER
LOOK AT YOU!! ALL DAY LONG YOU SIT ON YOUR ASS!! YOU'RE WELL ON YOUR WAY TO A BAD HEART, MY SON!!
CHOKE!
I DON'T SEE ANY WAY OUT FOR YOU, FOONT! YOU'LL DIE IN MIDDLE AGE OF A HEART ATTACK JUST BEFORE THE RED CHINESE TAKE OVER THIS COUNTRY! TOO BAD YOU WON'T LIVE TO SEE IT!!
KEEP ON TRUCKIN
WHO CARES?!
INCREDIBLE!
FOONT, YOU'RE USELESS!! GOOD BYE!!
HE'S RIGHT
SLAM
OH WELL... WHERE WAS I?
GURLS

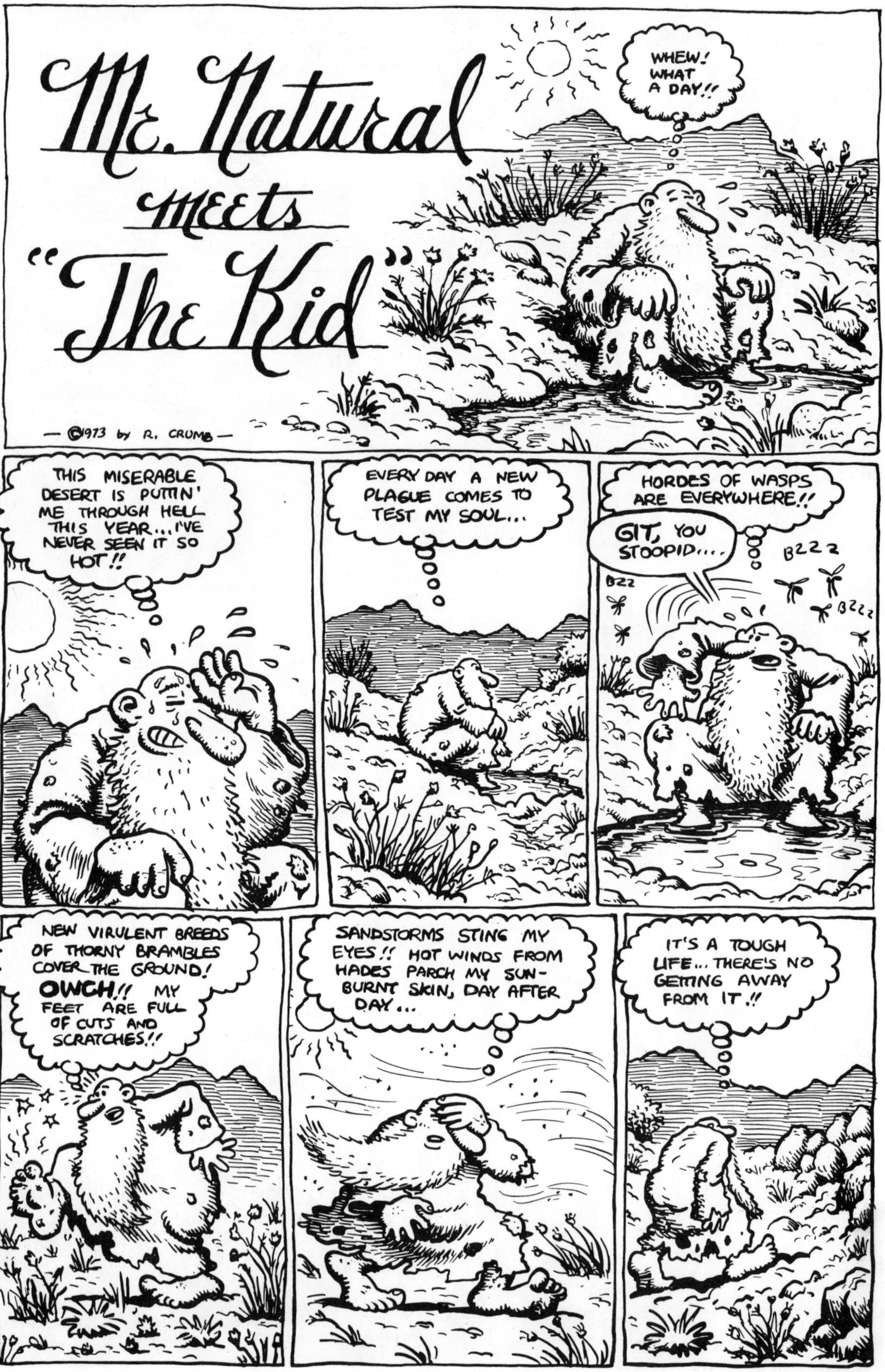
Mr. Natural meets "The Kid"
WHEW! WHAT A DAY!!
©1973 by R. CRUMB
THIS MISERABLE DESERT IS PUTTIN' ME THROUGH HELL THIS YEAR... I'VE NEVER SEEN IT SO HOT!!
EVERY DAY A NEW PLAGUE COMES TO TEST MY SOUL...
HORDES OF WASPS ARE EVERYWHERE!!
GIT, YOU STOOPID....
BZZZ
BZZ
BZZZ
NEW VIRULENT BREEDS OF THORNY BRAMBLES COVER THE GROUND! OWCH!! MY FEET ARE FULL OF CUTS AND SCRATCHES!!
SANDSTORMS STING MY EYES!! HOT WINDS FROM HADES PARCH MY SUN-BURNT SKIN, DAY AFTER DAY...
IT'S A TOUGH LIFE... THERE'S NO GETTING AWAY FROM IT.!!

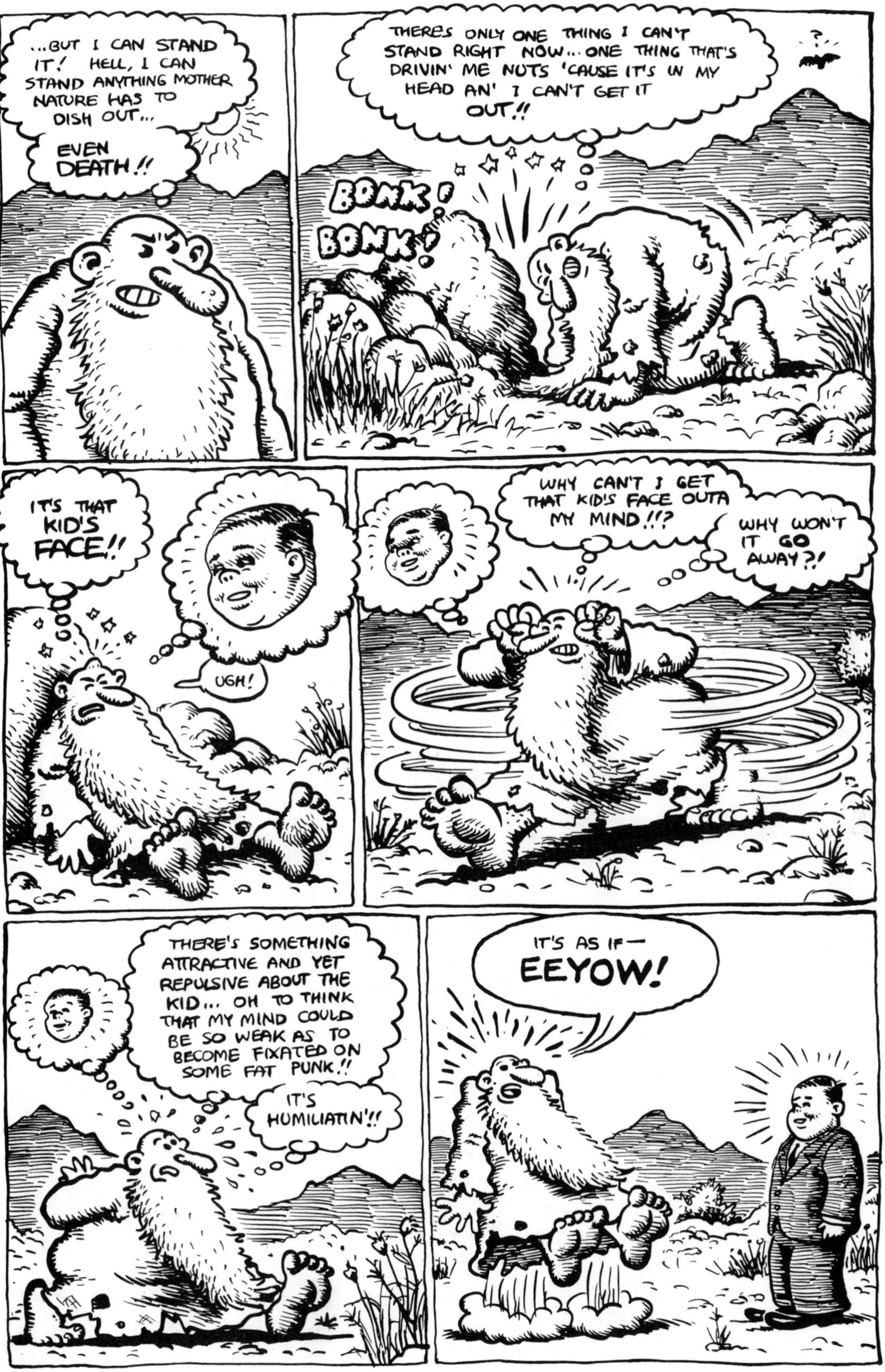

...BUT I CAN STAND IT! HELL, I CAN STAND ANYTHING MOTHER NATURE HAS TO DISH OUT...
EVEN DEATH!!
THERE'S ONLY ONE THING I CAN'T STAND RIGHT NOW... ONE THING THAT'S DRIVIN' ME NUTS 'CAUSE IT'S IN MY HEAD AN' I CAN'T GET IT OUT!!
?
BONK!
BONK!
IT'S THAT KID'S FACE!!
UGH!
WHY CAN'T I GET THAT KID'S FACE OUTA MY MIND!!?
WHY WON'T IT GO AWAY?!
THERE'S SOMETHING ATTRACTIVE AND YET REPULSIVE ABOUT THE KID... OH TO THINK THAT MY MIND COULD BE SO WEAK AS TO BECOME FIXATED ON SOME FAT PUNK!!
IT'S HUMILIATIN'!!
IT'S AS IF—
EEYOW!

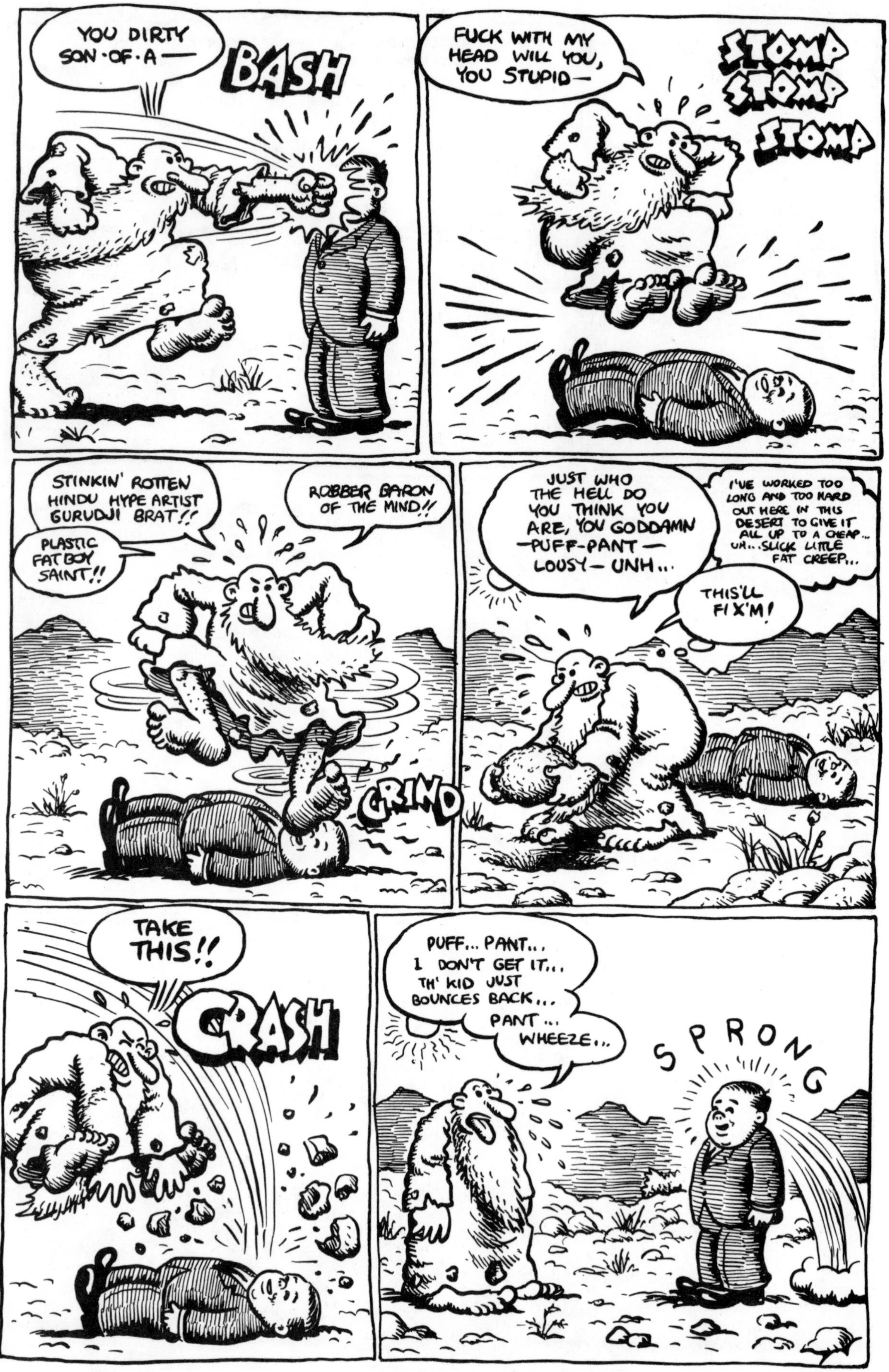

YOU DIRTY SON-OF-A —
BASH
FUCK WITH MY HEAD WILL YOU, YOU STUPID—
STOMP STOMP STOMP
STINKIN' ROTTEN HINDU HYPE ARTIST GURUDJI BRAT!!
PLASTIC FATBOY SAINT!!
ROBBER BARON OF THE MIND!!
GRIND
JUST WHO THE HELL DO YOU THINK YOU ARE, YOU GODDAMN —PUFF-PANT— LOUSY— UNH...
I'VE WORKED TOO LONG AND TOO HARD OUT HERE IN THIS DESERT TO GIVE IT ALL UP TO A CHEAP... UH... SLICK LITTLE FAT CREEP...
THIS'LL FIX'M!
TAKE THIS!!
CRASH
PUFF... PANT... I DON'T GET IT... TH' KID JUST BOUNCES BACK... PANT... WHEEZE...
SPRONG

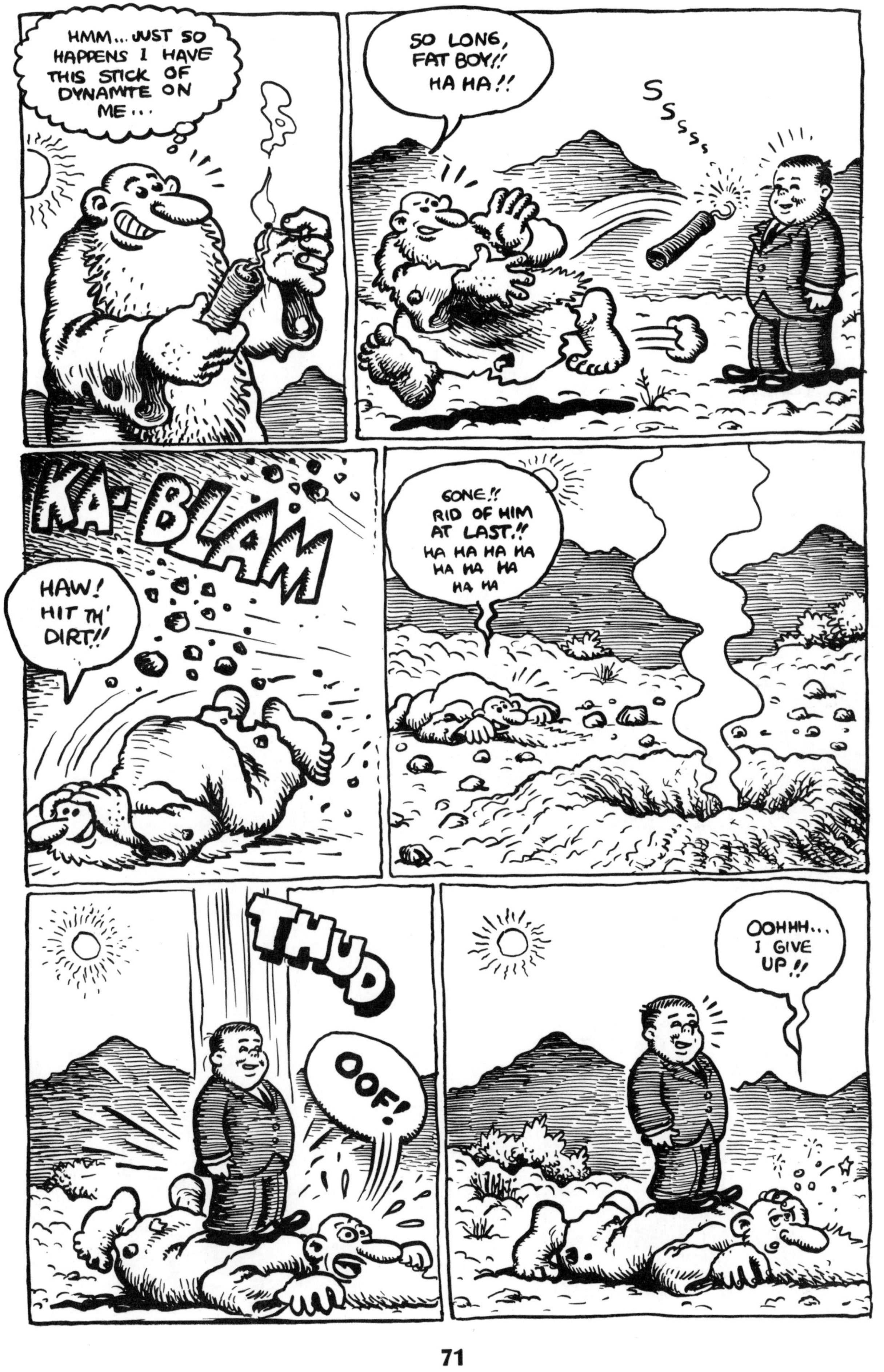
HMM... JUST SO HAPPENS I HAVE THIS STICK OF DYNAMITE ON ME...
SO LONG, FAT BOY!! HA HA!!
SSsss
KA-BLAM
HAW! HIT TH' DIRT!!
GONE!! RID OF HIM AT LAST!! HA HA HA HA HA HA HA HA HA
THUD
OOF!
OOHHH... I GIVE UP!!

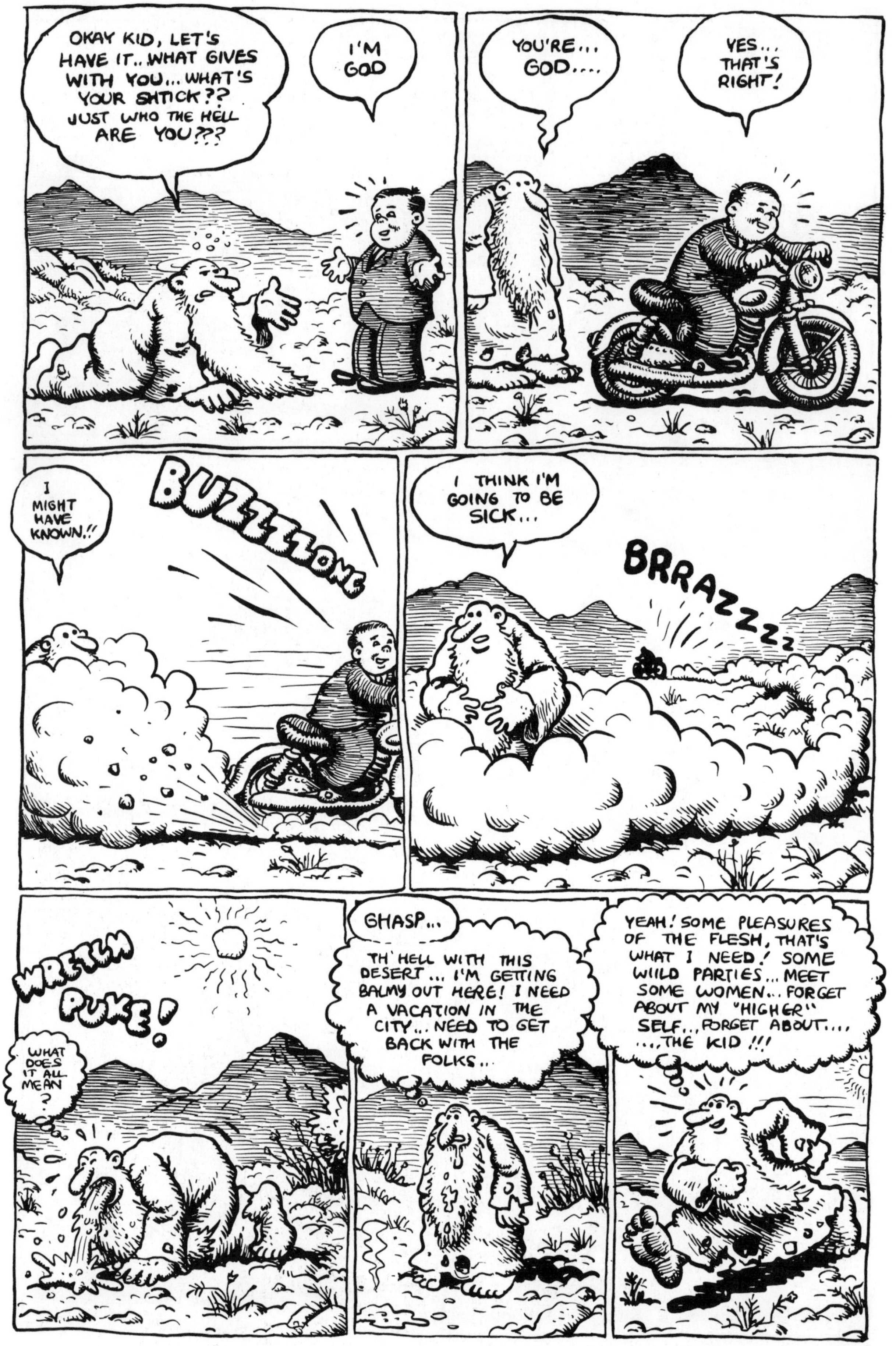

OKAY KID, LET'S HAVE IT.. WHAT GIVES WITH YOU... WHAT'S YOUR SHTICK?? JUST WHO THE HELL ARE YOU???
I'M GOD
YOU'RE... GOD....
YES... THAT'S RIGHT!
I MIGHT HAVE KNOWN!!
BUZZZZZONG
I THINK I'M GOING TO BE SICK...
BRRAZZZZZ
WRETCH
PUKE!
WHAT DOES IT ALL MEAN ?
GHASP...
TH' HELL WITH THIS DESERT... I'M GETTING BALMY OUT HERE! I NEED A VACATION IN THE CITY... NEED TO GET BACK WITH THE FOLKS...
YEAH! SOME PLEASURES OF THE FLESH, THAT'S WHAT I NEED! SOME WILD PARTIES... MEET SOME WOMEN... FORGET ABOUT MY "HIGHER" SELF... FORGET ABOUT.... ....THE KID!!!

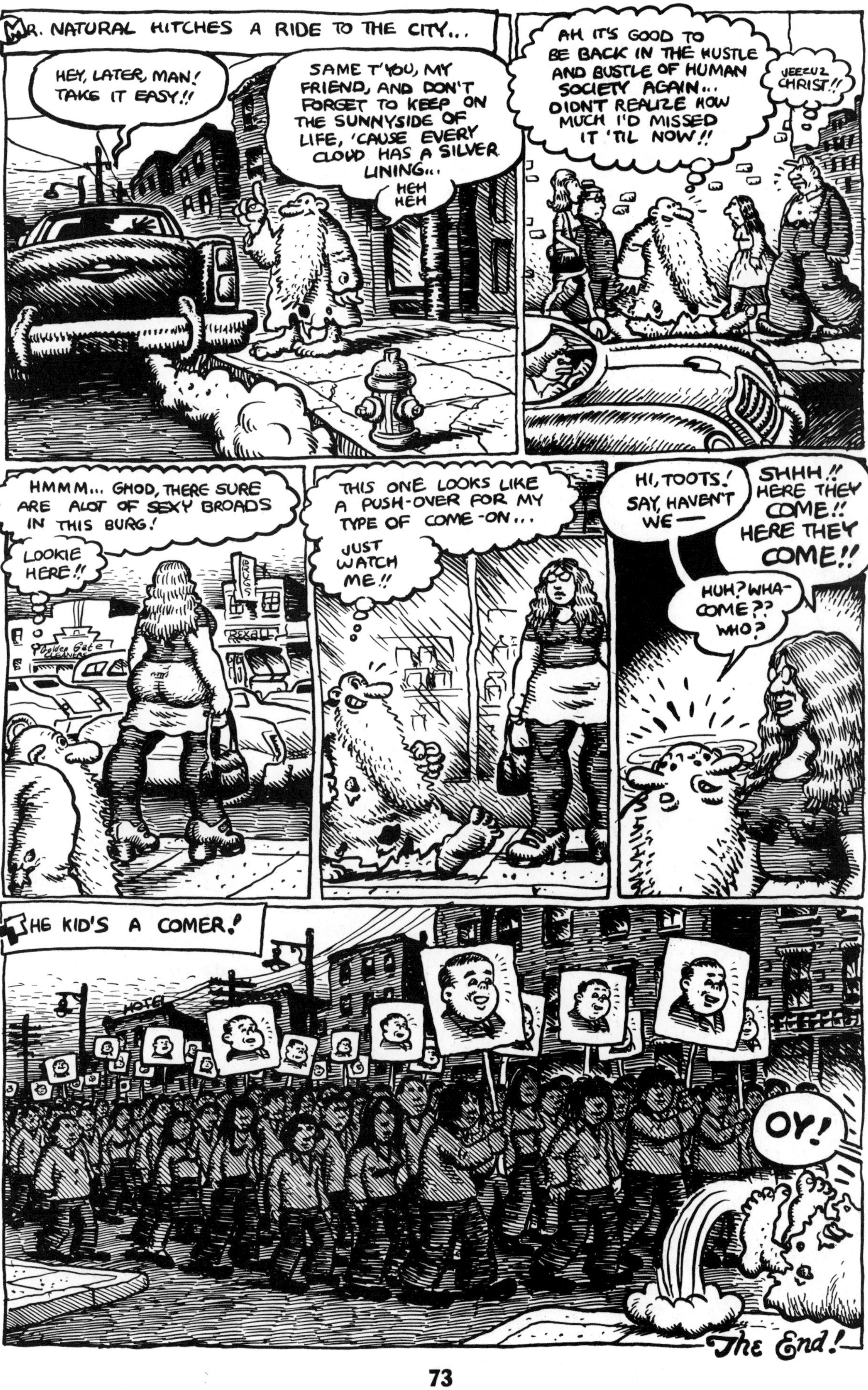

MR. NATURAL HITCHES A RIDE TO THE CITY...
HEY, LATER, MAN! TAKE IT EASY!!
SAME T'YOU, MY FRIEND, AND DON'T FORGET TO KEEP ON THE SUNNYSIDE OF LIFE, 'CAUSE EVERY CLOUD HAS A SILVER LINING...
HEH HEH
AH IT'S GOOD TO BE BACK IN THE HUSTLE AND BUSTLE OF HUMAN SOCIETY AGAIN... DIDN'T REALIZE HOW MUCH I'D MISSED IT 'TIL NOW!!
JEEZUZ CHRIST!!
HMMM... GHOD, THERE SURE ARE ALOT OF SEXY BROADS IN THIS BURG!
LOOKIE HERE!!
DRUGS
REXALL
Golden Gate CLEANERS
THIS ONE LOOKS LIKE A PUSH-OVER FOR MY TYPE OF COME-ON...
JUST WATCH ME!!
HI, TOOTS! SAY, HAVEN'T WE—
SHHH!! HERE THEY COME!! HERE THEY COME!!
HUH? WHA-COME?? WHO?
THE KID'S A COMER!
HOTEL
OY!
The End!

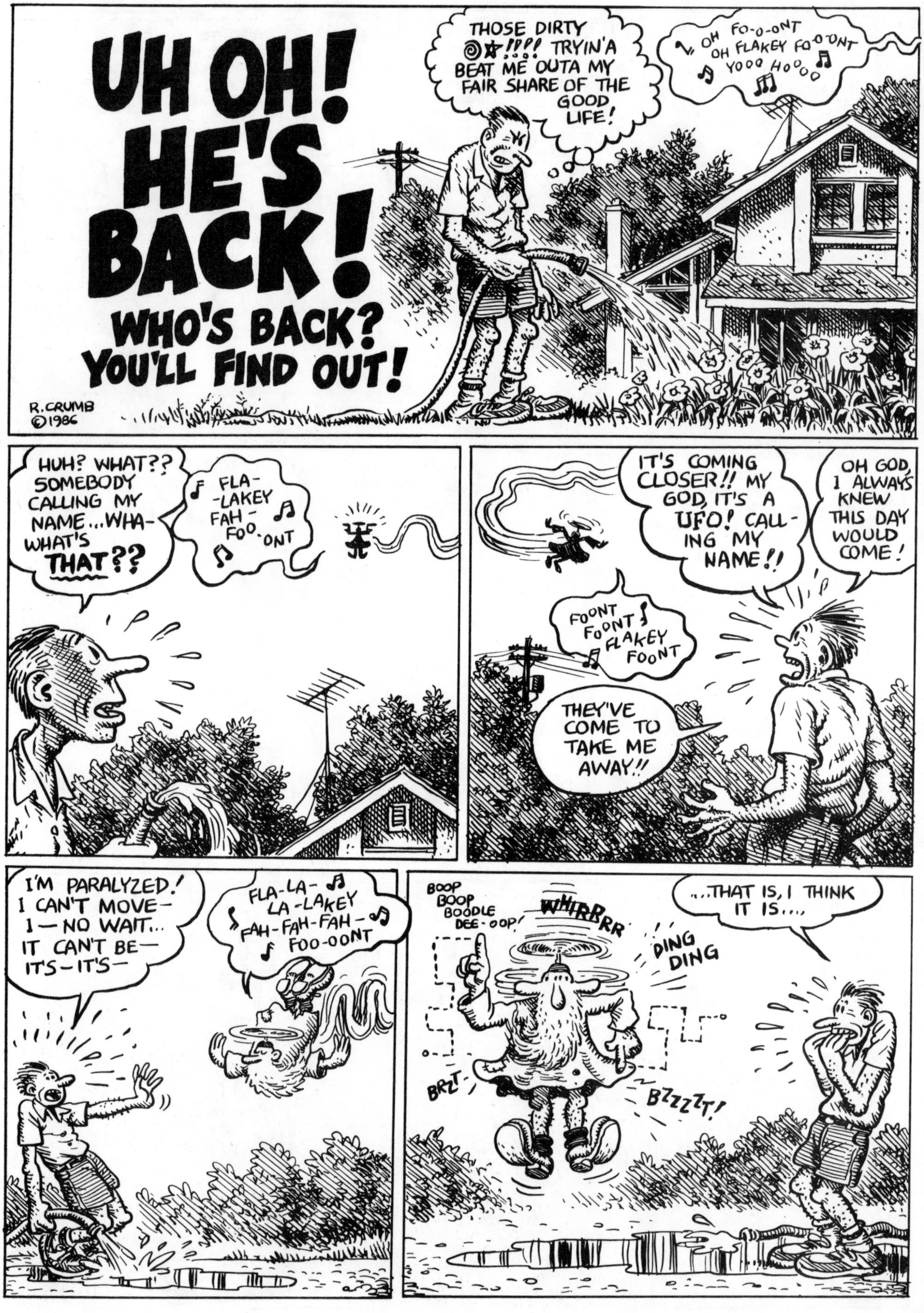
UH OH! HE'S BACK!
WHO'S BACK? YOU'LL FIND OUT!
R. CRUMB ©1986
THOSE DIRTY @☆!!?! TRYIN'A BEAT ME OUTA MY FAIR SHARE OF THE GOOD LIFE!
OH FO-O-ONT OH FLAKEY FO-O-ONT YOOO HOOOO
HUH? WHAT?? SOMEBODY CALLING MY NAME...WHA-WHAT'S THAT??
FLA- -LAKEY FAH - FOO-ONT
IT'S COMING CLOSER!! MY GOD, IT'S A UFO! CALL-ING MY NAME!!
OH GOD, I ALWAYS KNEW THIS DAY WOULD COME!
FOONT FOONT FLAKEY FOONT
THEY'VE COME TO TAKE ME AWAY!!
I'M PARALYZED! I CAN'T MOVE- I—NO WAIT... IT CAN'T BE— IT'S—IT'S—
FLA-LA- LA-LAKEY FAH-FAH-FAH- FOO-OONT
BOOP BOOP BOODLE DEE-OOP!
WHIRRRR
DING DING
BRZT
BZZZZT!
...THAT IS, I THINK IT IS....

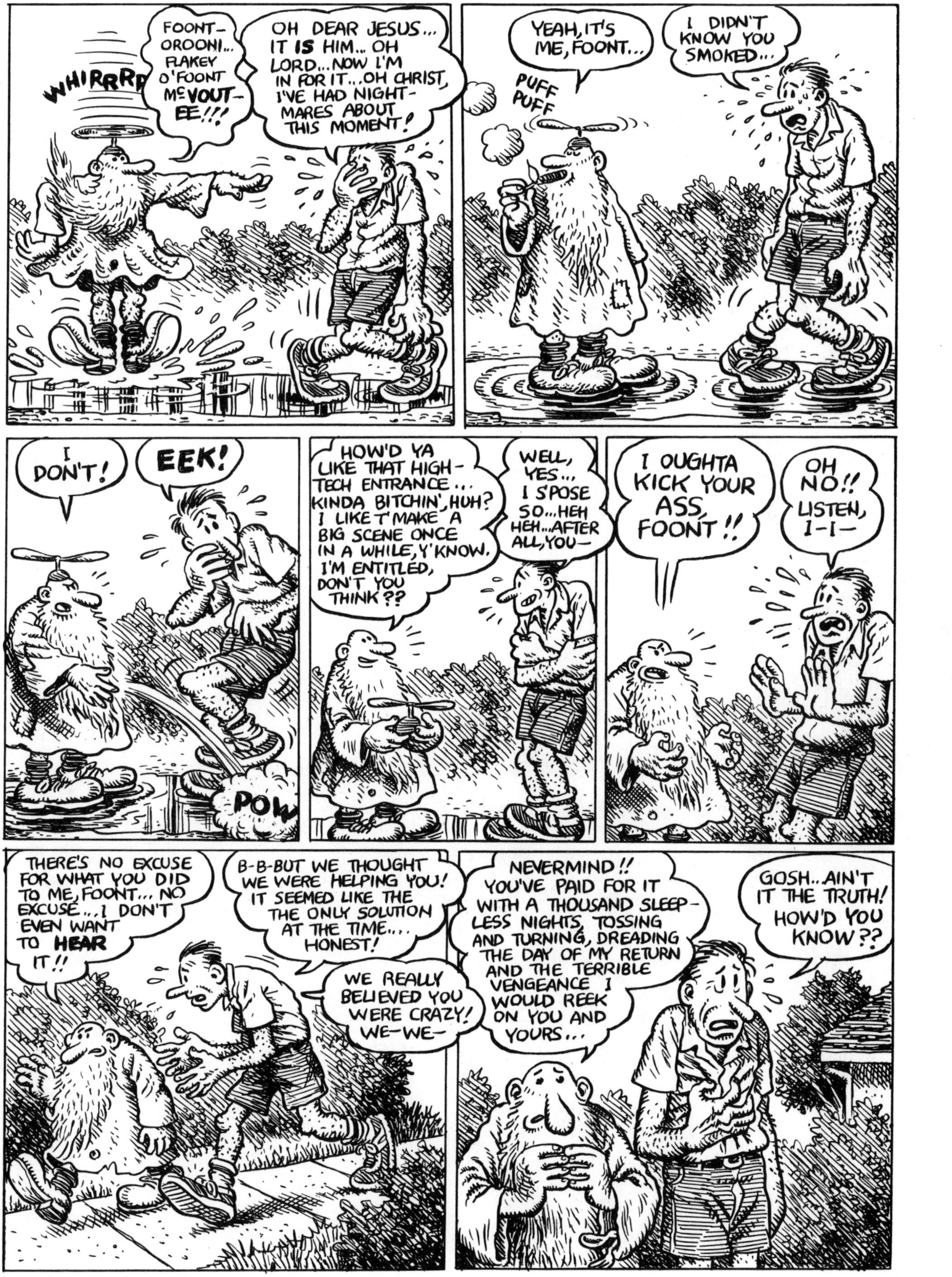
WHIRRRP
FOONT-OROONI... FLAKEY O'FOONT McVOUT-EE!!!
OH DEAR JESUS... IT IS HIM... OH LORD... NOW I'M IN FOR IT... OH CHRIST, I'VE HAD NIGHT-MARES ABOUT THIS MOMENT!
YEAH, IT'S ME, FOONT...
I DIDN'T KNOW YOU SMOKED...
PUFF PUFF
I DON'T!
EEK!
POW
HOW'D YA LIKE THAT HIGH-TECH ENTRANCE... KINDA BITCHIN', HUH? I LIKE T' MAKE A BIG SCENE ONCE IN A WHILE, Y'KNOW. I'M ENTITLED, DON'T YOU THINK??
WELL, YES... I S'POSE SO... HEH HEH... AFTER ALL, YOU—
I OUGHTA KICK YOUR ASS, FOONT!!
OH NO!! LISTEN, I-I—
THERE'S NO EXCUSE FOR WHAT YOU DID TO ME, FOONT... NO EXCUSE... I DON'T EVEN WANT TO HEAR IT!!
B-B-BUT WE THOUGHT WE WERE HELPING YOU! IT SEEMED LIKE THE THE ONLY SOLUTION AT THE TIME.... HONEST!
WE REALLY BELIEVED YOU WERE CRAZY! WE-WE-
NEVERMIND!! YOU'VE PAID FOR IT WITH A THOUSAND SLEEP-LESS NIGHTS, TOSSING AND TURNING, DREADING THE DAY OF MY RETURN AND THE TERRIBLE VENGEANCE I WOULD REEK ON YOU AND YOURS...
GOSH.. AIN'T IT THE TRUTH! HOW'D YOU KNOW??

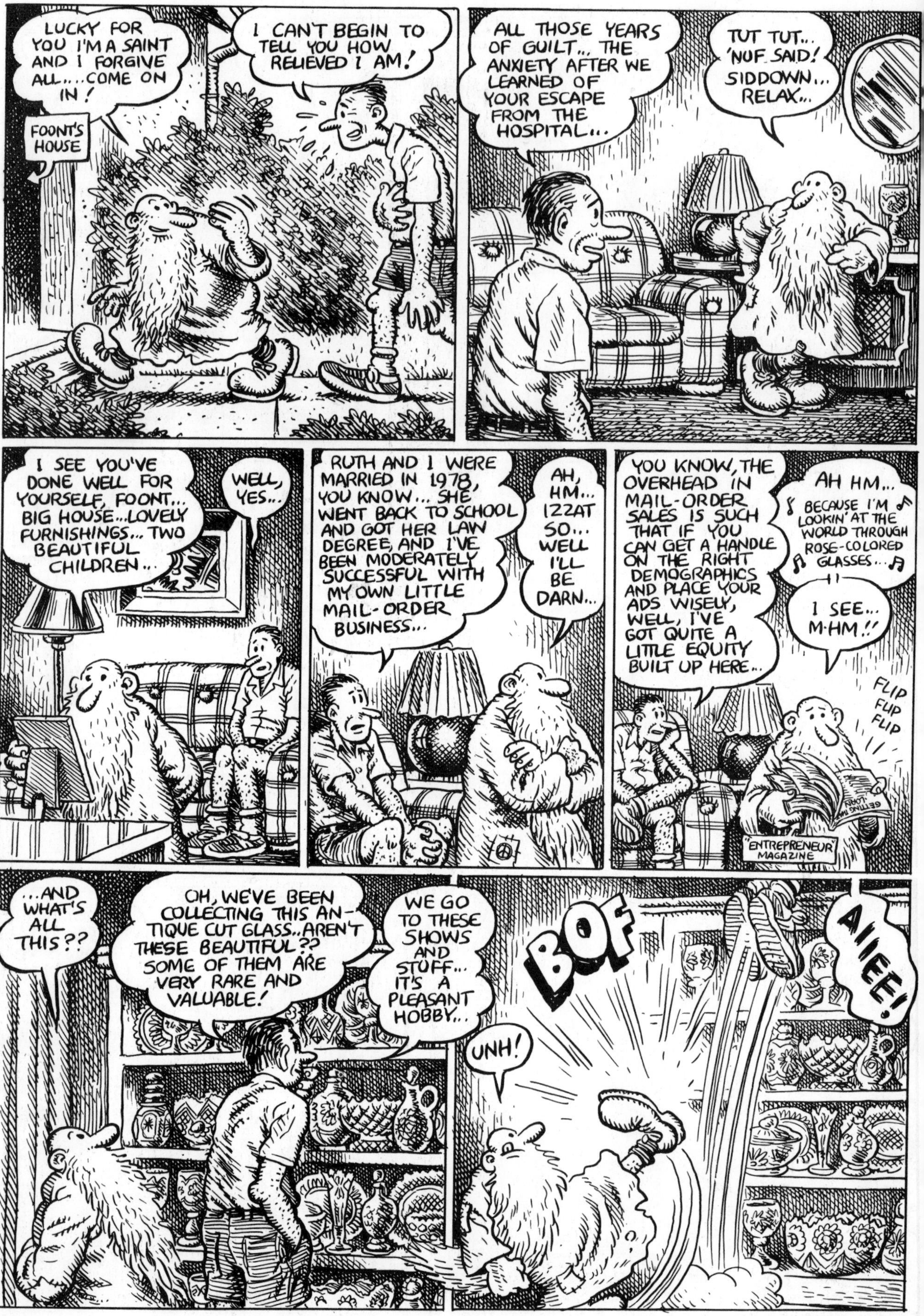
LUCKY FOR YOU I'M A SAINT AND I FORGIVE ALL....COME ON IN!
FOONT'S HOUSE
I CAN'T BEGIN TO TELL YOU HOW RELIEVED I AM!
ALL THOSE YEARS OF GUILT... THE ANXIETY AFTER WE LEARNED OF YOUR ESCAPE FROM THE HOSPITAL...
TUT TUT... 'NUF SAID! SIDDOWN... RELAX...
I SEE YOU'VE DONE WELL FOR YOURSELF, FOONT... BIG HOUSE...LOVELY FURNISHINGS... TWO BEAUTIFUL CHILDREN...
WELL, YES...
RUTH AND I WERE MARRIED IN 1978, YOU KNOW... SHE WENT BACK TO SCHOOL AND GOT HER LAW DEGREE, AND I'VE BEEN MODERATELY SUCCESSFUL WITH MY OWN LITTLE MAIL-ORDER BUSINESS...
AH, HM... IZZAT SO... WELL I'LL BE DARN...
YOU KNOW, THE OVERHEAD IN MAIL-ORDER SALES IS SUCH THAT IF YOU CAN GET A HANDLE ON THE RIGHT DEMOGRAPHICS AND PLACE YOUR ADS WISELY, WELL, I'VE GOT QUITE A LITTLE EQUITY BUILT UP HERE...
AH HM...
BECAUSE I'M LOOKIN' AT THE WORLD THROUGH ROSE-COLORED GLASSES...
I SEE... M-HM!!
FLIP FLIP FLIP
"ENTREPRENEUR" MAGAZINE
...AND WHAT'S ALL THIS??
OH, WE'VE BEEN COLLECTING THIS ANTIQUE CUT GLASS..AREN'T THESE BEAUTIFUL?? SOME OF THEM ARE VERY RARE AND VALUABLE!
WE GO TO THESE SHOWS AND STUFF... IT'S A PLEASANT HOBBY...
BOF
UNH!
AIIEE!

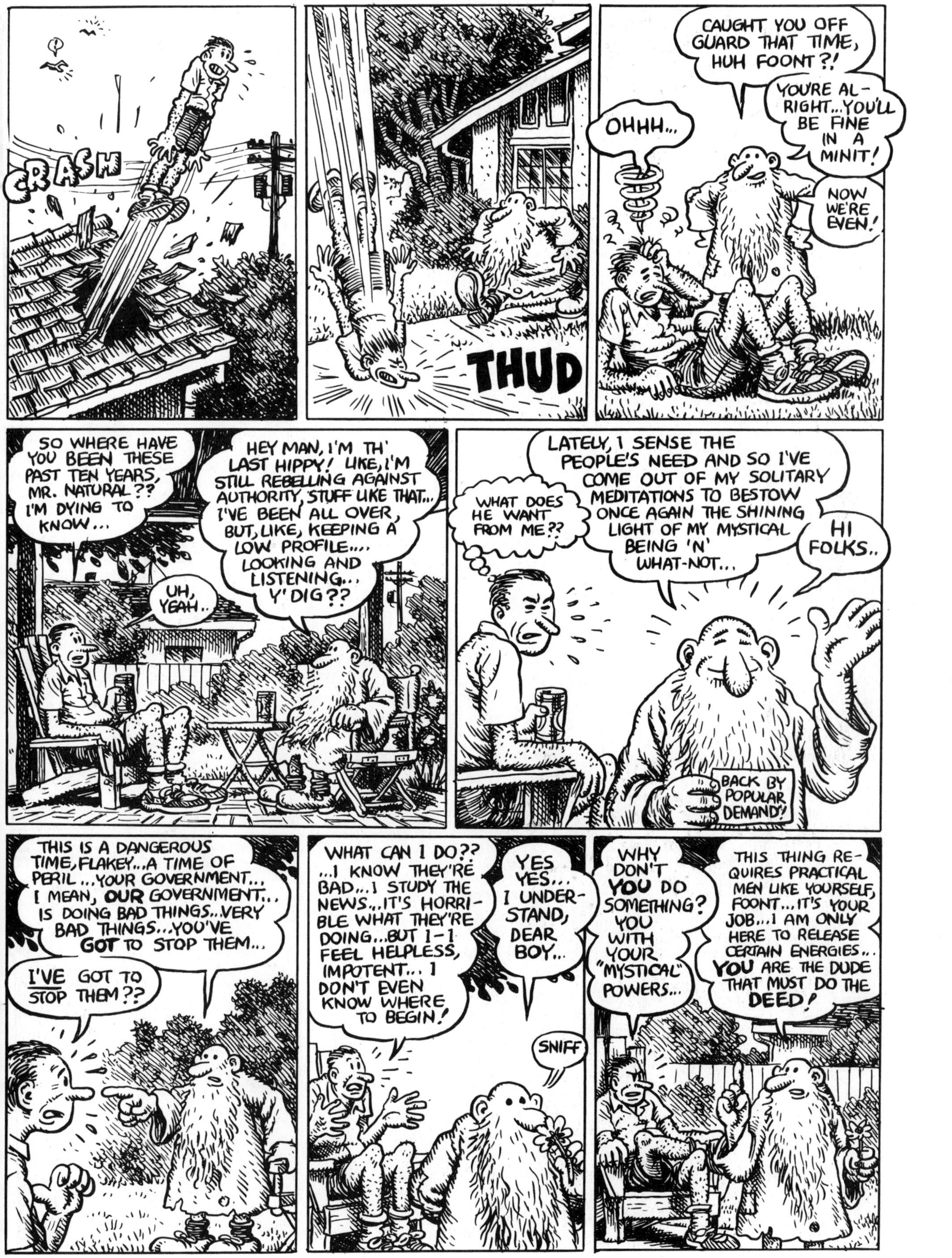
CRASH
THUD
CAUGHT YOU OFF GUARD THAT TIME, HUH FOONT?!
YOU'RE AL-RIGHT...YOU'LL BE FINE IN A MINIT!
OHHH...
NOW WE'RE EVEN!
SO WHERE HAVE YOU BEEN THESE PAST TEN YEARS, MR. NATURAL?? I'M DYING TO KNOW...
HEY MAN, I'M TH' LAST HIPPY! LIKE, I'M STILL REBELLING AGAINST AUTHORITY, STUFF LIKE THAT... I'VE BEEN ALL OVER, BUT, LIKE, KEEPING A LOW PROFILE.... LOOKING AND LISTENING... Y'DIG??
UH, YEAH..
LATELY, I SENSE THE PEOPLE'S NEED AND SO I'VE COME OUT OF MY SOLITARY MEDITATIONS TO BESTOW ONCE AGAIN THE SHINING LIGHT OF MY MYSTICAL BEING 'N' WHAT-NOT...
WHAT DOES HE WANT FROM ME??
HI FOLKS..
BACK BY POPULAR DEMAND!
THIS IS A DANGEROUS TIME, FLAKEY...A TIME OF PERIL...YOUR GOVERNMENT... I MEAN, **OUR** GOVERNMENT... IS DOING BAD THINGS...VERY BAD THINGS...YOU'VE **GOT** TO STOP THEM...
I'VE GOT TO STOP THEM??
WHAT CAN I DO?? ...I KNOW THEY'RE BAD...I STUDY THE NEWS...IT'S HORRIBLE WHAT THEY'RE DOING...BUT I-I FEEL HELPLESS, IMPOTENT... I DON'T EVEN KNOW WHERE TO BEGIN!
YES YES... I UNDERSTAND, DEAR BOY...
SNIFF
WHY DON'T **YOU** DO SOMETHING? YOU WITH YOUR "MYSTICAL" POWERS...
THIS THING REQUIRES PRACTICAL MEN LIKE YOURSELF, FOONT...IT'S YOUR JOB...I AM ONLY HERE TO RELEASE CERTAIN ENERGIES... **YOU** ARE THE DUDE THAT MUST DO THE **DEED**!

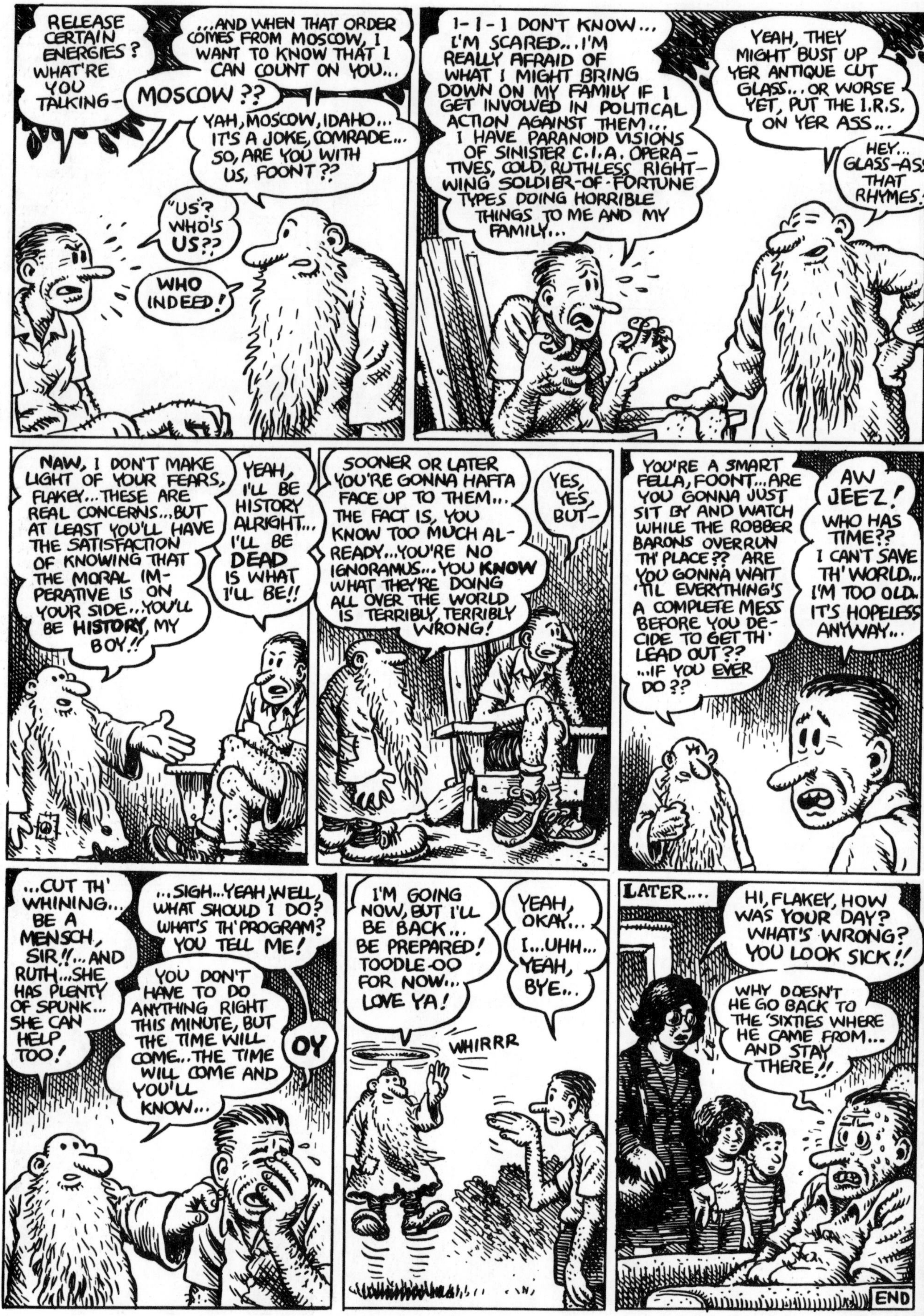
RELEASE CERTAIN ENERGIES? WHAT'RE YOU TALKING-
...AND WHEN THAT ORDER COMES FROM MOSCOW, I WANT TO KNOW THAT I CAN COUNT ON YOU...
MOSCOW??
YAH, MOSCOW, IDAHO... IT'S A JOKE, COMRADE... SO, ARE YOU WITH US, FOONT??
"US? WHO'S US??
WHO INDEED!
I-I-I DON'T KNOW... I'M SCARED...I'M REALLY AFRAID OF WHAT I MIGHT BRING DOWN ON MY FAMILY IF I GET INVOLVED IN POLITICAL ACTION AGAINST THEM... I HAVE PARANOID VISIONS OF SINISTER C.I.A. OPERA-TIVES, COLD, RUTHLESS RIGHT-WING SOLDIER-OF-FORTUNE TYPES DOING HORRIBLE THINGS TO ME AND MY FAMILY...
YEAH, THEY MIGHT BUST UP YER ANTIQUE CUT GLASS... OR WORSE YET, PUT THE I.R.S. ON YER ASS...
HEY... GLASS-ASS THAT RHYMES!
NAW, I DON'T MAKE LIGHT OF YOUR FEARS, FLAKEY... THESE ARE REAL CONCERNS...BUT AT LEAST YOU'LL HAVE THE SATISFACTION OF KNOWING THAT THE MORAL IM-PERATIVE IS ON YOUR SIDE...YOU'LL BE HISTORY, MY BOY!!
YEAH, I'LL BE HISTORY ALRIGHT... I'LL BE DEAD IS WHAT I'LL BE!!
SOONER OR LATER YOU'RE GONNA HAFTA FACE UP TO THEM... THE FACT IS, YOU KNOW TOO MUCH AL-READY...YOU'RE NO IGNORAMUS... YOU KNOW WHAT THEY'RE DOING ALL OVER THE WORLD IS TERRIBLY, TERRIBLY WRONG!
YES, YES, BUT-
YOU'RE A SMART FELLA, FOONT... ARE YOU GONNA JUST SIT BY AND WATCH WHILE THE ROBBER BARONS OVERRUN TH' PLACE?? ARE YOU GONNA WAIT 'TIL EVERYTHING'S A COMPLETE MESS BEFORE YOU DE-CIDE TO GET TH' LEAD OUT?? ...IF YOU EVER DO??
AW JEEZ! WHO HAS TIME?? I CAN'T SAVE TH' WORLD... I'M TOO OLD. IT'S HOPELESS ANYWAY...
...CUT TH' WHINING... BE A MENSCH, SIR!!... AND RUTH...SHE HAS PLENTY OF SPUNK... SHE CAN HELP TOO!
...SIGH...YEAH, WELL, WHAT SHOULD I DO? WHAT'S TH' PROGRAM? YOU TELL ME!
YOU DON'T HAVE TO DO ANYTHING RIGHT THIS MINUTE, BUT THE TIME WILL COME...THE TIME WILL COME AND YOU'LL KNOW...
OY
I'M GOING NOW, BUT I'LL BE BACK... BE PREPARED! TOODLE-OO FOR NOW... LOVE YA!
YEAH, OKAY... I...UHH... YEAH, BYE...
WHIRRR
LATER....
HI, FLAKEY, HOW WAS YOUR DAY? WHAT'S WRONG? YOU LOOK SICK!!
WHY DOESN'T HE GO BACK TO THE 'SIXTIES WHERE HE CAME FROM... AND STAY THERE!!
END

HERE HE COMES AGAIN!

R. CRUMB
©1986

WHAT?? ALREADY??

I CAN SEE HE DOESN'T INTEND TO GIVE ME ANY PEACE...AND HERE I'M TRYIN'A RELAX BEFORE RUTH AND THE KIDS GET BACK FROM TH' MOVIES...

☺✱!!!

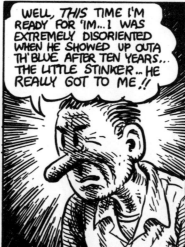

WELL, *THIS* TIME I'M READY FOR 'IM...I WAS EXTREMELY DISORIENTED WHEN HE SHOWED UP OUTA TH' BLUE AFTER TEN YEARS...THE LITTLE STINKER...HE REALLY GOT TO ME!!

BUT SINCE LAST WEEK I'VE HAD SOME TIME TO THINK AND I'VE GOT A FEW THINGS TO TELL *HIM*, GODDAMMIT!

DING DONG KNOCK KNOCK DING DONG

I'M COMING! HOLD YER HORSES!

SAY, LISTEN, WHY DON'T YOU GO BACK TO THE 'SIXTIES WHERE YOU BELONG...GET A JOB...YOU'RE A *BUM!* GO PEDDLE YOUR NONSENSE ELSEWHERE!!

BASICALLY, YOU HAVE NOTHING TO SAY TO ME ANYMORE...YOUR METHODS DON'T BUTTER NO PARSNIPS IN *THIS* DAY AND AGE...YOU'RE A HAS-BEEN...AN ANACHRONISM!!

YOU'RE JUST ANOTHER 'SIXTIES BURN-OUT STREET-CRAZY...YOU PROBABLY LIVE ON WELFARE...AID-TO-THE-TOTALLY-SPACED-OUT!!

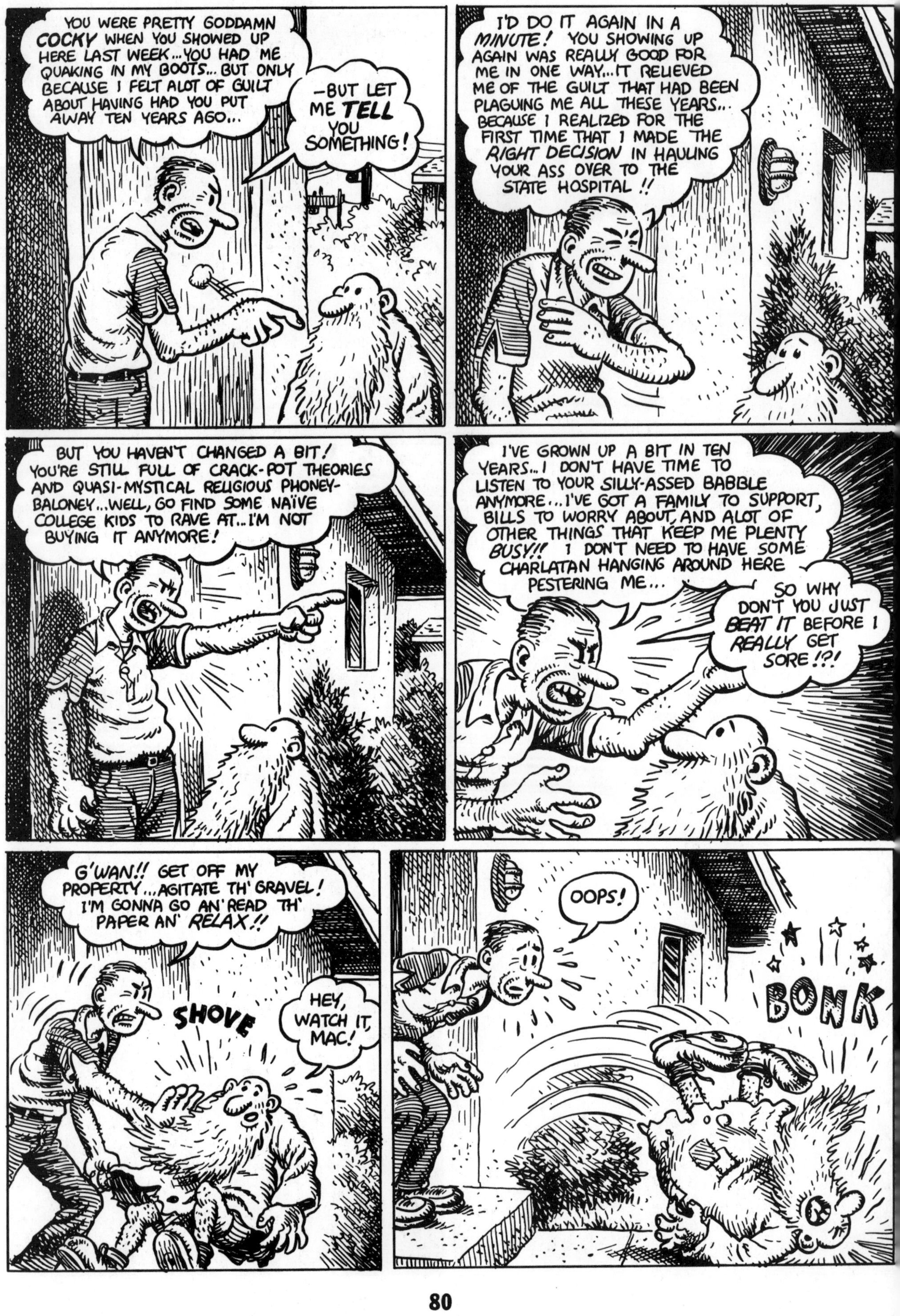
YOU WERE PRETTY GODDAMN COCKY WHEN YOU SHOWED UP HERE LAST WEEK...YOU HAD ME QUAKING IN MY BOOTS... BUT ONLY BECAUSE I FELT ALOT OF GUILT ABOUT HAVING HAD YOU PUT AWAY TEN YEARS AGO...
—BUT LET ME TELL YOU SOMETHING!
I'D DO IT AGAIN IN A MINUTE! YOU SHOWING UP AGAIN WAS REALLY GOOD FOR ME IN ONE WAY...IT RELIEVED ME OF THE GUILT THAT HAD BEEN PLAGUING ME ALL THESE YEARS.. BECAUSE I REALIZED FOR THE FIRST TIME THAT I MADE THE RIGHT DECISION IN HAULING YOUR ASS OVER TO THE STATE HOSPITAL !!
BUT YOU HAVEN'T CHANGED A BIT! YOU'RE STILL FULL OF CRACK-POT THEORIES AND QUASI-MYSTICAL RELIGIOUS PHONEY-BALONEY...WELL, GO FIND SOME NAÏVE COLLEGE KIDS TO RAVE AT...I'M NOT BUYING IT ANYMORE!
I'VE GROWN UP A BIT IN TEN YEARS..I DON'T HAVE TIME TO LISTEN TO YOUR SILLY-ASSED BABBLE ANYMORE...I'VE GOT A FAMILY TO SUPPORT, BILLS TO WORRY ABOUT, AND ALOT OF OTHER THINGS THAT KEEP ME PLENTY BUSY!! I DON'T NEED TO HAVE SOME CHARLATAN HANGING AROUND HERE PESTERING ME...
SO WHY DON'T YOU JUST BEAT IT BEFORE I REALLY GET SORE!?!
G'WAN!! GET OFF MY PROPERTY...AGITATE TH' GRAVEL! I'M GONNA GO AN' READ TH' PAPER AN' RELAX!!
SHOVE
HEY, WATCH IT, MAC!
OOPS!
BONK

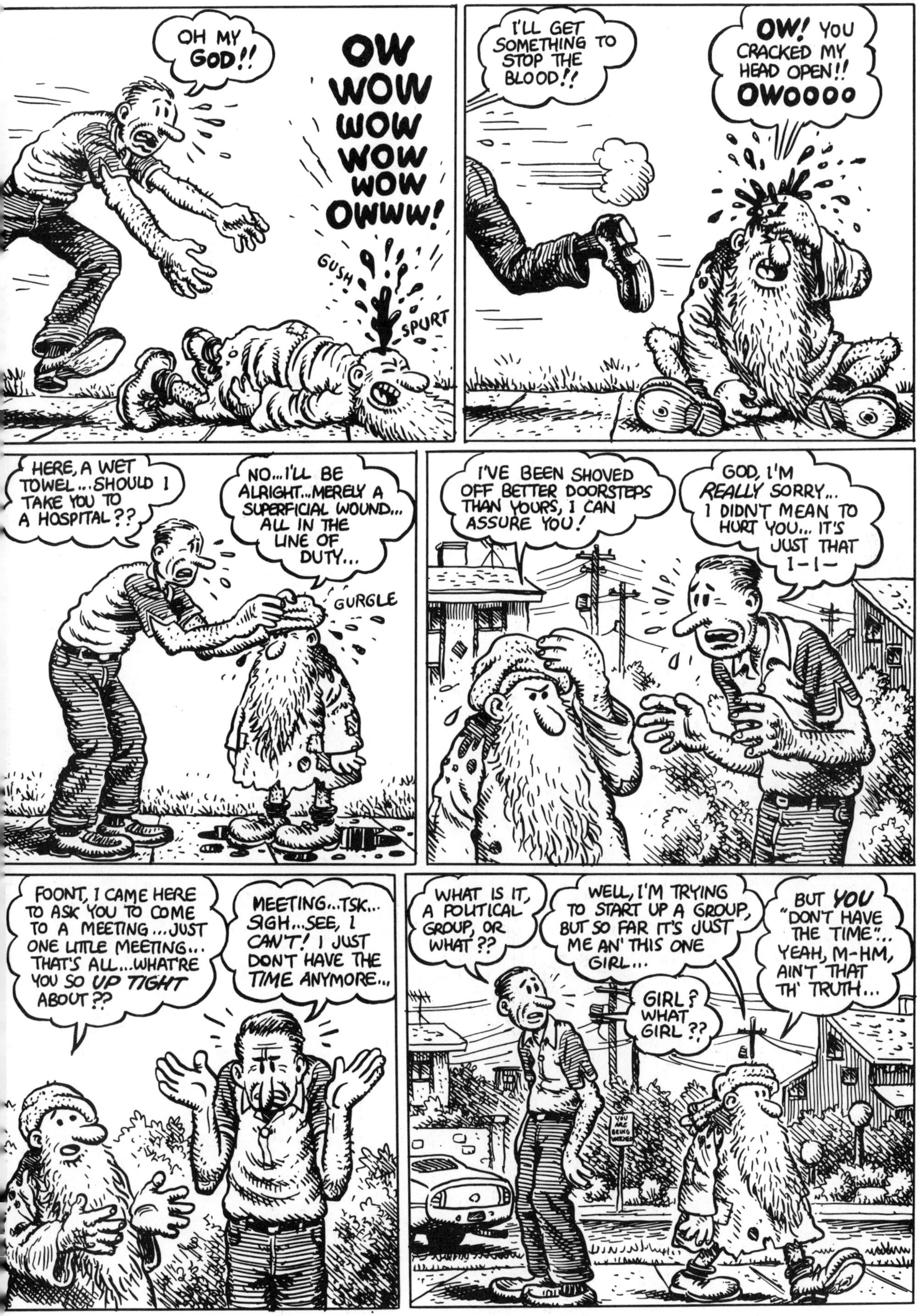
OH MY GOD!!
OW WOW WOW WOW WOW OWWW!
GUSH
SPURT
I'LL GET SOMETHING TO STOP THE BLOOD!!
OW! YOU CRACKED MY HEAD OPEN!! OWOOOO
HERE, A WET TOWEL... SHOULD I TAKE YOU TO A HOSPITAL??
NO... I'LL BE ALRIGHT... MERELY A SUPERFICIAL WOUND... ALL IN THE LINE OF DUTY...
GURGLE
I'VE BEEN SHOVED OFF BETTER DOORSTEPS THAN YOURS, I CAN ASSURE YOU!
GOD, I'M REALLY SORRY... I DIDN'T MEAN TO HURT YOU... IT'S JUST THAT I-I-
FOONT, I CAME HERE TO ASK YOU TO COME TO A MEETING... JUST ONE LITTLE MEETING... THAT'S ALL... WHAT'RE YOU SO UP TIGHT ABOUT??
MEETING... TSK... SIGH... SEE, I CAN'T! I JUST DON'T HAVE THE TIME ANYMORE...
WHAT IS IT, A POLITICAL GROUP, OR WHAT??
WELL, I'M TRYING TO START UP A GROUP, BUT SO FAR IT'S JUST ME AN' THIS ONE GIRL...
GIRL? WHAT GIRL??
BUT YOU "DON'T HAVE THE TIME"... YEAH, M-HM, AIN'T THAT TH' TRUTH...

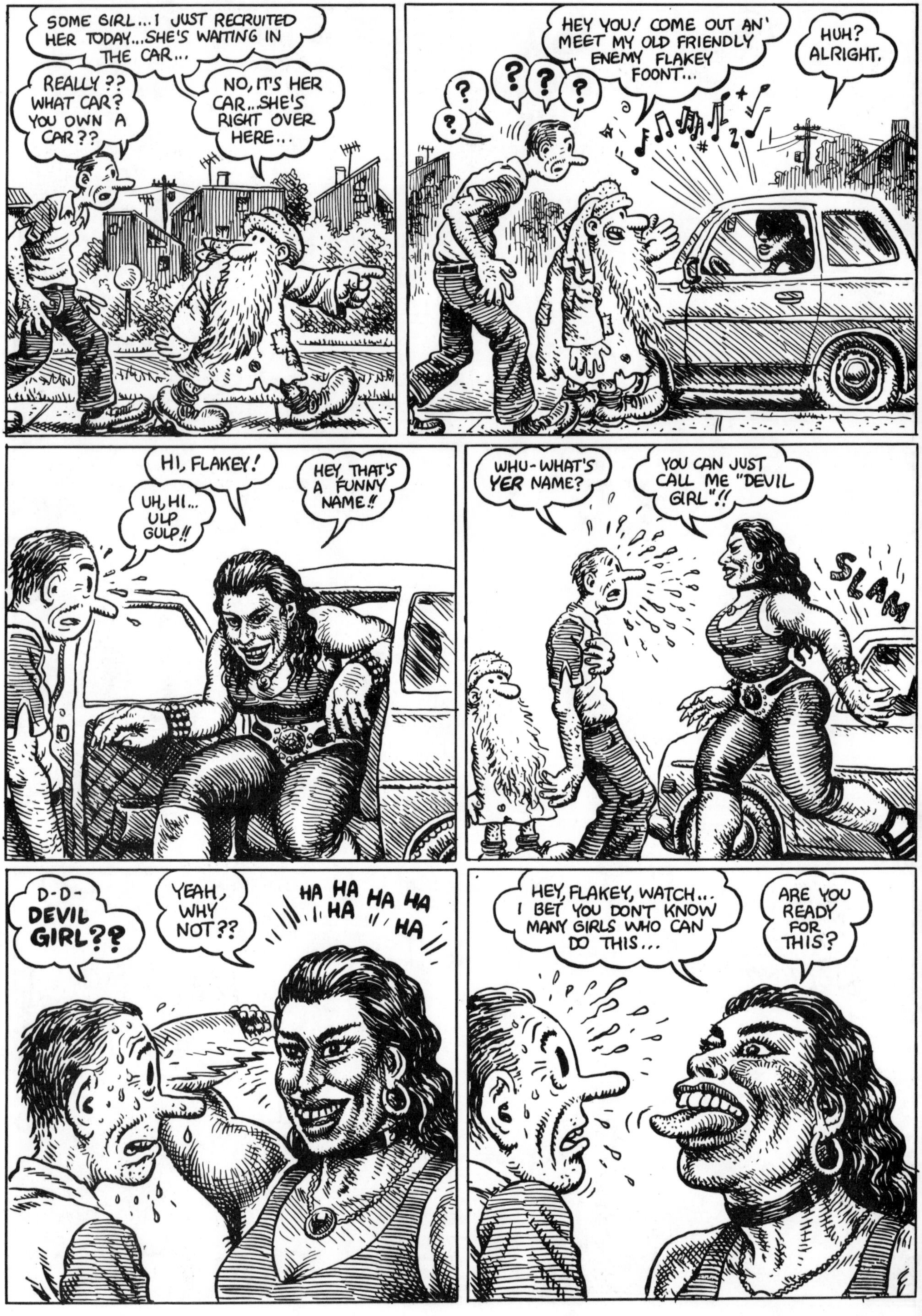
SOME GIRL... I JUST RECRUITED HER TODAY... SHE'S WAITING IN THE CAR...
REALLY?? WHAT CAR? YOU OWN A CAR??
NO, IT'S HER CAR... SHE'S RIGHT OVER HERE...
HEY YOU! COME OUT AN' MEET MY OLD FRIENDLY ENEMY FLAKEY FOONT...
HUH? ALRIGHT.
HI, FLAKEY!
UH, HI... ULP GULP!!
HEY, THAT'S A FUNNY NAME!!
WHU-WHAT'S YER NAME?
YOU CAN JUST CALL ME "DEVIL GIRL"!!
SLAM
D-D-DEVIL GIRL??
YEAH, WHY NOT??
HA HA HA HA HA HA HA
HEY, FLAKEY, WATCH... I BET YOU DON'T KNOW MANY GIRLS WHO CAN DO THIS...
ARE YOU READY FOR THIS?

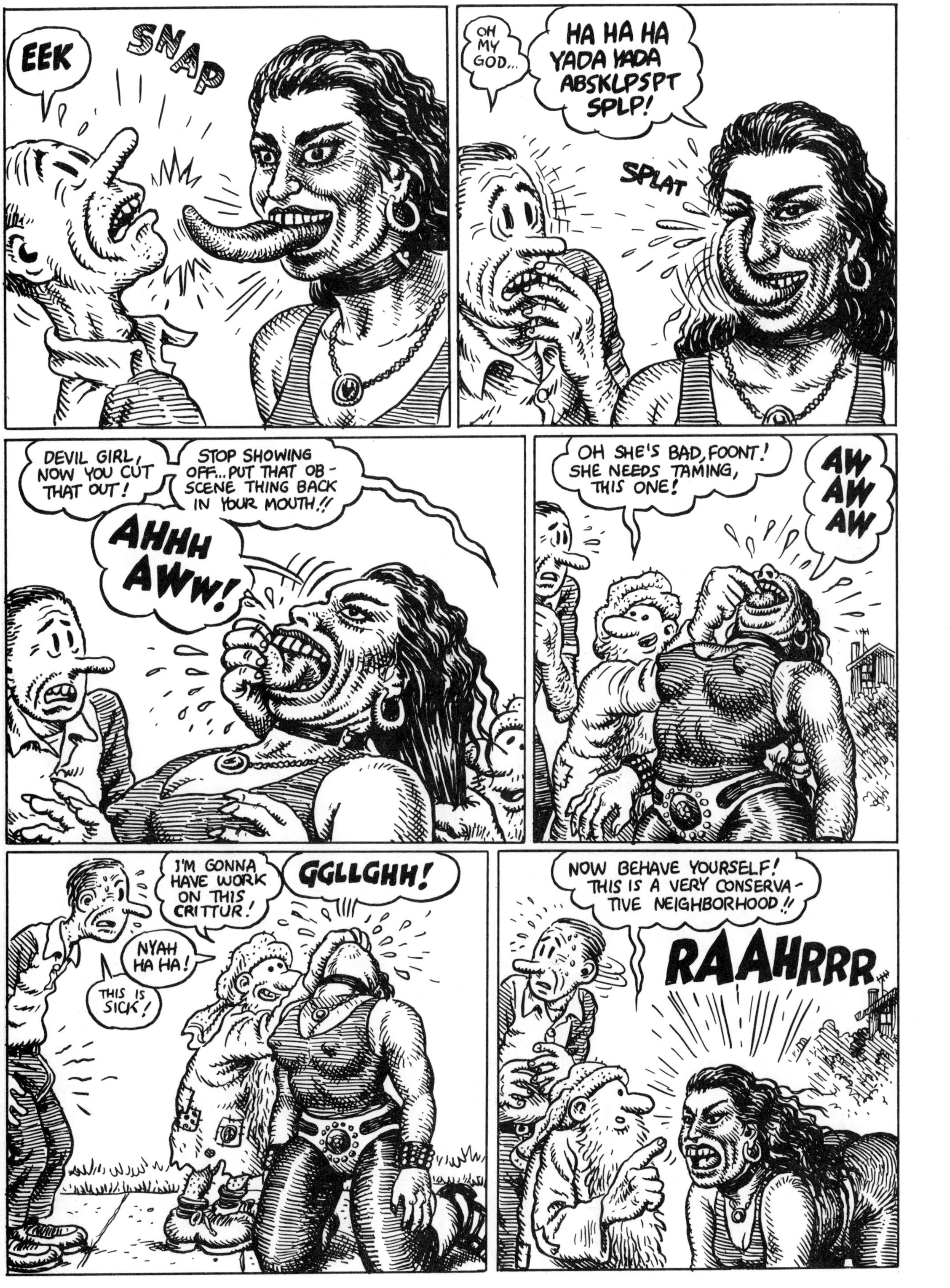
EEK
SNAP
OH MY GOD...
HA HA HA YADA YADA ABSKLPSPT SPLP!
SPLAT
DEVIL GIRL, NOW YOU CUT THAT OUT!
STOP SHOWING OFF... PUT THAT OB-SCENE THING BACK IN YOUR MOUTH!!
AHHH AWW!
OH SHE'S BAD, FOONT! SHE NEEDS TAMING, THIS ONE!
AW AW AW
I'M GONNA HAVE WORK ON THIS CRITTUR!
GGLLGHH!
NYAH HA HA!
THIS IS SICK!
NOW BEHAVE YOURSELF! THIS IS A VERY CONSERVA-TIVE NEIGHBORHOOD!!
RAAHRRR

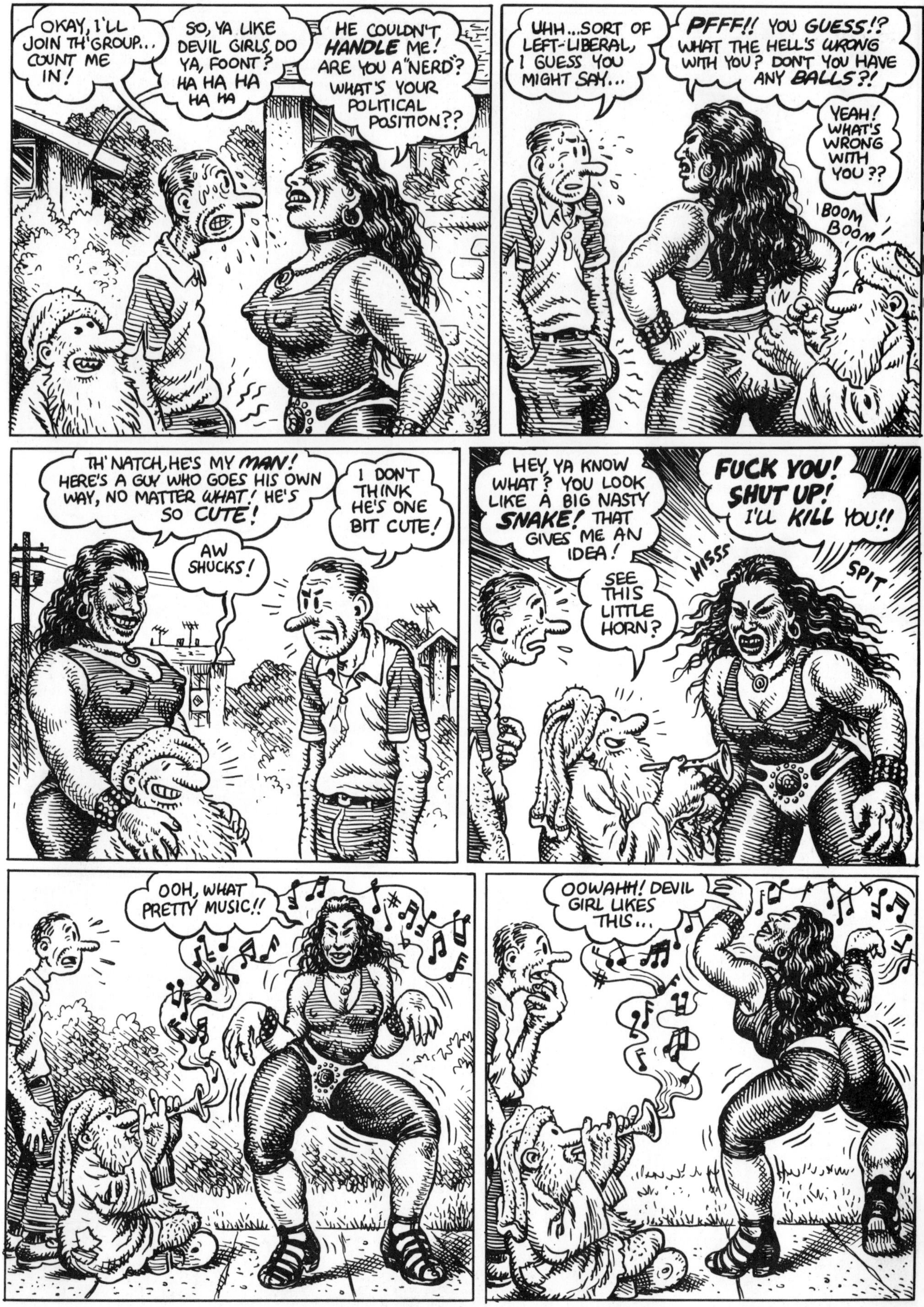
OKAY, I'LL JOIN TH' GROUP... COUNT ME IN!
SO, YA LIKE DEVIL GIRLS, DO YA, FOONT? HA HA HA HA HA
HE COULDN'T HANDLE ME! ARE YOU A "NERD"? WHAT'S YOUR POLITICAL POSITION??
UHH...SORT OF LEFT-LIBERAL, I GUESS YOU MIGHT SAY...
PFFF!! YOU GUESS!? WHAT THE HELL'S WRONG WITH YOU? DON'T YOU HAVE ANY BALLS?!
YEAH! WHAT'S WRONG WITH YOU??
BOOM BOOM
TH' NATCH, HE'S MY MAN! HERE'S A GUY WHO GOES HIS OWN WAY, NO MATTER WHAT! HE'S SO CUTE!
I DON'T THINK HE'S ONE BIT CUTE!
AW SHUCKS!
HEY, YA KNOW WHAT? YOU LOOK LIKE A BIG NASTY SNAKE! THAT GIVES ME AN IDEA!
FUCK YOU! SHUT UP! I'LL KILL YOU!!
SEE THIS LITTLE HORN?
HISSS
SPIT
OOH, WHAT PRETTY MUSIC!!
OOWAHH! DEVIL GIRL LIKES THIS...

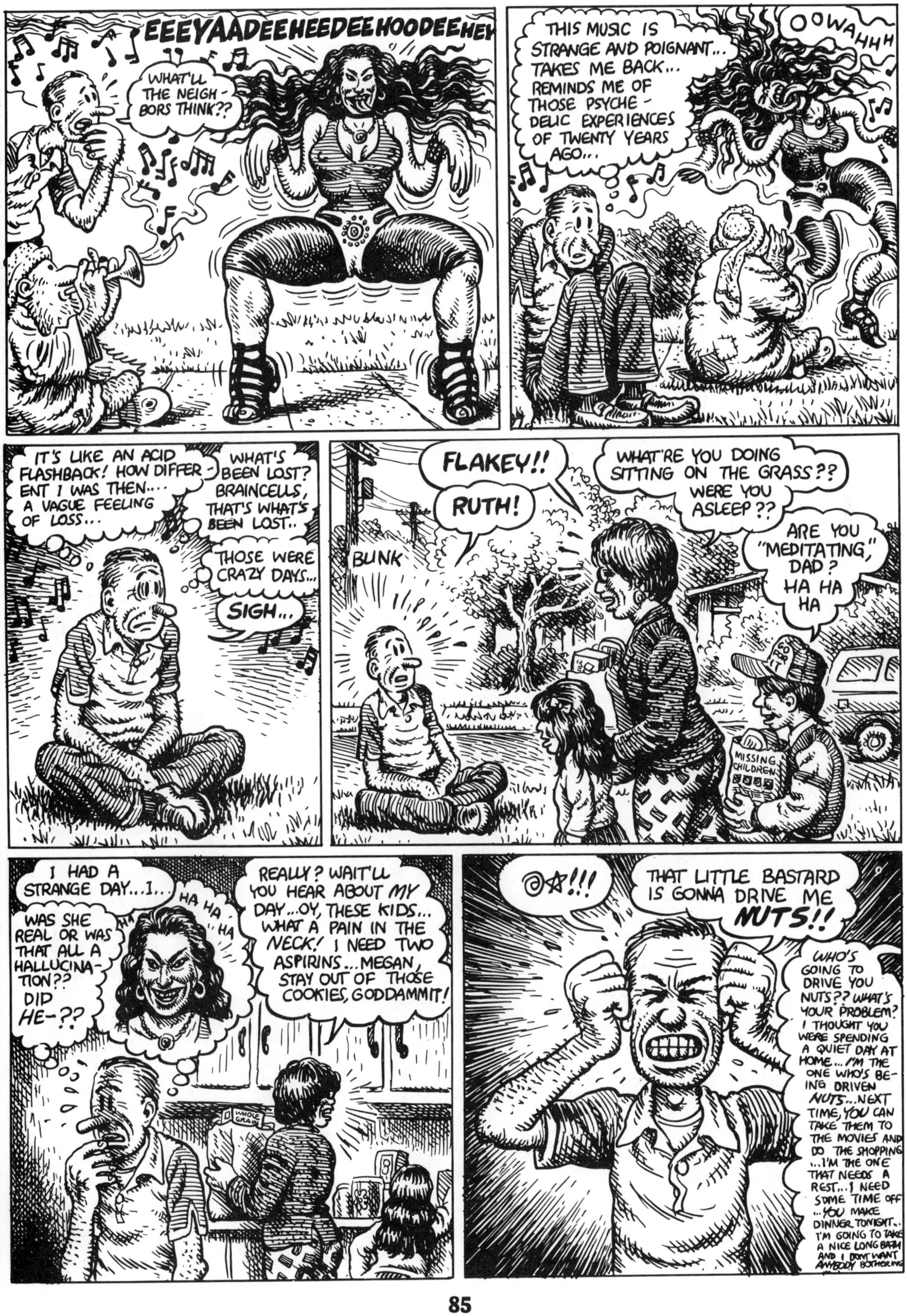

EEEYAADEEHEEDEEHOODEEHEY
WHAT'LL THE NEIGHBORS THINK??
THIS MUSIC IS STRANGE AND POIGNANT... TAKES ME BACK... REMINDS ME OF THOSE PSYCHEDELIC EXPERIENCES OF TWENTY YEARS AGO...
OOWAHHH
IT'S LIKE AN ACID FLASHBACK! HOW DIFFERENT I WAS THEN... A VAGUE FEELING OF LOSS...
WHAT'S BEEN LOST? BRAINCELLS, THAT'S WHAT'S BEEN LOST..
THOSE WERE CRAZY DAYS...
SIGH...
BUNK
FLAKEY!!
RUTH!
WHAT'RE YOU DOING SITTING ON THE GRASS?? WERE YOU ASLEEP??
ARE YOU "MEDITATING," DAD? HA HA HA
MISSING CHILDREN
I HAD A STRANGE DAY...I...
WAS SHE REAL OR WAS THAT ALL A HALLUCINATION?? DID HE-??
HA HA HA HA
REALLY? WAIT'LL YOU HEAR ABOUT MY DAY...OY, THESE KIDS... WHAT A PAIN IN THE NECK! I NEED TWO ASPIRINS...MEGAN, STAY OUT OF THOSE COOKIES, GODDAMMIT!
WHOLE GRAIN
@☆!!!
THAT LITTLE BASTARD IS GONNA DRIVE ME NUTS!!
WHO'S GOING TO DRIVE YOU NUTS?? WHAT'S YOUR PROBLEM? I THOUGHT YOU WERE SPENDING A QUIET DAY AT HOME... I'M THE ONE WHO'S BEING DRIVEN NUTS...NEXT TIME, YOU CAN TAKE THEM TO THE MOVIES AND DO THE SHOPPING ...I'M THE ONE THAT NEEDS A REST...I NEED SOME TIME OFF ...YOU MAKE DINNER TONIGHT.. I'M GOING TO TAKE A NICE LONG BATH AND I DON'T WANT ANYBODY BOTHERING

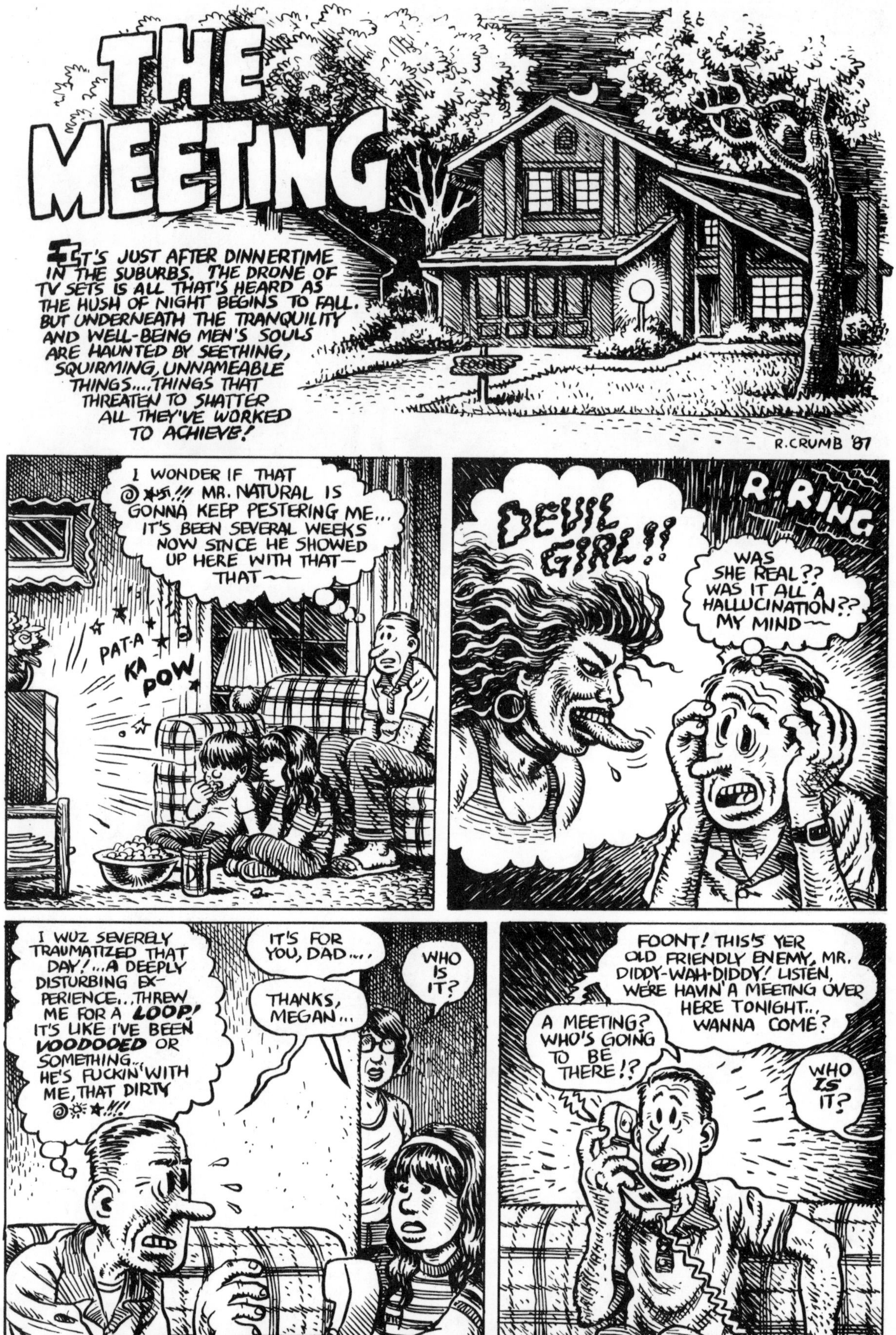
THE MEETING
IT'S JUST AFTER DINNERTIME IN THE SUBURBS. THE DRONE OF TV SETS IS ALL THAT'S HEARD AS THE HUSH OF NIGHT BEGINS TO FALL. BUT UNDERNEATH THE TRANQUILITY AND WELL-BEING MEN'S SOULS ARE HAUNTED BY SEETHING, SQUIRMING, UNNAMEABLE THINGS.... THINGS THAT THREATEN TO SHATTER ALL THEY'VE WORKED TO ACHIEVE!
FOONT
R. CRUMB '87
I WONDER IF THAT @*#!!! MR. NATURAL IS GONNA KEEP PESTERING ME... IT'S BEEN SEVERAL WEEKS NOW SINCE HE SHOWED UP HERE WITH THAT— THAT—
PAT-A KA POW
DEVIL GIRL!!
R-RING
WAS SHE REAL?? WAS IT ALL A HALLUCINATION?? MY MIND—
I WUZ SEVERELY TRAUMATIZED THAT DAY!... A DEEPLY DISTURBING EX-PERIENCE... THREW ME FOR A LOOP! IT'S LIKE I'VE BEEN VOODOOED OR SOMETHING... HE'S FUCKIN' WITH ME, THAT DIRTY @*#!!!
IT'S FOR YOU, DAD....
WHO IS IT?
THANKS, MEGAN...
FOONT! THIS'S YER OLD FRIENDLY ENEMY, MR. DIDDY-WAH-DIDDY! LISTEN, WE'RE HAVIN' A MEETING OVER HERE TONIGHT... WANNA COME?
A MEETING? WHO'S GOING TO BE THERE!?
WHO IS IT?

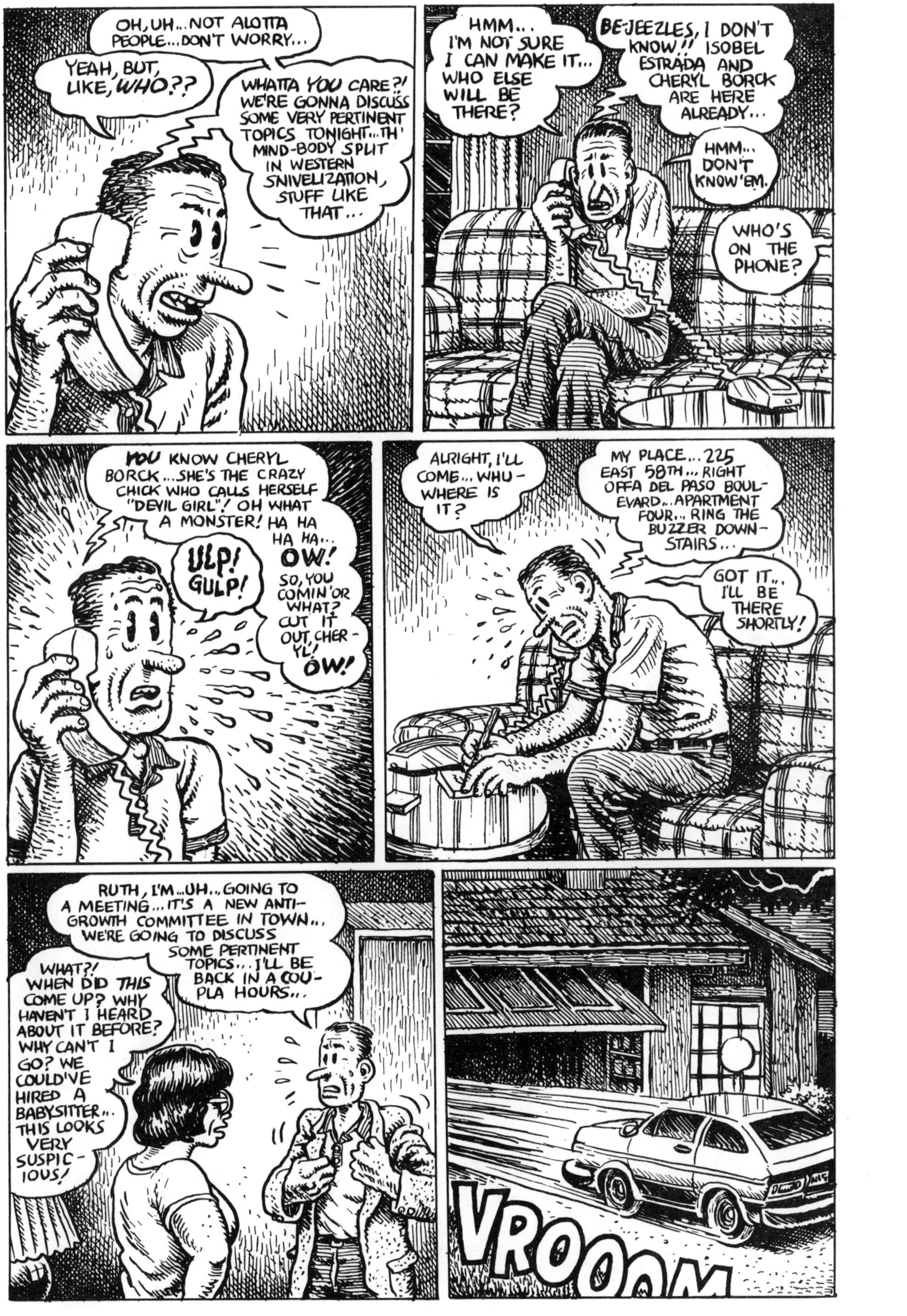

OH, UH... NOT ALOTTA PEOPLE... DON'T WORRY...
YEAH, BUT, LIKE, WHO??
WHATTA YOU CARE?! WE'RE GONNA DISCUSS SOME VERY PERTINENT TOPICS TONIGHT... TH' MIND-BODY SPLIT IN WESTERN SNIVELIZATION, STUFF LIKE THAT...
HMM... I'M NOT SURE I CAN MAKE IT... WHO ELSE WILL BE THERE?
BE-JEEZLES, I DON'T KNOW!! ISOBEL ESTRADA AND CHERYL BORCK ARE HERE ALREADY...
HMM... DON'T KNOW 'EM.
WHO'S ON THE PHONE?
YOU KNOW CHERYL BORCK... SHE'S THE CRAZY CHICK WHO CALLS HERSELF "DEVIL GIRL"! OH WHAT A MONSTER! HA HA HA HA... OW! SO, YOU COMIN' OR WHAT? CUT IT OUT, CHERYL! OW!
ULP! GULP!
ALRIGHT, I'LL COME... WHU-WHERE IS IT?
MY PLACE... 225 EAST 58TH... RIGHT OFFA DEL PASO BOULEVARD... APARTMENT FOUR... RING THE BUZZER DOWNSTAIRS...
GOT IT... I'LL BE THERE SHORTLY!
RUTH, I'M... UH... GOING TO A MEETING... IT'S A NEW ANTI-GROWTH COMMITTEE IN TOWN... WE'RE GOING TO DISCUSS SOME PERTINENT TOPICS... I'LL BE BACK IN A COUPLA HOURS...
WHAT?! WHEN DID THIS COME UP? WHY HAVEN'T I HEARD ABOUT IT BEFORE? WHY CAN'T I GO? WE COULD'VE HIRED A BABYSITTER... THIS LOOKS VERY SUSPICIOUS!
VROOOM

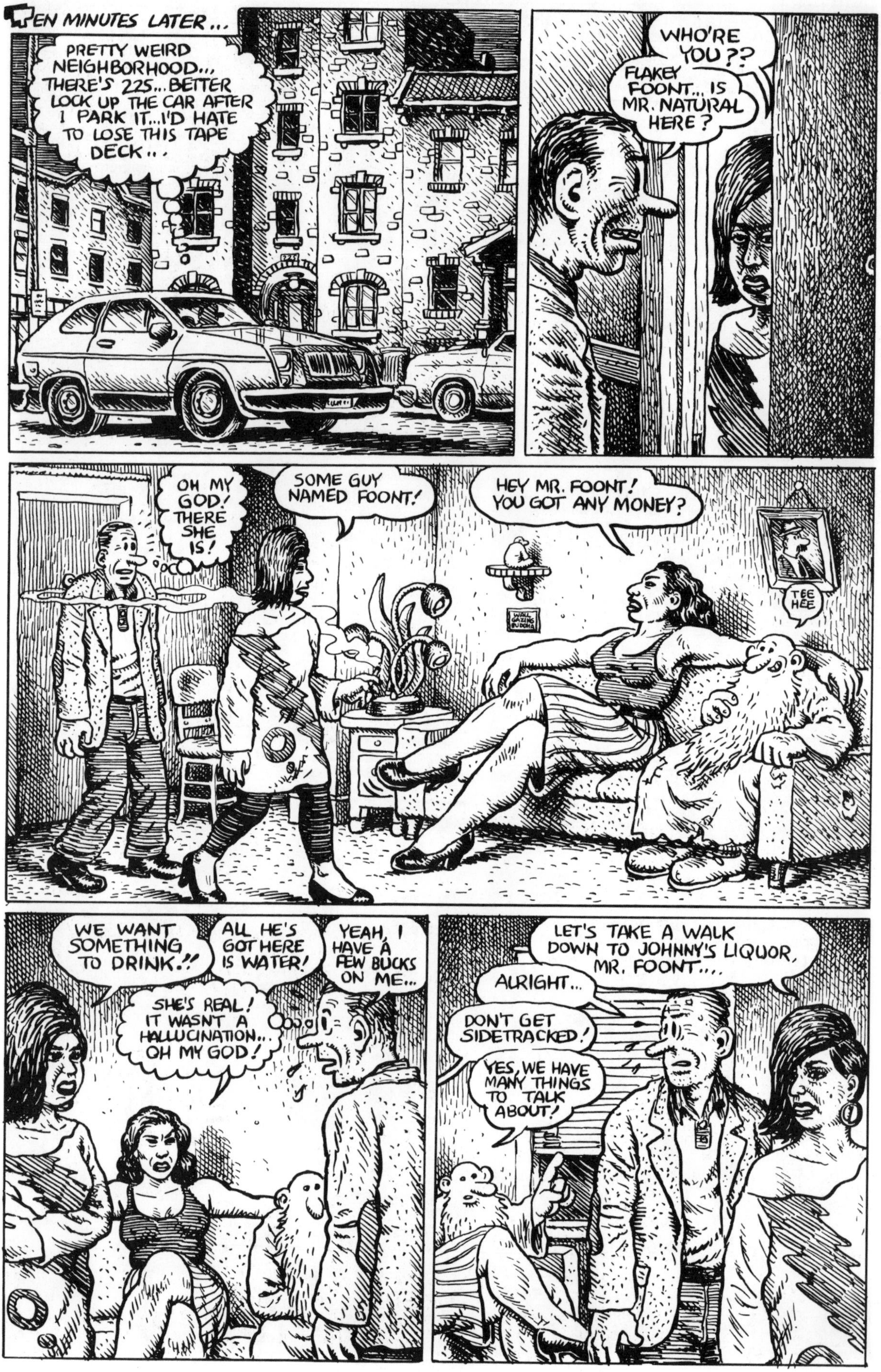
TEN MINUTES LATER...
PRETTY WEIRD NEIGHBORHOOD.., THERE'S 225...BETTER LOCK UP THE CAR AFTER I PARK IT...I'D HATE TO LOSE THIS TAPE DECK...
WHO'RE YOU??
FLAKEY FOONT... IS MR. NATURAL HERE?
OH MY GOD! THERE SHE IS!
SOME GUY NAMED FOONT!
HEY MR. FOONT! YOU GOT ANY MONEY?
WALL GAZING BUDDHA
TEE HEE
WE WANT SOMETHING TO DRINK.!!
ALL HE'S GOT HERE IS WATER!
YEAH, I HAVE A FEW BUCKS ON ME...
SHE'S REAL! IT WASN'T A HALLUCINATION.. OH MY GOD!
LET'S TAKE A WALK DOWN TO JOHNNY'S LIQUOR, MR. FOONT....
ALRIGHT...
DON'T GET SIDETRACKED!
YES, WE HAVE MANY THINGS TO TALK ABOUT!

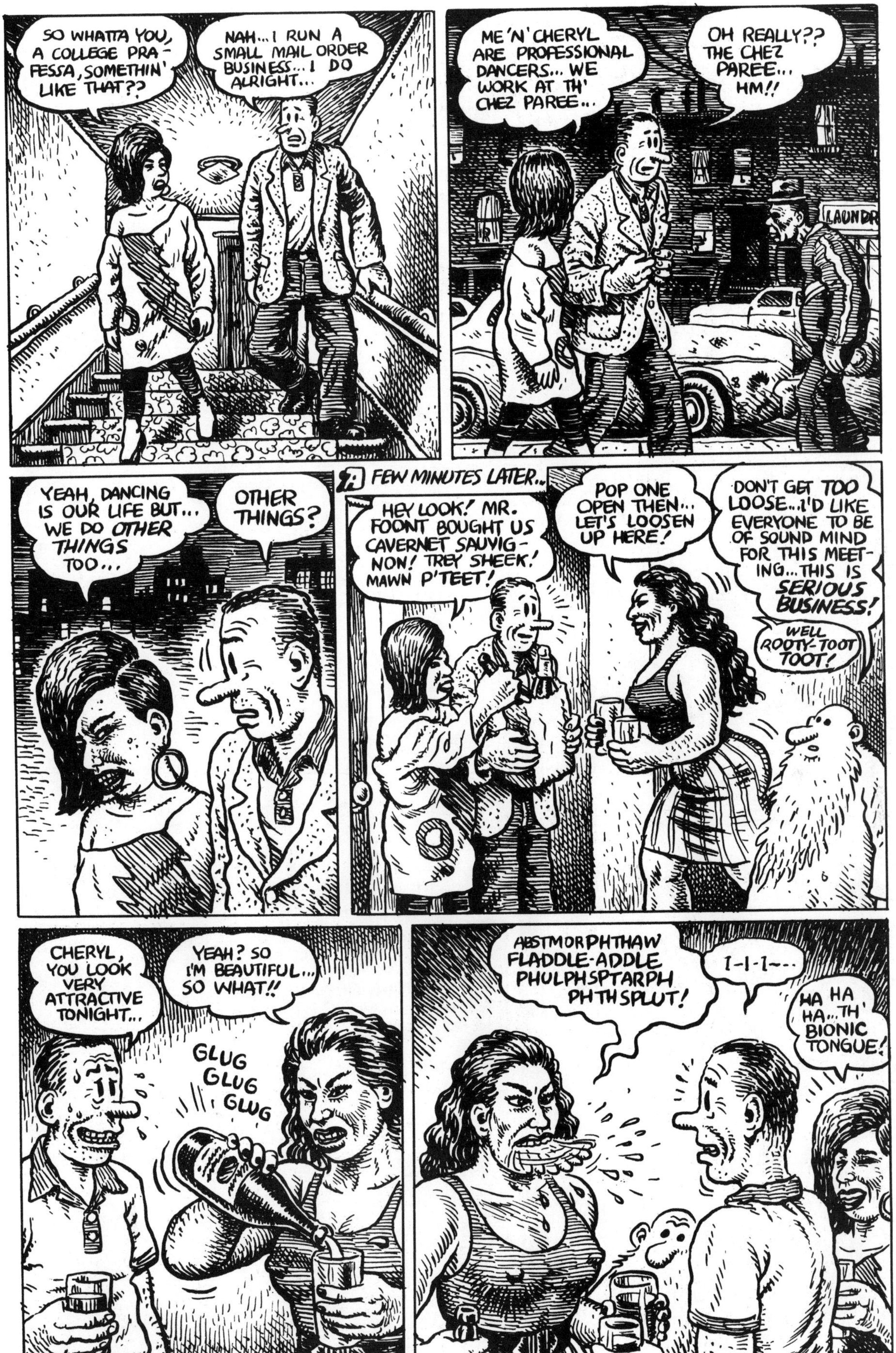
SO WHATTA YOU, A COLLEGE PRA-FESSA, SOMETHIN' LIKE THAT??
NAH... I RUN A SMALL MAIL ORDER BUSINESS... I DO ALRIGHT...
ME 'N' CHERYL ARE PROFESSIONAL DANCERS... WE WORK AT TH' CHEZ PAREE...
OH REALLY?? THE CHEZ PAREE... HM!!
LAUNDR
YEAH, DANCING IS OUR LIFE BUT... WE DO OTHER THINGS TOO...
OTHER THINGS?
A FEW MINUTES LATER...
HEY LOOK! MR. FOONT BOUGHT US CAVERNET SAUVIG-NON! TREY SHEEK! MAWN P'TEET!
POP ONE OPEN THEN... LET'S LOOSEN UP HERE!
DON'T GET TOO LOOSE... I'D LIKE EVERYONE TO BE OF SOUND MIND FOR THIS MEET-ING... THIS IS SERIOUS BUSINESS!
WELL ROOTY-TOOT TOOT!
CHERYL, YOU LOOK VERY ATTRACTIVE TONIGHT...
YEAH? SO I'M BEAUTIFUL... SO WHAT!!
GLUG GLUG GLUG
ABSTMORPHTHAW FLADDLE-ADDLE PHULPHSPTARPH PHTHSPLUT!
I-I-I---
HA HA HA... TH' BIONIC TONGUE!

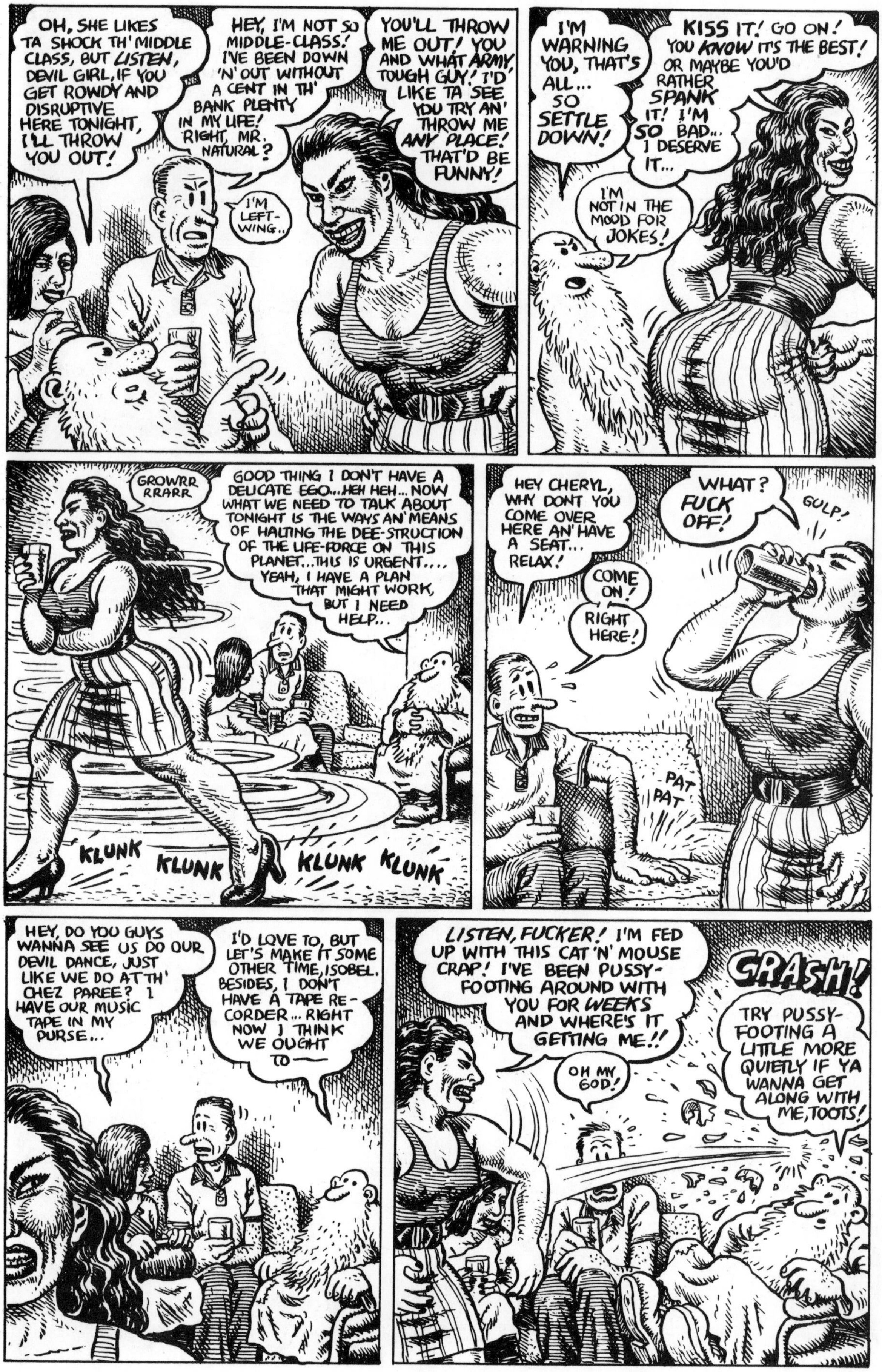

OH, SHE LIKES TA SHOCK TH' MIDDLE CLASS, BUT LISTEN, DEVIL GIRL, IF YOU GET ROWDY AND DISRUPTIVE HERE TONIGHT, I'LL THROW YOU OUT!
HEY, I'M NOT SO MIDDLE-CLASS! I'VE BEEN DOWN 'N' OUT WITHOUT A CENT IN TH' BANK PLENTY IN MY LIFE! RIGHT, MR. NATURAL?
I'M LEFT-WING...
YOU'LL THROW ME OUT! YOU AND WHAT ARMY, TOUGH GUY! I'D LIKE TA SEE YOU TRY AN' THROW ME ANY PLACE! THAT'D BE FUNNY!
I'M WARNING YOU, THAT'S ALL... SO SETTLE DOWN!
KISS IT! GO ON! YOU KNOW IT'S THE BEST! OR MAYBE YOU'D RATHER SPANK IT! I'M SO BAD... I DESERVE IT...
I'M NOT IN THE MOOD FOR JOKES!
GROWRR RRARR
GOOD THING I DON'T HAVE A DELICATE EGO... HEH HEH... NOW WHAT WE NEED TO TALK ABOUT TONIGHT IS THE WAYS AN' MEANS OF HALTING THE DEE-STRUCTION OF THE LIFE-FORCE ON THIS PLANET... THIS IS URGENT.... YEAH, I HAVE A PLAN THAT MIGHT WORK, BUT I NEED HELP...
KLUNK KLUNK KLUNK KLUNK
HEY CHERYL, WHY DONT YOU COME OVER HERE AN' HAVE A SEAT... RELAX!
COME ON! RIGHT HERE!
WHAT? FUCK OFF!
GULP!
PAT PAT
HEY, DO YOU GUYS WANNA SEE US DO OUR DEVIL DANCE, JUST LIKE WE DO AT TH' CHEZ PAREE? I HAVE OUR MUSIC TAPE IN MY PURSE...
I'D LOVE TO, BUT LET'S MAKE IT SOME OTHER TIME, ISOBEL. BESIDES, I DON'T HAVE A TAPE RE-CORDER... RIGHT NOW I THINK WE OUGHT TO—
LISTEN, FUCKER! I'M FED UP WITH THIS CAT 'N' MOUSE CRAP! I'VE BEEN PUSSY-FOOTING AROUND WITH YOU FOR WEEKS AND WHERE'S IT GETTING ME!!
OH MY GOD!
CRASH!
TRY PUSSY-FOOTING A LITTLE MORE QUIETLY IF YA WANNA GET ALONG WITH ME, TOOTS!

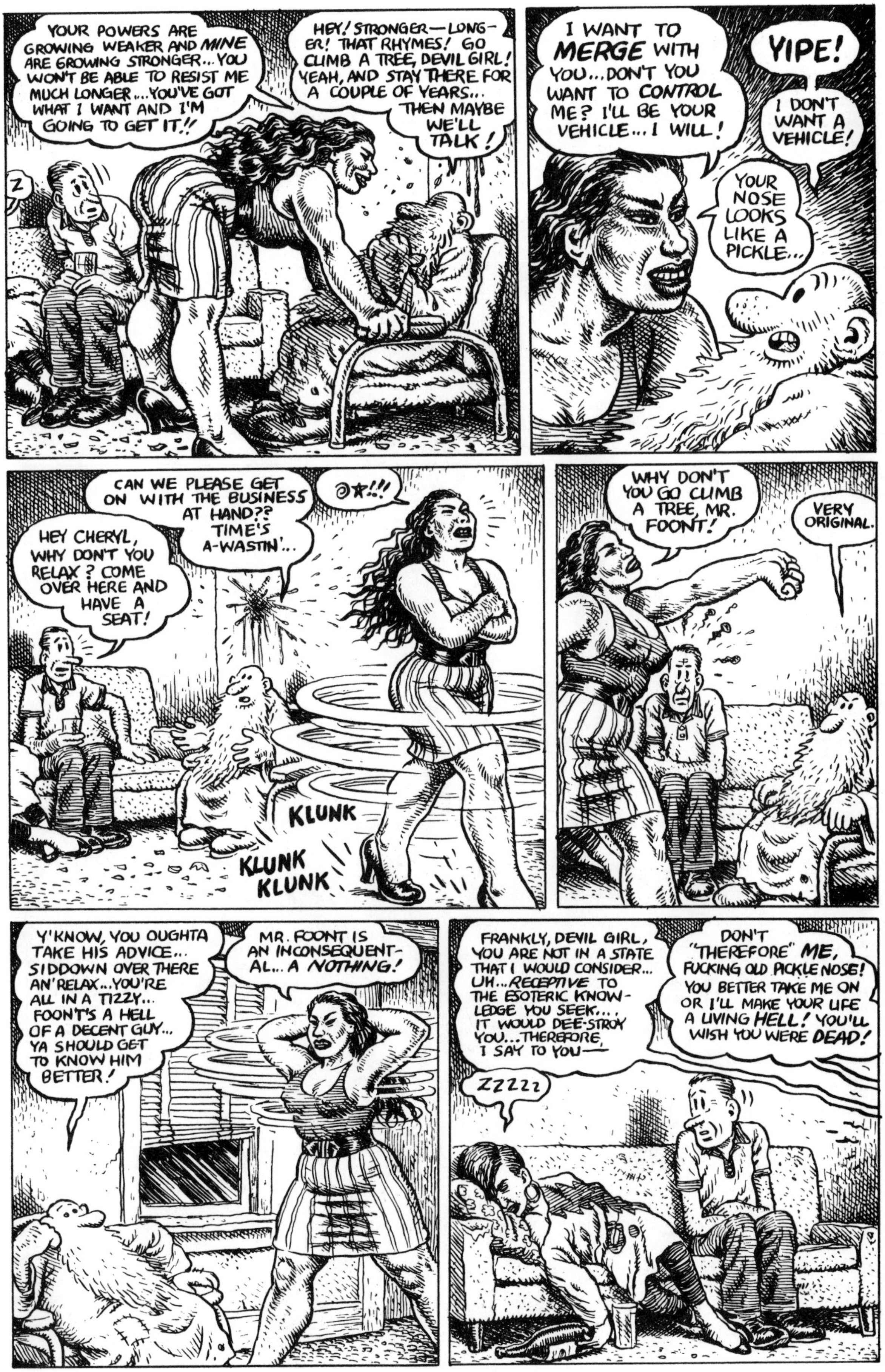
YOUR POWERS ARE GROWING WEAKER AND MINE ARE GROWING STRONGER... YOU WON'T BE ABLE TO RESIST ME MUCH LONGER... YOU'VE GOT WHAT I WANT AND I'M GOING TO GET IT!!
HEY! STRONGER—LONGER! THAT RHYMES! GO CLIMB A TREE, DEVIL GIRL! YEAH, AND STAY THERE FOR A COUPLE OF YEARS... THEN MAYBE WE'LL TALK!
Z
I WANT TO MERGE WITH YOU... DON'T YOU WANT TO CONTROL ME? I'LL BE YOUR VEHICLE... I WILL!
YIPE!
I DON'T WANT A VEHICLE!
YOUR NOSE LOOKS LIKE A PICKLE...
CAN WE PLEASE GET ON WITH THE BUSINESS AT HAND?? TIME'S A-WASTIN'...
@☆!!!
HEY CHERYL, WHY DON'T YOU RELAX? COME OVER HERE AND HAVE A SEAT!
KLUNK
KLUNK KLUNK
WHY DON'T YOU GO CLIMB A TREE, MR. FOONT!
VERY ORIGINAL.
Y'KNOW, YOU OUGHTA TAKE HIS ADVICE... SIDDOWN OVER THERE AN' RELAX... YOU'RE ALL IN A TIZZY... FOONT'S A HELL OF A DECENT GUY... YA SHOULD GET TO KNOW HIM BETTER!
MR. FOONT IS AN INCONSEQUENTAL... A NOTHING!
FRANKLY, DEVIL GIRL, YOU ARE NOT IN A STATE THAT I WOULD CONSIDER... UH... RECEPTIVE TO THE ESOTERIC KNOWLEDGE YOU SEEK... IT WOULD DEE-STROY YOU... THEREFORE, I SAY TO YOU—
DON'T "THEREFORE" ME, FUCKING OLD PICKLE NOSE! YOU BETTER TAKE ME ON OR I'LL MAKE YOUR LIFE A LIVING HELL! YOU'LL WISH YOU WERE DEAD!
ZZZZZ

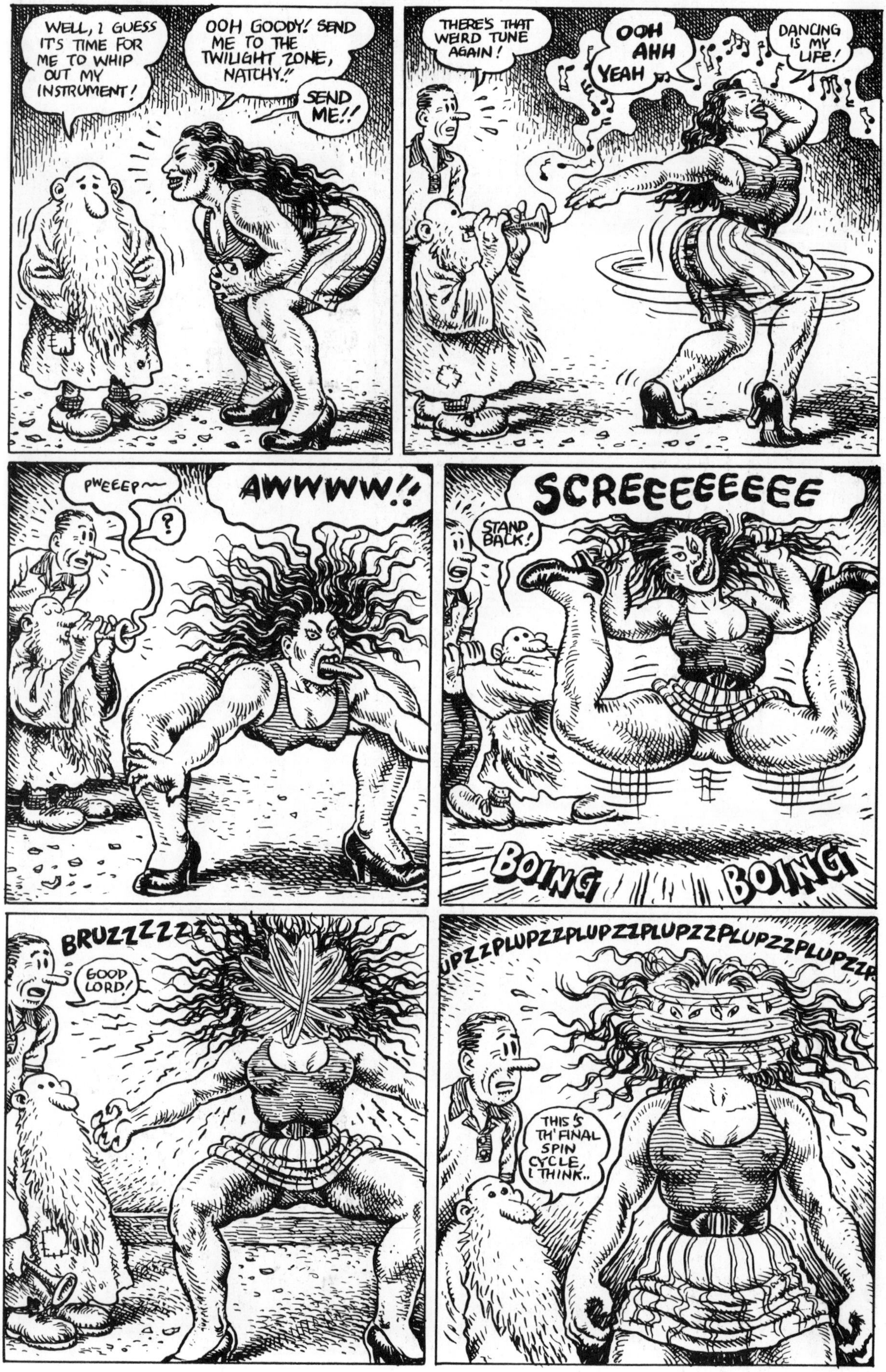
WELL, I GUESS IT'S TIME FOR ME TO WHIP OUT MY INSTRUMENT!
OOH GOODY! SEND ME TO THE TWILIGHT ZONE, NATCHY!!
SEND ME!!
THERE'S THAT WEIRD TUNE AGAIN!
OOH AHH YEAH
DANCING IS MY LIFE!
PWEEEP~
?
AWWWW!!
SCREEEEEEEEE
STAND BACK!
BOING
BOING
BRUZZZZZZ
GOOD LORD!
UPZZPLUPZZPLUPZZPLUPZZPLUPZZPLUPZZP
THIS'S TH' FINAL SPIN CYCLE, I THINK..

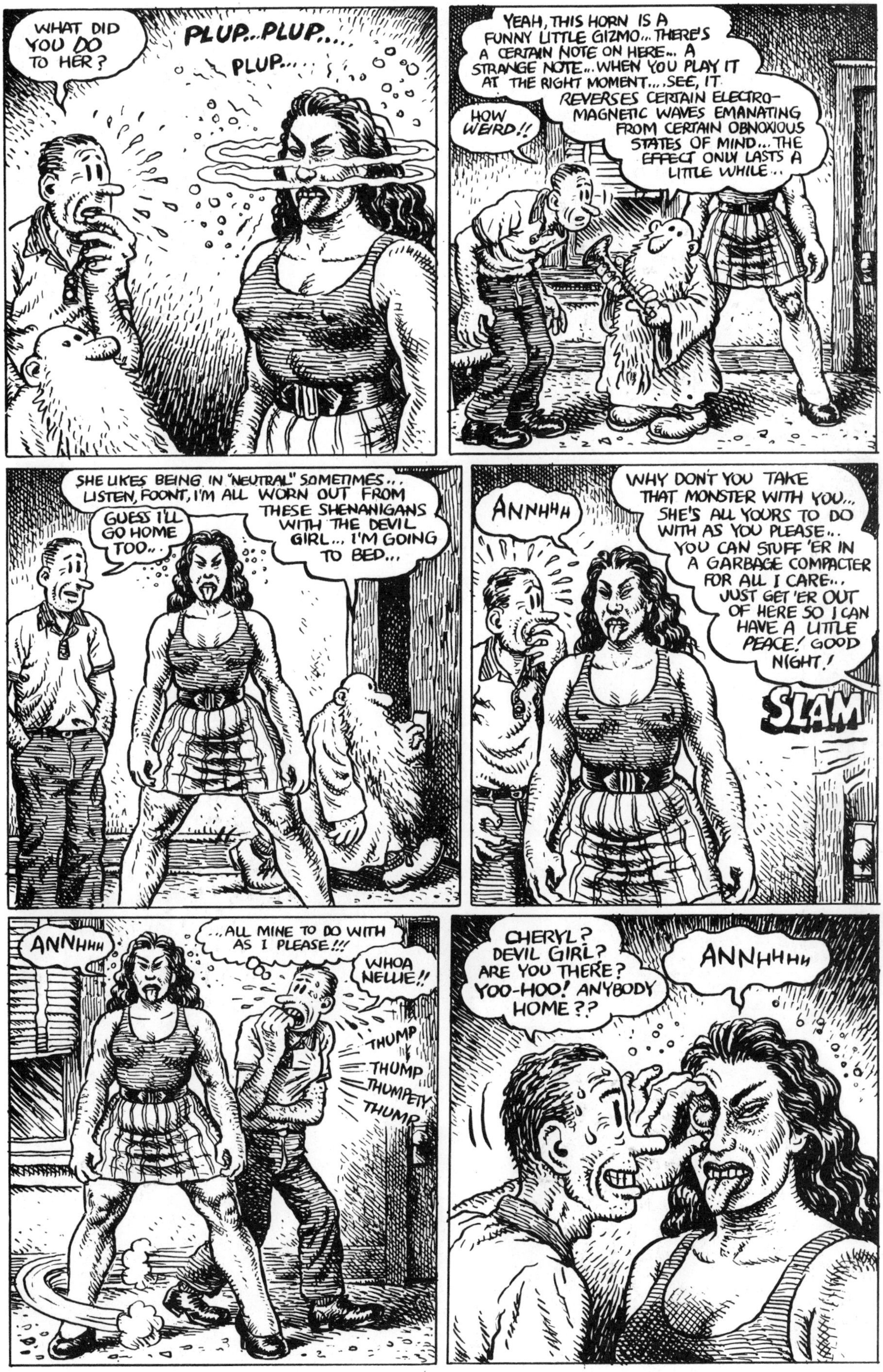
WHAT DID YOU DO TO HER?
PLUP...PLUP.... PLUP...
YEAH, THIS HORN IS A FUNNY LITTLE GIZMO... THERE'S A CERTAIN NOTE ON HERE... A STRANGE NOTE... WHEN YOU PLAY IT AT THE RIGHT MOMENT..., SEE, IT REVERSES CERTAIN ELECTRO-MAGNETIC WAVES EMANATING FROM CERTAIN OBNOXIOUS STATES OF MIND... THE EFFECT ONLY LASTS A LITTLE WHILE...
HOW WEIRD!!
SHE LIKES BEING IN "NEUTRAL" SOMETIMES... LISTEN, FOONT, I'M ALL WORN OUT FROM THESE SHENANIGANS WITH THE DEVIL GIRL... I'M GOING TO BED...
GUESS I'LL GO HOME TOO...
ANNHHH
WHY DON'T YOU TAKE THAT MONSTER WITH YOU... SHE'S ALL YOURS TO DO WITH AS YOU PLEASE... YOU CAN STUFF 'ER IN A GARBAGE COMPACTER FOR ALL I CARE... JUST GET 'ER OUT OF HERE SO I CAN HAVE A LITTLE PEACE! GOOD NIGHT!
SLAM
ANNHHH
...ALL MINE TO DO WITH AS I PLEASE!!!
WHOA NELLIE!!
THUMP THUMP THUMPETY THUMP
CHERYL? DEVIL GIRL? ARE YOU THERE? YOO-HOO! ANYBODY HOME??
ANNHHHHH

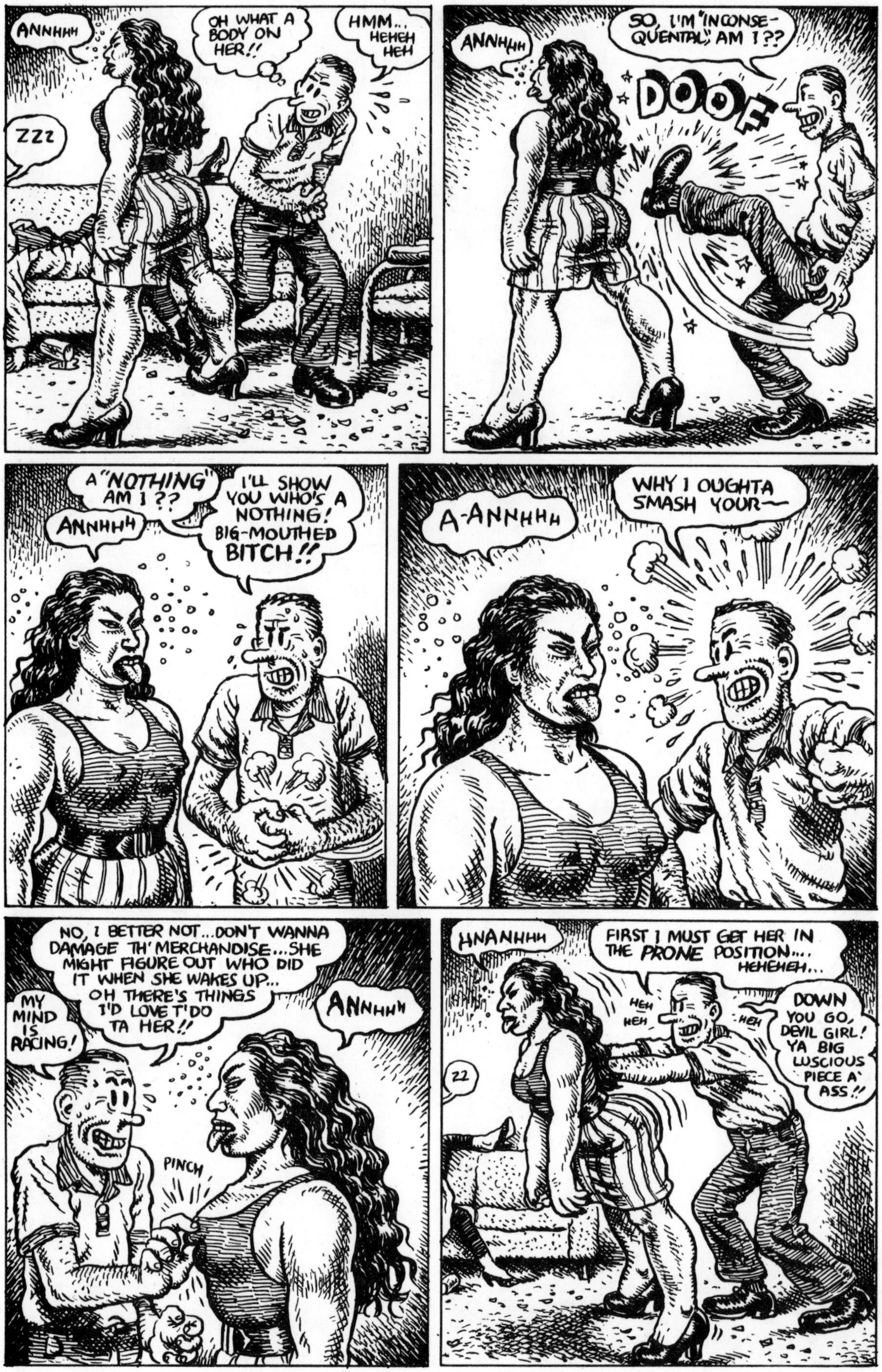
ANNHHH
OH WHAT A BODY ON HER!!
HMM... HEHEH HEH
ZZZ
ANNHHH
SO, I'M "INCONSE-QUENTIAL," AM I??
DOOF
A "NOTHING" AM I??
ANNHHH
I'LL SHOW YOU WHO'S A NOTHING! BIG-MOUTHED BITCH!!
A-ANNHHH
WHY I OUGHTA SMASH YOUR—
NO, I BETTER NOT...DON'T WANNA DAMAGE TH' MERCHANDISE...SHE MIGHT FIGURE OUT WHO DID IT WHEN SHE WAKES UP... OH THERE'S THINGS I'D LOVE T'DO TA HER!!
MY MIND IS RACING!
ANNHHH
PINCH
HNANHHH
FIRST I MUST GET HER IN THE PRONE POSITION.... HEHEHEH...
HEH HEH
HEH
DOWN YOU GO, DEVIL GIRL! YA BIG LUSCIOUS PIECE A' ASS!!
ZZ

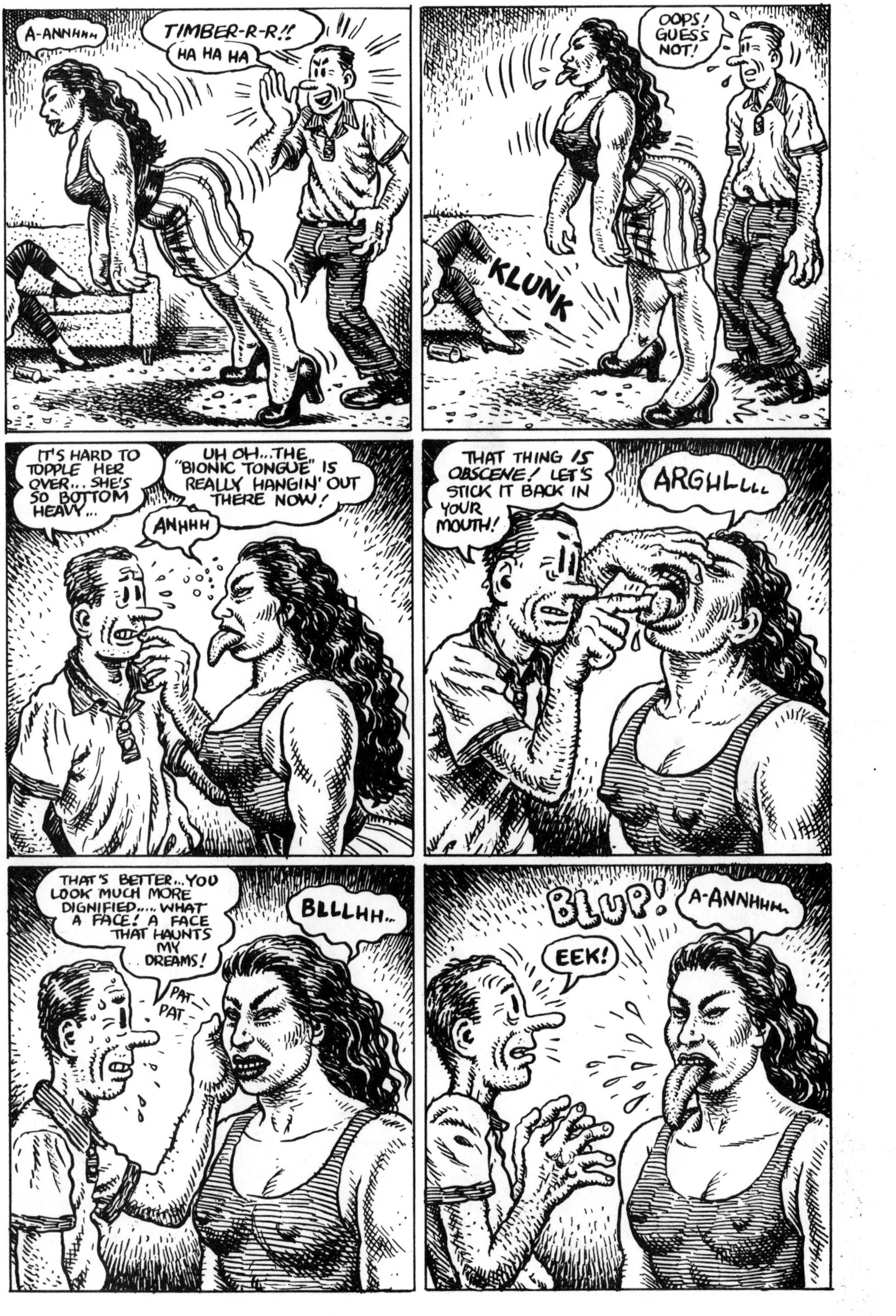
A-ANNHHH
TIMBER-R-R!!
HA HA HA
OOPS! GUESS NOT!
KLUNK
IT'S HARD TO TOPPLE HER OVER... SHE'S SO BOTTOM HEAVY...
UH OH...THE "BIONIC TONGUE" IS REALLY HANGIN' OUT THERE NOW!
ANHHH
THAT THING IS OBSCENE! LET'S STICK IT BACK IN YOUR MOUTH!
ARGHLLLL
THAT'S BETTER...YOU LOOK MUCH MORE DIGNIFIED.... WHAT A FACE! A FACE THAT HAUNTS MY DREAMS!
BLLLHH..
PAT PAT
BLUP!
A-ANNHHH
EEK!

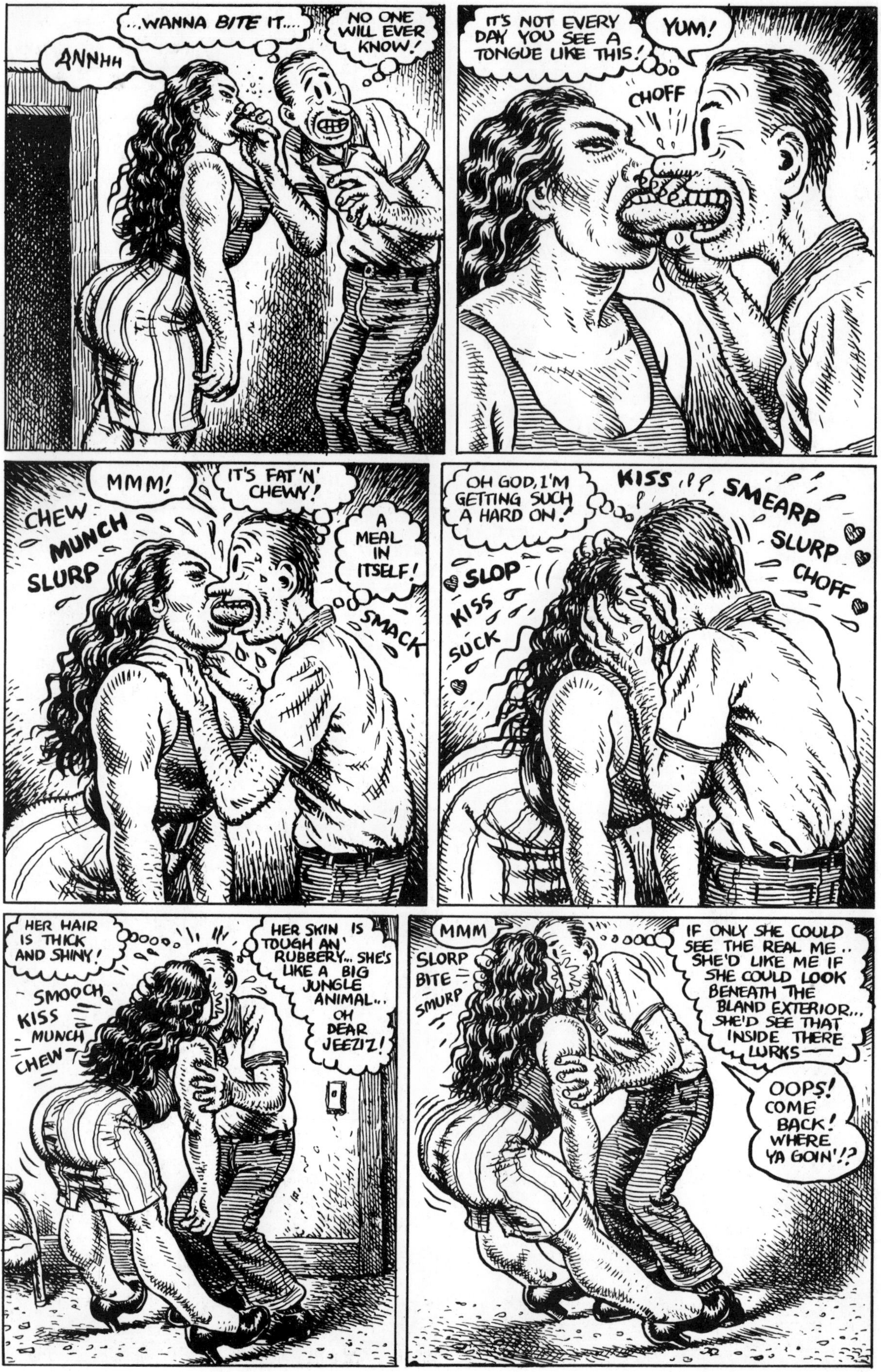
ANNHH
...WANNA BITE IT....
NO ONE WILL EVER KNOW!
IT'S NOT EVERY DAY YOU SEE A TONGUE LIKE THIS!
YUM!
CHOFF
MMM!
IT'S FAT 'N' CHEWY!
CHEW
MUNCH
SLURP
A MEAL IN ITSELF!
SMACK
OH GOD, I'M GETTING SUCH A HARD ON!
KISS
SMEARP
SLURP
CHOFF
SLOP
KISS
SUCK
HER HAIR IS THICK AND SHINY!
HER SKIN IS TOUGH AN' RUBBERY... SHE'S LIKE A BIG JUNGLE ANIMAL... OH DEAR JEEZIZ!
SMOOCH
KISS
MUNCH
CHEW
MMM
SLORP
BITE
SMURP
IF ONLY SHE COULD SEE THE REAL ME.. SHE'D LIKE ME IF SHE COULD LOOK BENEATH THE BLAND EXTERIOR... SHE'D SEE THAT INSIDE THERE LURKS —
OOPS! COME BACK! WHERE YA GOIN'!?

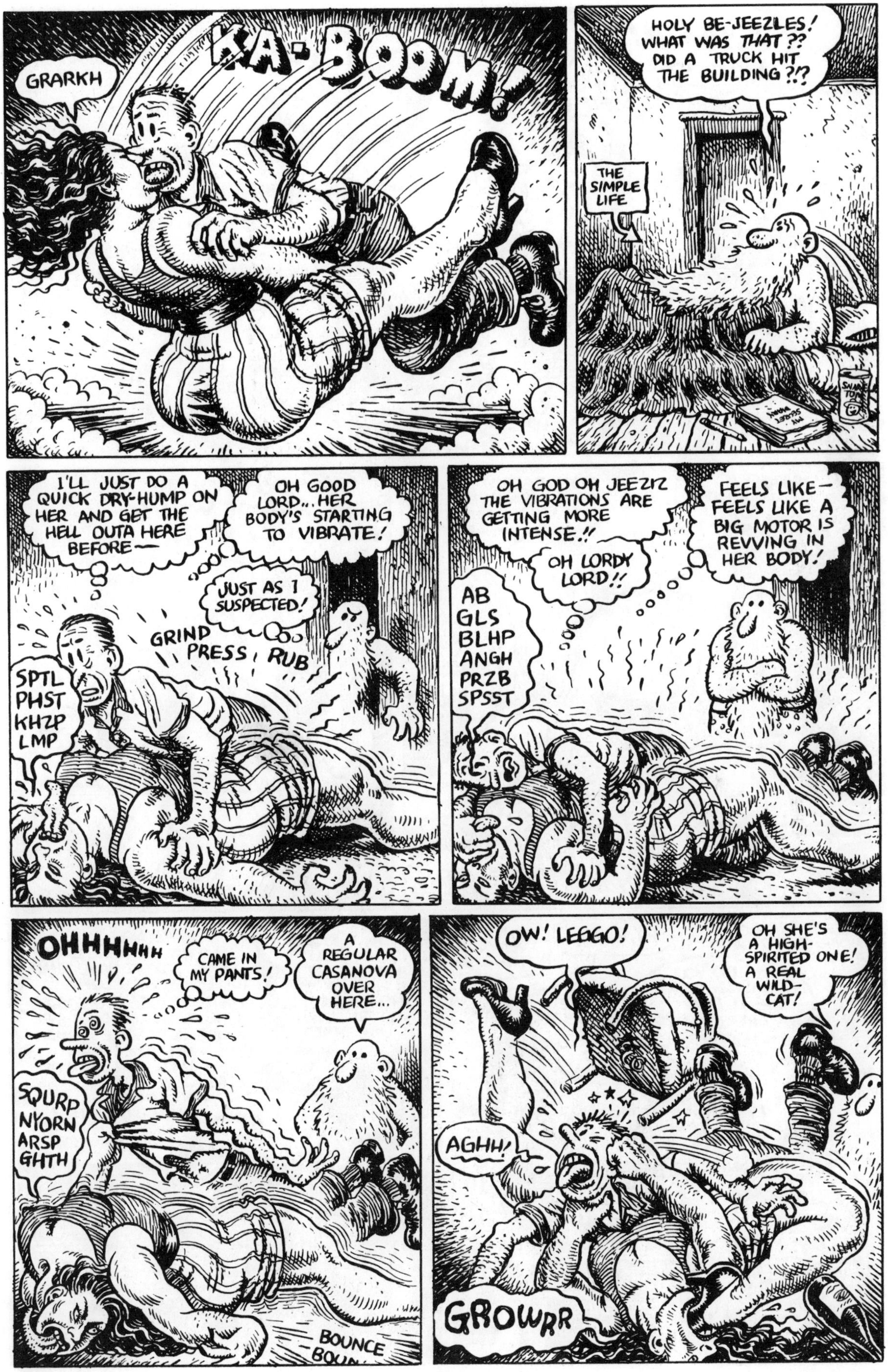
GRARKH
KA-BOOM!
HOLY BE-JEEZLES! WHAT WAS THAT?? DID A TRUCK HIT THE BUILDING?!?
THE SIMPLE LIFE
I'LL JUST DO A QUICK DRY-HUMP ON HER AND GET THE HELL OUTA HERE BEFORE—
OH GOOD LORD... HER BODY'S STARTING TO VIBRATE!
JUST AS I SUSPECTED!
GRIND PRESS RUB
SPTL PHST KHZP LMP
OH GOD OH JEEZ!Z THE VIBRATIONS ARE GETTING MORE INTENSE!!
FEELS LIKE— FEELS LIKE A BIG MOTOR IS REVVING IN HER BODY!
OH LORDY LORD!!
AB GLS BLHP ANGH PRZB SPSST
OHHHHHH
CAME IN MY PANTS!
A REGULAR CASANOVA OVER HERE...
SQURP NYORN ARSP GHTH
BOUNCE
OW! LEGGO!
OH SHE'S A HIGH-SPIRITED ONE! A REAL WILD-CAT!
AGHH!
GROWRR

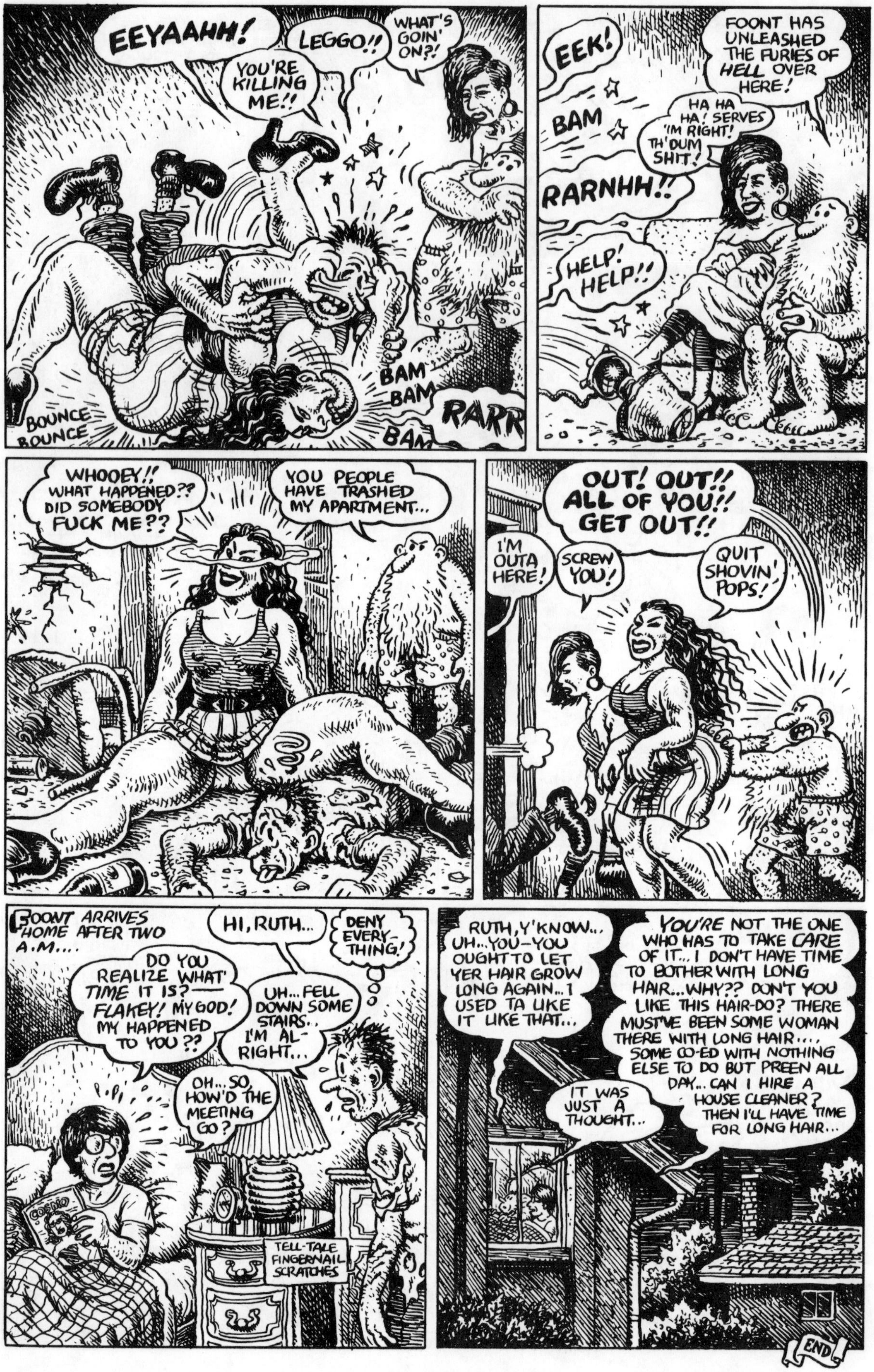
EEYAAHH!
YOU'RE KILLING ME!!
LEGGO!!
WHAT'S GOIN' ON?!
BOUNCE BOUNCE
BAM BAM BAM
RARR
EEK!
FOONT HAS UNLEASHED THE FURIES OF HELL OVER HERE!
BAM
HA HA HA! SERVES 'IM RIGHT! TH' DUM SHIT!
RARNHH!!
HELP! HELP!!
WHOOEY!! WHAT HAPPENED?? DID SOMEBODY FUCK ME??
YOU PEOPLE HAVE TRASHED MY APARTMENT...
OUT! OUT!! ALL OF YOU!! GET OUT!!
I'M OUTA HERE!
SCREW YOU!
QUIT SHOVIN' POPS!
FOONT ARRIVES HOME AFTER TWO A.M....
HI, RUTH...
DENY EVERY-THING!
DO YOU REALIZE WHAT TIME IT IS?— FLAKEY! MY GOD! MY HAPPENED TO YOU??
UH... FELL DOWN SOME STAIRS.. I'M AL-RIGHT...
OH... SO, HOW'D THE MEETING GO?
COSMO
TELL-TALE FINGERNAIL SCRATCHES
RUTH, Y'KNOW... UH... YOU-YOU OUGHT TO LET YER HAIR GROW LONG AGAIN... I USED TA LIKE IT LIKE THAT...
YOU'RE NOT THE ONE WHO HAS TO TAKE CARE OF IT... I DON'T HAVE TIME TO BOTHER WITH LONG HAIR... WHY?? DON'T YOU LIKE THIS HAIR-DO? THERE MUST'VE BEEN SOME WOMAN THERE WITH LONG HAIR..., SOME CO-ED WITH NOTHING ELSE TO DO BUT PREEN ALL DAY... CAN I HIRE A HOUSE CLEANER? THEN I'LL HAVE TIME FOR LONG HAIR...
IT WAS JUST A THOUGHT...
END

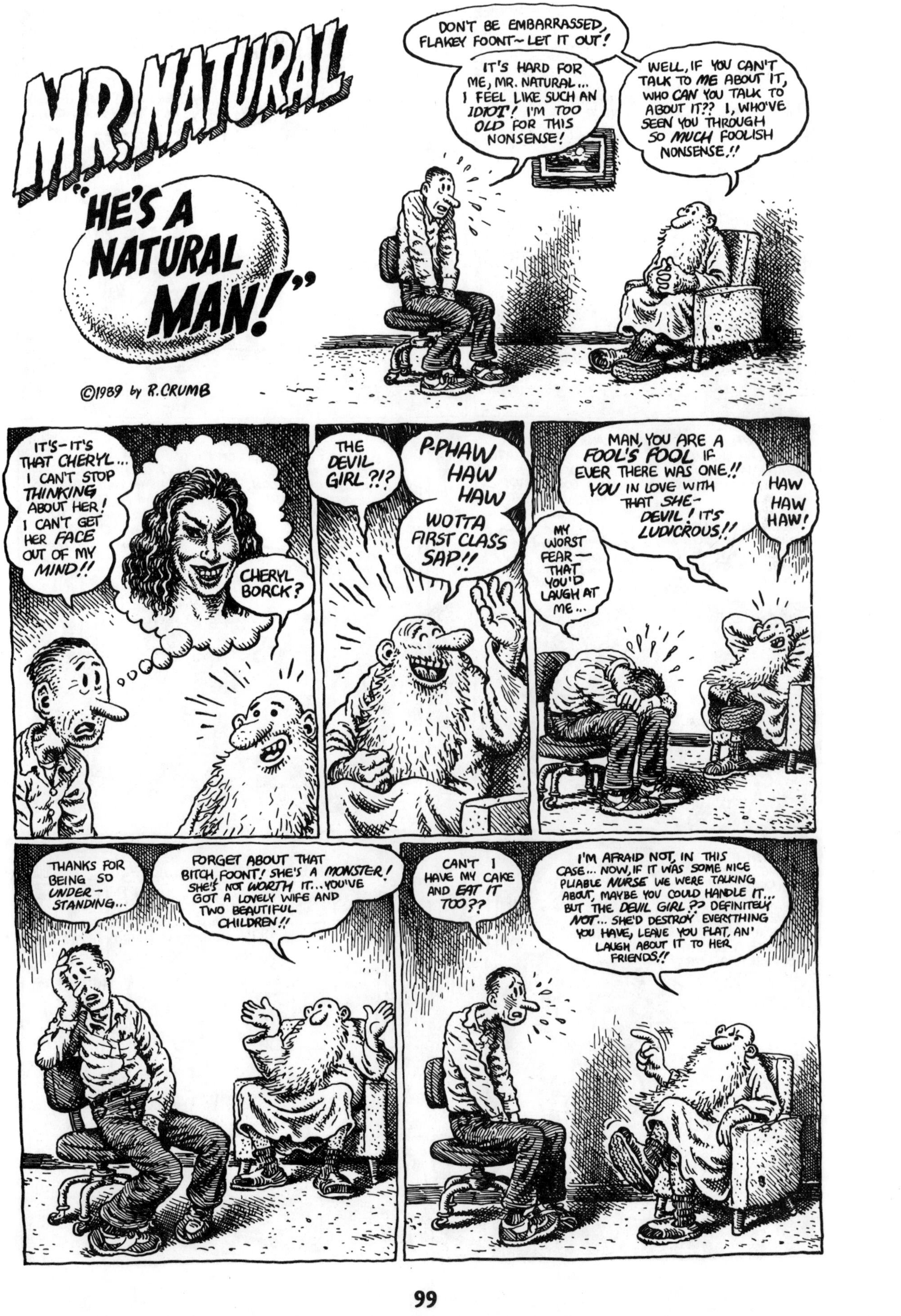
MR. NATURAL
"HE'S A NATURAL MAN!"
©1989 by R. CRUMB
DON'T BE EMBARRASSED, FLAKEY FOONT~ LET IT OUT!
IT'S HARD FOR ME, MR. NATURAL... I FEEL LIKE SUCH AN IDIOT! I'M TOO OLD FOR THIS NONSENSE!
WELL, IF YOU CAN'T TALK TO ME ABOUT IT, WHO CAN YOU TALK TO ABOUT IT?? I, WHO'VE SEEN YOU THROUGH SO MUCH FOOLISH NONSENSE!!
IT'S– IT'S THAT CHERYL... I CAN'T STOP THINKING ABOUT HER! I CAN'T GET HER FACE OUT OF MY MIND!!
CHERYL BORCK?
THE DEVIL GIRL?!?
P-PHAW HAW HAW
WOTTA FIRST CLASS SAP!!
MAN, YOU ARE A FOOL'S FOOL IF EVER THERE WAS ONE!! YOU IN LOVE WITH THAT SHE-DEVIL! IT'S LUDICROUS!!
HAW HAW HAW!
MY WORST FEAR— THAT YOU'D LAUGH AT ME...
THANKS FOR BEING SO UNDER-STANDING...
FORGET ABOUT THAT BITCH, FOONT! SHE'S A MONSTER! SHE'S NOT WORTH IT... YOU'VE GOT A LOVELY WIFE AND TWO BEAUTIFUL CHILDREN!!
CAN'T I HAVE MY CAKE AND EAT IT TOO??
I'M AFRAID NOT, IN THIS CASE... NOW, IF IT WAS SOME NICE PLIABLE NURSE WE WERE TALKING ABOUT, MAYBE YOU COULD HANDLE IT... BUT THE DEVIL GIRL?? DEFINITELY NOT... SHE'D DESTROY EVERYTHING YOU HAVE, LEAVE YOU FLAT, AN' LAUGH ABOUT IT TO HER FRIENDS!!

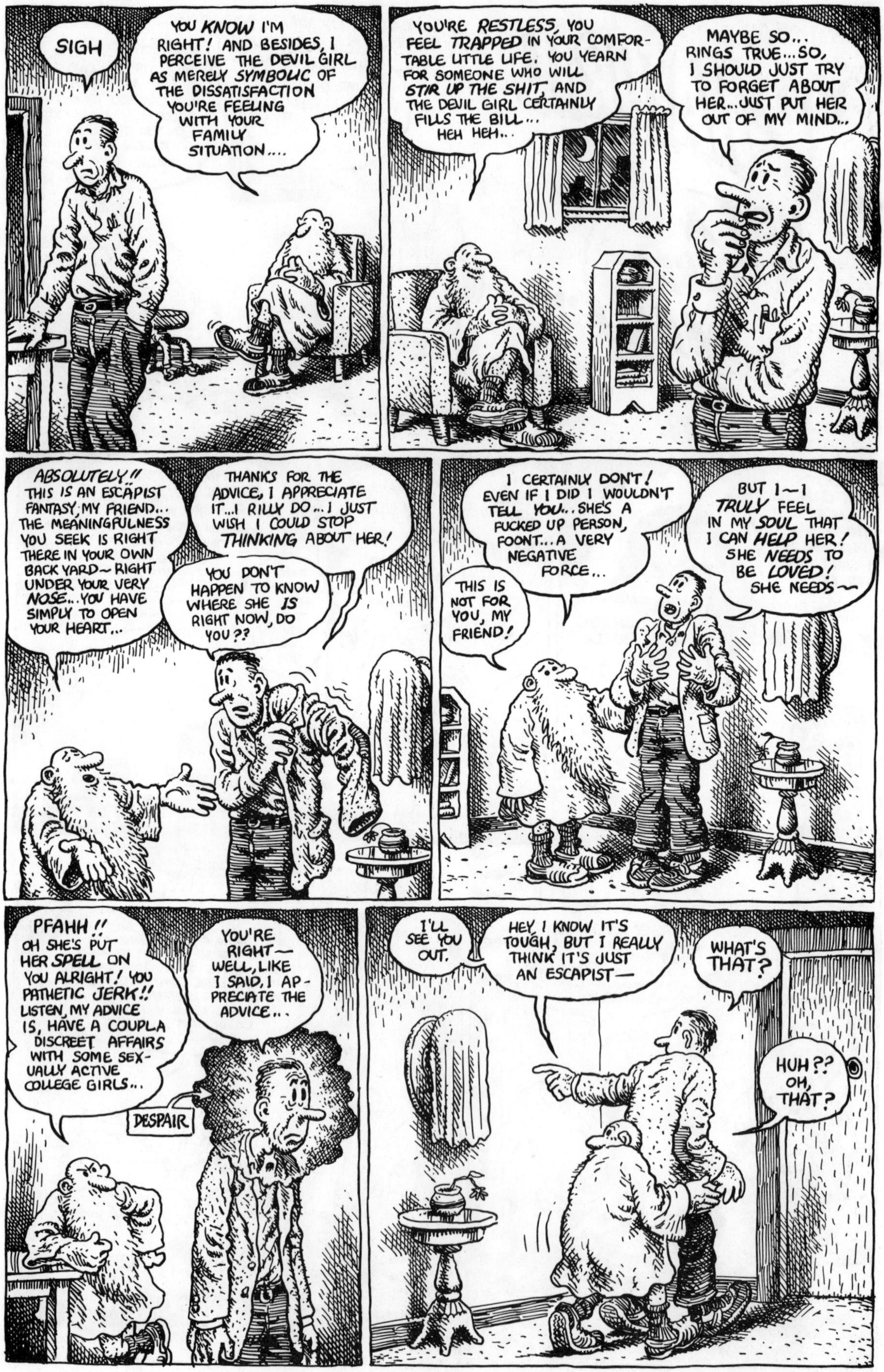
SIGH
YOU KNOW I'M RIGHT! AND BESIDES, I PERCEIVE THE DEVIL GIRL AS MERELY SYMBOLIC OF THE DISSATISFACTION YOU'RE FEELING WITH YOUR FAMILY SITUATION....
YOU'RE RESTLESS, YOU FEEL TRAPPED IN YOUR COMFORTABLE LITTLE LIFE. YOU YEARN FOR SOMEONE WHO WILL STIR UP THE SHIT, AND THE DEVIL GIRL CERTAINLY FILLS THE BILL... HEH HEH..
MAYBE SO... RINGS TRUE... SO, I SHOULD JUST TRY TO FORGET ABOUT HER... JUST PUT HER OUT OF MY MIND...
ABSOLUTELY!! THIS IS AN ESCÄPIST FANTASY, MY FRIEND... THE MEANINGFULNESS YOU SEEK IS RIGHT THERE IN YOUR OWN BACK YARD~ RIGHT UNDER YOUR VERY NOSE... YOU HAVE SIMPLY TO OPEN YOUR HEART...
THANKS FOR THE ADVICE, I APPRECIATE IT... I RILLY DO... I JUST WISH I COULD STOP THINKING ABOUT HER!
YOU DON'T HAPPEN TO KNOW WHERE SHE IS RIGHT NOW, DO YOU??
I CERTAINLY DON'T! EVEN IF I DID I WOULDN'T TELL YOU.. SHE'S A FUCKED UP PERSON, FOONT... A VERY NEGATIVE FORCE...
THIS IS NOT FOR YOU, MY FRIEND!
BUT I~I TRULY FEEL IN MY SOUL THAT I CAN HELP HER! SHE NEEDS TO BE LOVED! SHE NEEDS~
PFAHH!! OH SHE'S PUT HER SPELL ON YOU ALRIGHT! YOU PATHETIC JERK!! LISTEN, MY ADVICE IS, HAVE A COUPLA DISCREET AFFAIRS WITH SOME SEXUALLY ACTIVE COLLEGE GIRLS...
YOU'RE RIGHT— WELL, LIKE I SAID, I APPRECIATE THE ADVICE...
DESPAIR
I'LL SEE YOU OUT.
HEY, I KNOW IT'S TOUGH, BUT I REALLY THINK IT'S JUST AN ESCAPIST—
WHAT'S THAT?
HUH?? OH, THAT?

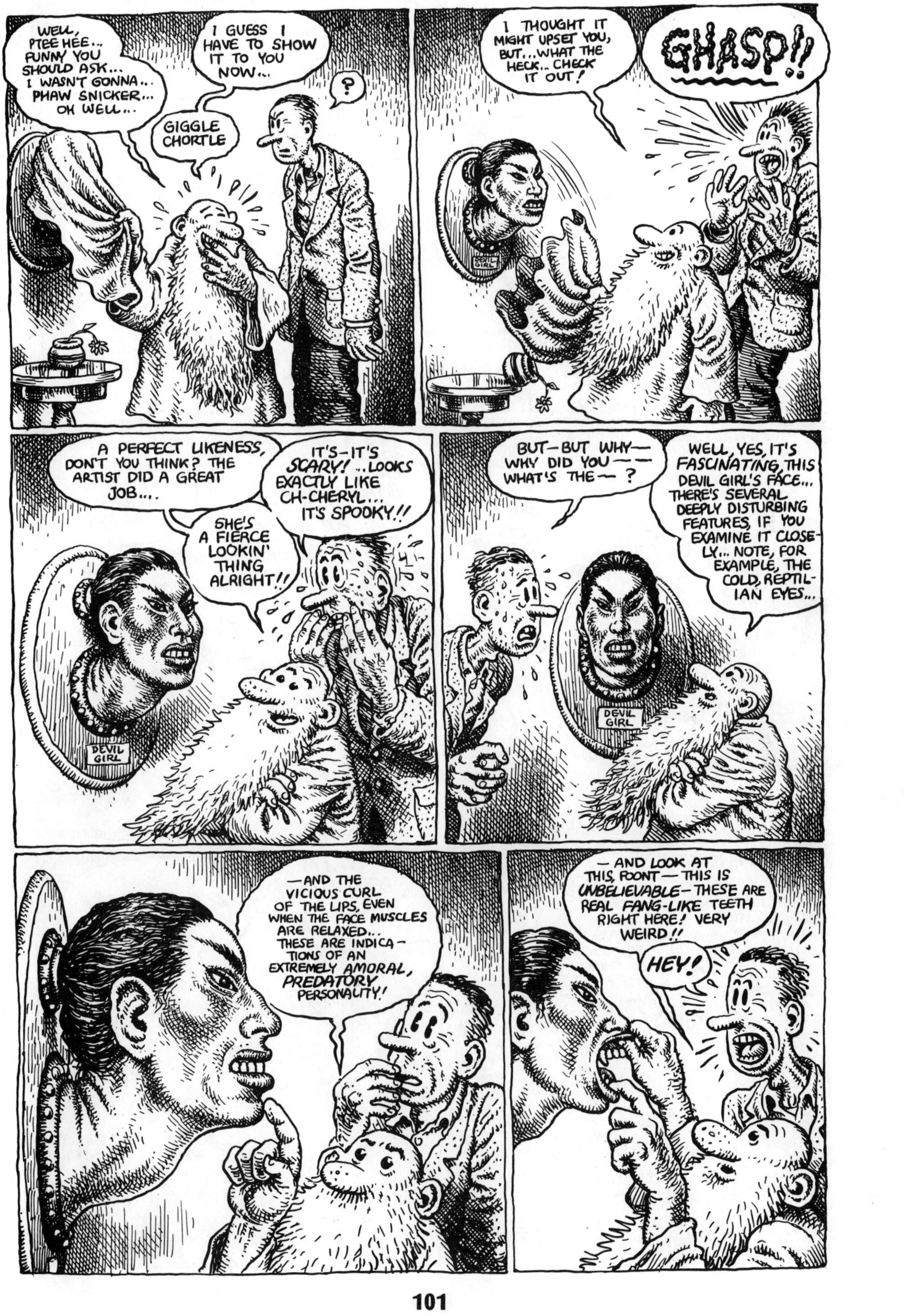
WELL, PTEE HÉE... FUNNY YOU SHOULD ASK... I WASN'T GONNA... PHAW SNICKER... OH WELL...
I GUESS I HAVE TO SHOW IT TO YOU NOW...
GIGGLE CHORTLE
?
I THOUGHT IT MIGHT UPSET YOU, BUT... WHAT THE HECK.. CHECK IT OUT!
GHASP!!
DEVIL GIRL
A PERFECT LIKENESS, DON'T YOU THINK? THE ARTIST DID A GREAT JOB....
IT'S-IT'S SCARY! ...LOOKS EXACTLY LIKE CH-CHERYL... IT'S SPOOKY!!
SHE'S A FIERCE LOOKIN' THING ALRIGHT!!
DEVIL GIRL
BUT-BUT WHY- WHY DID YOU-- WHAT'S THE-- ?
WELL, YES, IT'S FASCINATING, THIS DEVIL GIRL'S FACE... THERE'S SEVERAL DEEPLY DISTURBING FEATURES, IF YOU EXAMINE IT CLOSELY... NOTE, FOR EXAMPLE, THE COLD, REPTILIAN EYES...
DEVIL GIRL
—AND THE VICIOUS CURL OF THE LIPS, EVEN WHEN THE FACE MUSCLES ARE RELAXED... THESE ARE INDICATIONS OF AN EXTREMELY AMORAL, PREDATORY PERSONALITY!
—AND LOOK AT THIS, FOONT— THIS IS UNBELIEVABLE— THESE ARE REAL FANG-LIKE TEETH RIGHT HERE! VERY WEIRD!!
HEY!

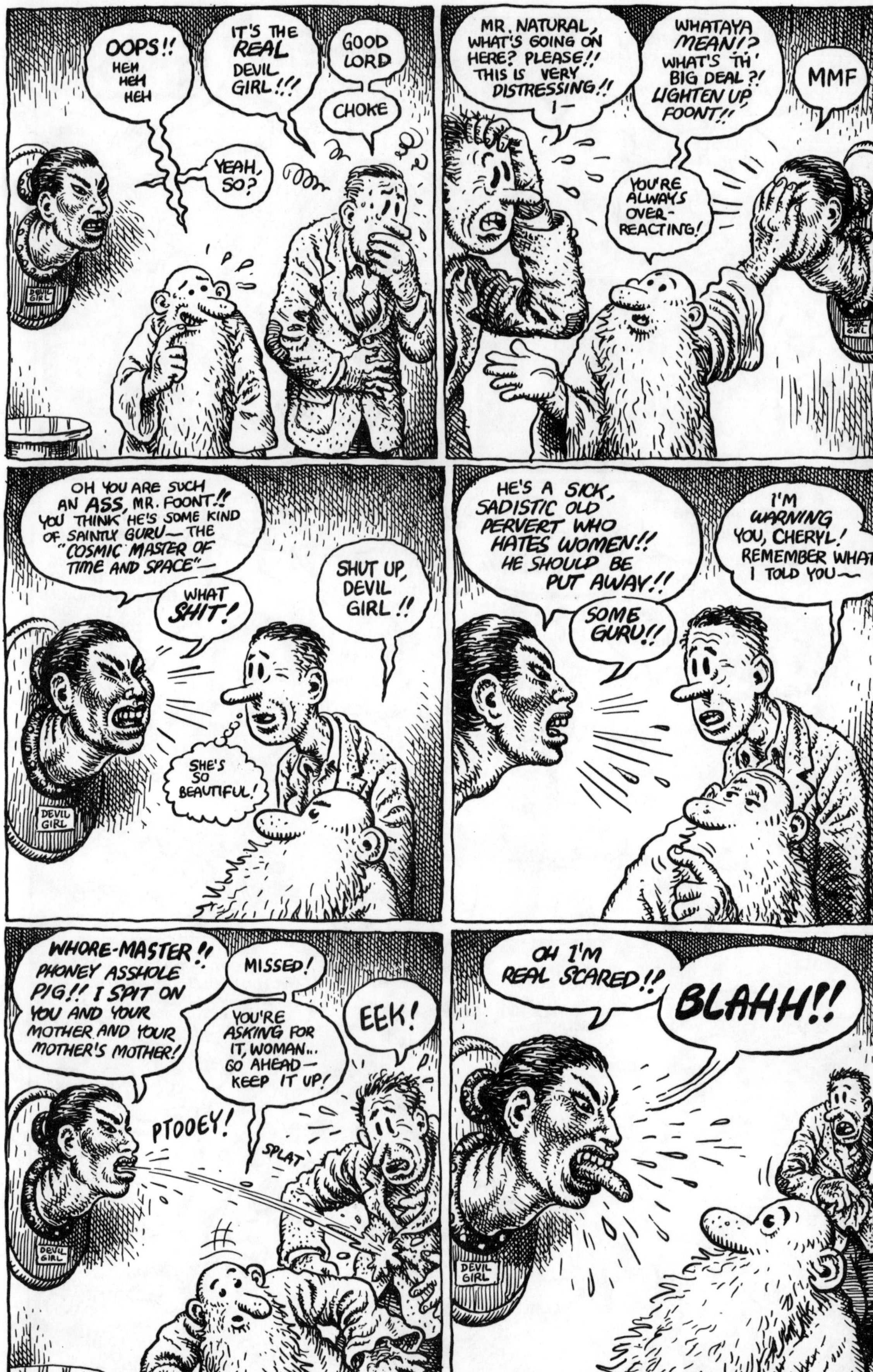
OOPS!! HEH HEH HEH
IT'S THE REAL DEVIL GIRL!!!
GOOD LORD
CHOKE
YEAH, SO?
MR. NATURAL, WHAT'S GOING ON HERE? PLEASE!! THIS IS VERY DISTRESSING!! I—
WHATAYA MEAN!? WHAT'S TH' BIG DEAL?! LIGHTEN UP FOONT!!
MMF
YOU'RE ALWAYS OVER-REACTING!
OH YOU ARE SUCH AN ASS, MR. FOONT!! YOU THINK HE'S SOME KIND OF SAINTLY GURU— THE "COSMIC MASTER OF TIME AND SPACE"—
WHAT SHIT!
SHUT UP, DEVIL GIRL!!
SHE'S SO BEAUTIFUL!
DEVIL GIRL
HE'S A SICK, SADISTIC OLD PERVERT WHO HATES WOMEN!! HE SHOULD BE PUT AWAY!!
SOME GURU!!
I'M WARNING YOU, CHERYL! REMEMBER WHAT I TOLD YOU~
WHORE-MASTER!! PHONEY ASSHOLE PIG!! I SPIT ON YOU AND YOUR MOTHER AND YOUR MOTHER'S MOTHER!
MISSED!
YOU'RE ASKING FOR IT, WOMAN... GO AHEAD— KEEP IT UP!
EEK!
PTOOEY!
SPLAT
DEVIL GIRL
OH I'M REAL SCARED!!
BLAHH!!
DEVIL GIRL

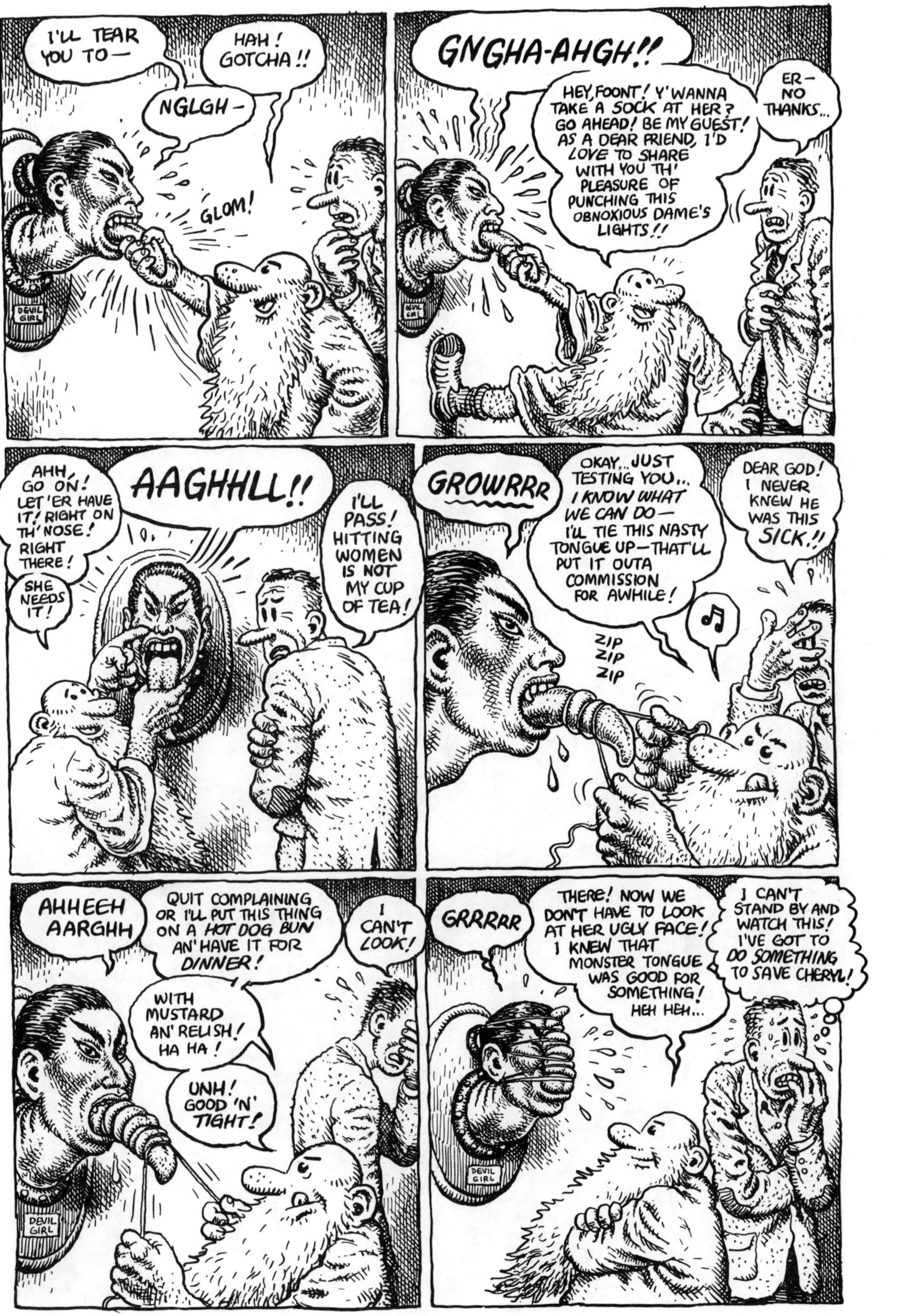
I'LL TEAR YOU TO—
HAH! GOTCHA!!
NGLGH—
GLOM!
DEVIL GIRL
GNGHA-AHGH!!
HEY, FOONT! Y'WANNA TAKE A SOCK AT HER? GO AHEAD! BE MY GUEST! AS A DEAR FRIEND, I'D LOVE TO SHARE WITH YOU TH' PLEASURE OF PUNCHING THIS OBNOXIOUS DAME'S LIGHTS!!
ER— NO THANKS...
AHH, GO ON! LET'ER HAVE IT! RIGHT ON TH' NOSE! RIGHT THERE!
SHE NEEDS IT!
AAGHHLL!!
I'LL PASS! HITTING WOMEN IS NOT MY CUP OF TEA!
GROWRRR
OKAY... JUST TESTING YOU... I KNOW WHAT WE CAN DO— I'LL TIE THIS NASTY TONGUE UP—THAT'LL PUT IT OUTA COMMISSION FOR AWHILE!
♪
ZIP ZIP ZIP
DEAR GOD! I NEVER KNEW HE WAS THIS SICK!!
AHHEEH AARGHH
QUIT COMPLAINING OR I'LL PUT THIS THING ON A HOT DOG BUN AN' HAVE IT FOR DINNER!
I CAN'T LOOK!
WITH MUSTARD AN' RELISH! HA HA!
UNH! GOOD 'N' TIGHT!
DEVIL GIRL
GRRRRR
THERE! NOW WE DON'T HAVE TO LOOK AT HER UGLY FACE! I KNEW THAT MONSTER TONGUE WAS GOOD FOR SOMETHING! HEH HEH...
I CAN'T STAND BY AND WATCH THIS! I'VE GOT TO DO SOMETHING TO SAVE CHERYL!
DEVIL GIRL

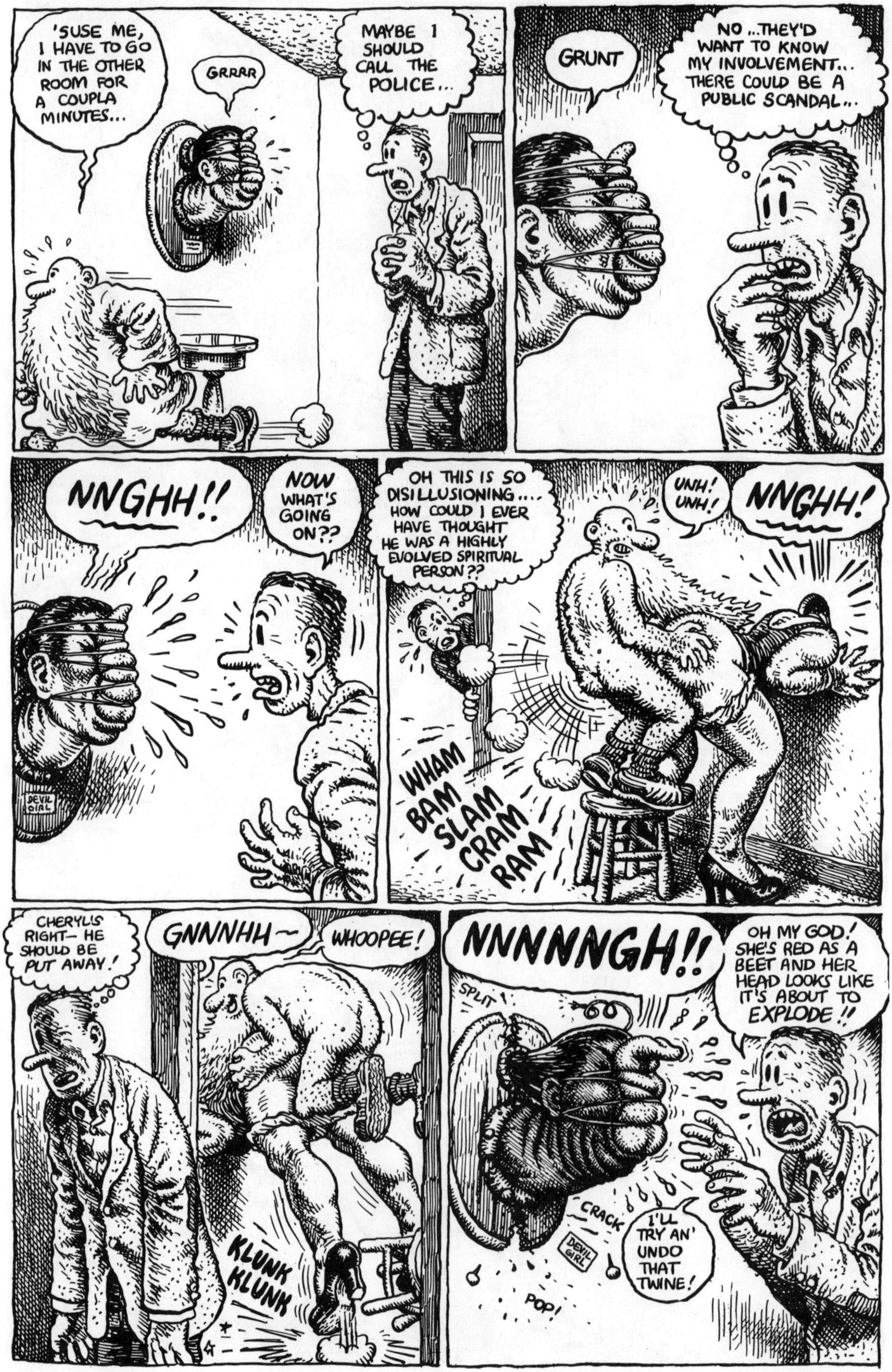
'SUSE ME, I HAVE TO GO IN THE OTHER ROOM FOR A COUPLA MINUTES...
GRRRR
MAYBE I SHOULD CALL THE POLICE...
GRUNT
NO...THEY'D WANT TO KNOW MY INVOLVEMENT... THERE COULD BE A PUBLIC SCANDAL...
NNGHH!!
NOW WHAT'S GOING ON??
DEVIL GIRL
OH THIS IS SO DISILLUSIONING... HOW COULD I EVER HAVE THOUGHT HE WAS A HIGHLY EVOLVED SPIRITUAL PERSON??
UNH! UNH!
NNGHH!
WHAM BAM SLAM CRAM RAM
CHERYL'S RIGHT— HE SHOULD BE PUT AWAY!
GNNNHH~
WHOOPEE!
KLUNK KLUNK
NNNNNNGH!!
OH MY GOD! SHE'S RED AS A BEET AND HER HEAD LOOKS LIKE IT'S ABOUT TO EXPLODE!!
SPLIT
CRACK
DEVIL GIRL
I'LL TRY AN' UNDO THAT TWINE!
POP!

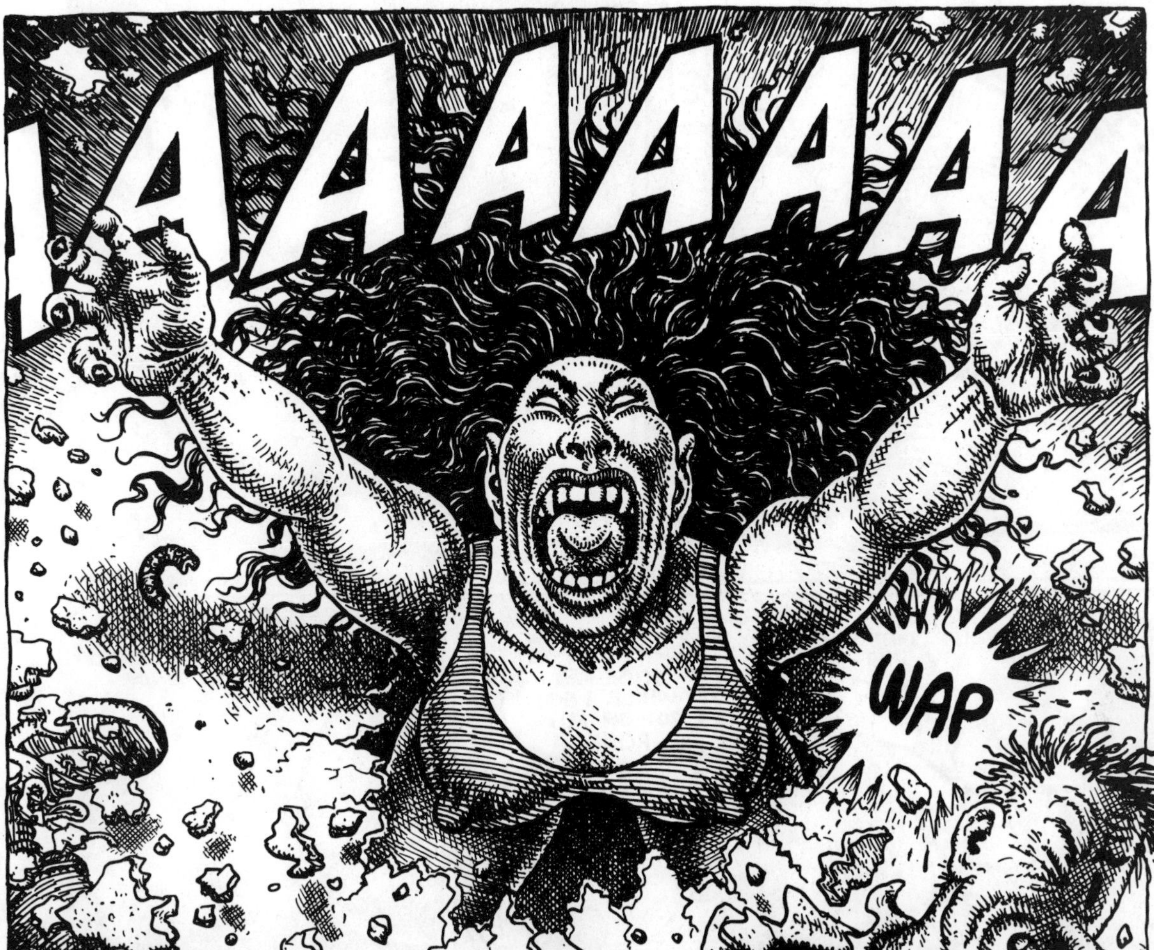
AAAAAAA
WAP

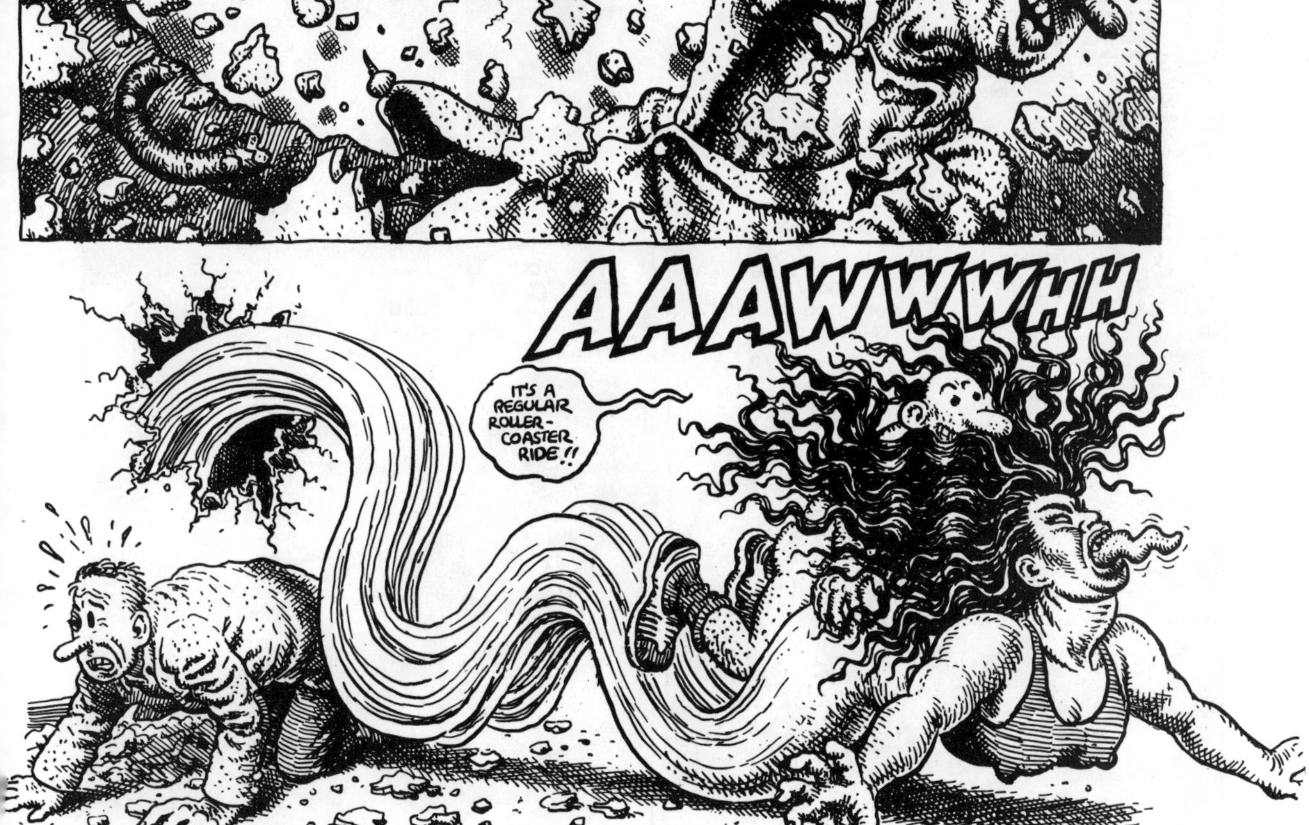
AAAWWWHH
IT'S A REGULAR ROLLER-COASTER RIDE!!

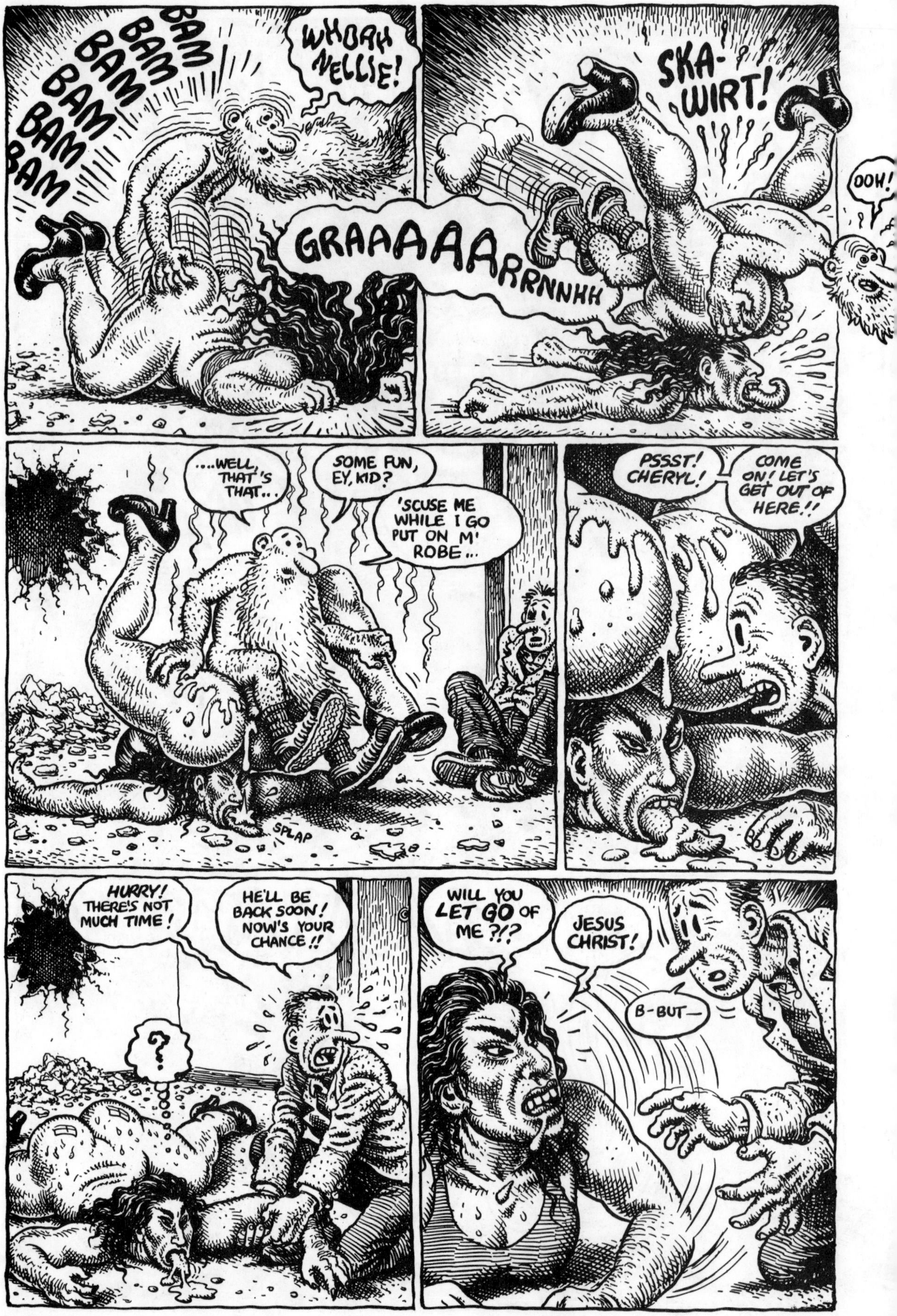
BAM BAM BAM BAM BAM BAM
WHOAH NELLIE!
GRAAAAAARRRNNHH
SKA-WIRT!
OOH!
...WELL, THAT'S THAT...
SOME FUN, EY, KID?
'SCUSE ME WHILE I GO PUT ON M' ROBE...
SPLAP
PSSST! CHERYL!
COME ON! LET'S GET OUT OF HERE!!
HURRY! THERE'S NOT MUCH TIME!
HE'LL BE BACK SOON! NOW'S YOUR CHANCE!!
?
WILL YOU LET GO OF ME?!?
JESUS CHRIST!
B-BUT—

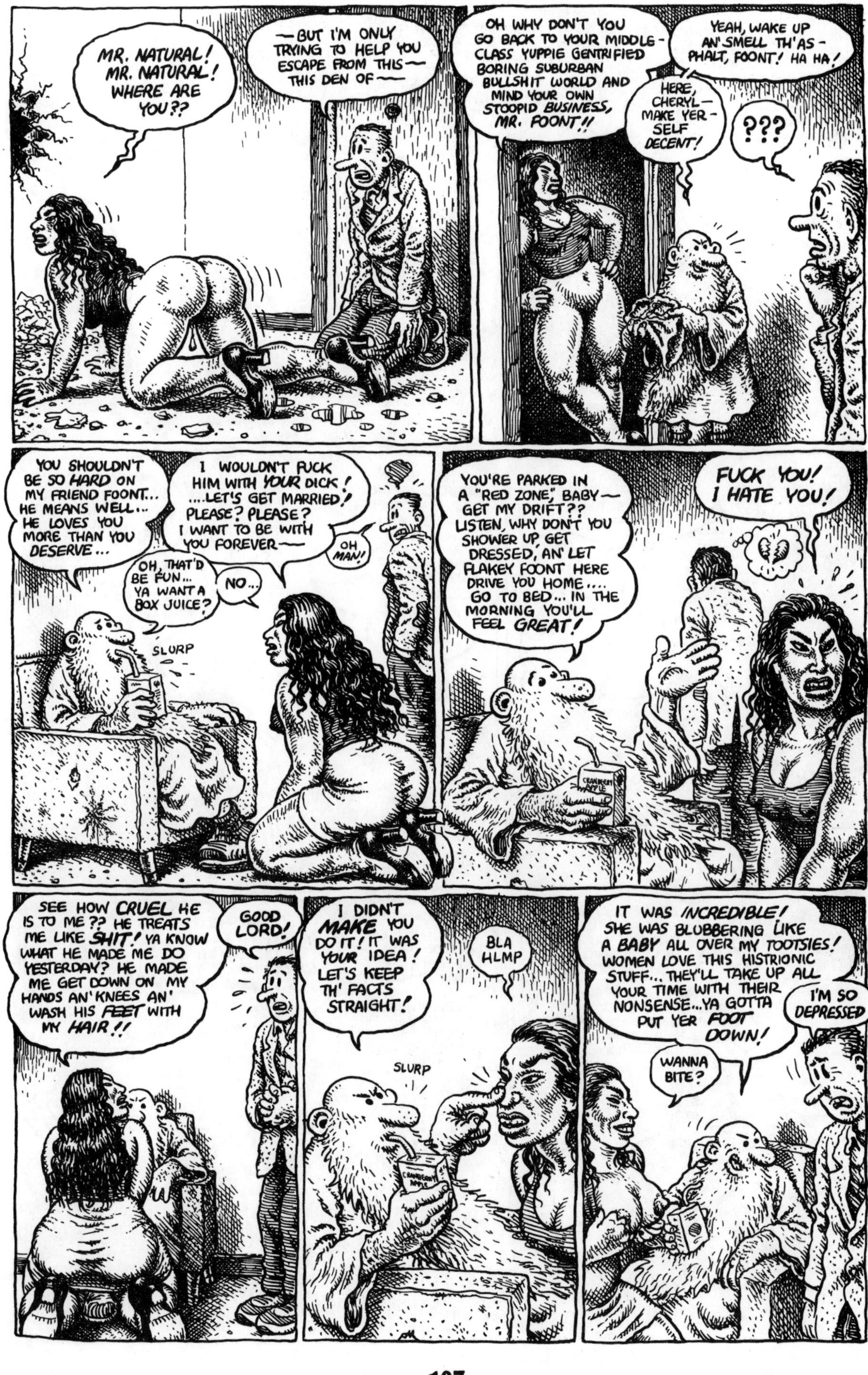
MR. NATURAL! MR. NATURAL! WHERE ARE YOU??
—BUT I'M ONLY TRYING TO HELP YOU ESCAPE FROM THIS— THIS DEN OF—
OH WHY DON'T YOU GO BACK TO YOUR MIDDLE-CLASS YUPPIE GENTRIFIED BORING SUBURBAN BULLSHIT WORLD AND MIND YOUR OWN STOOPID BUSINESS, MR. FOONT!!
YEAH, WAKE UP AN' SMELL TH' AS-PHALT, FOONT! HA HA!
HERE, CHERYL- MAKE YER-SELF DECENT!
???
YOU SHOULDN'T BE SO HARD ON MY FRIEND FOONT... HE MEANS WELL... HE LOVES YOU MORE THAN YOU DESERVE...
I WOULDN'T FUCK HIM WITH YOUR DICK! ...LET'S GET MARRIED! PLEASE? PLEASE? I WANT TO BE WITH YOU FOREVER—
OH MAN!
OH, THAT'D BE FUN... YA WANT A BOX JUICE?
NO...
SLURP
YOU'RE PARKED IN A "RED ZONE," BABY— GET MY DRIFT?? LISTEN, WHY DON'T YOU SHOWER UP, GET DRESSED, AN' LET FLAKEY FOONT HERE DRIVE YOU HOME.... GO TO BED... IN THE MORNING YOU'LL FEEL GREAT!
FUCK YOU! I HATE YOU!
CRANBERRY APPLE
SEE HOW CRUEL HE IS TO ME?? HE TREATS ME LIKE SHIT! YA KNOW WHAT HE MADE ME DO YESTERDAY? HE MADE ME GET DOWN ON MY HANDS AN' KNEES AN' WASH HIS FEET WITH MY HAIR!!
GOOD LORD!
I DIDN'T MAKE YOU DO IT! IT WAS YOUR IDEA! LET'S KEEP TH' FACTS STRAIGHT!
BLA HLMP
SLURP
IT WAS INCREDIBLE! SHE WAS BLUBBERING LIKE A BABY ALL OVER MY TOOTSIES! WOMEN LOVE THIS HISTRIONIC STUFF... THEY'LL TAKE UP ALL YOUR TIME WITH THEIR NONSENSE...YA GOTTA PUT YER FOOT DOWN!
I'M SO DEPRESSED
WANNA BITE?

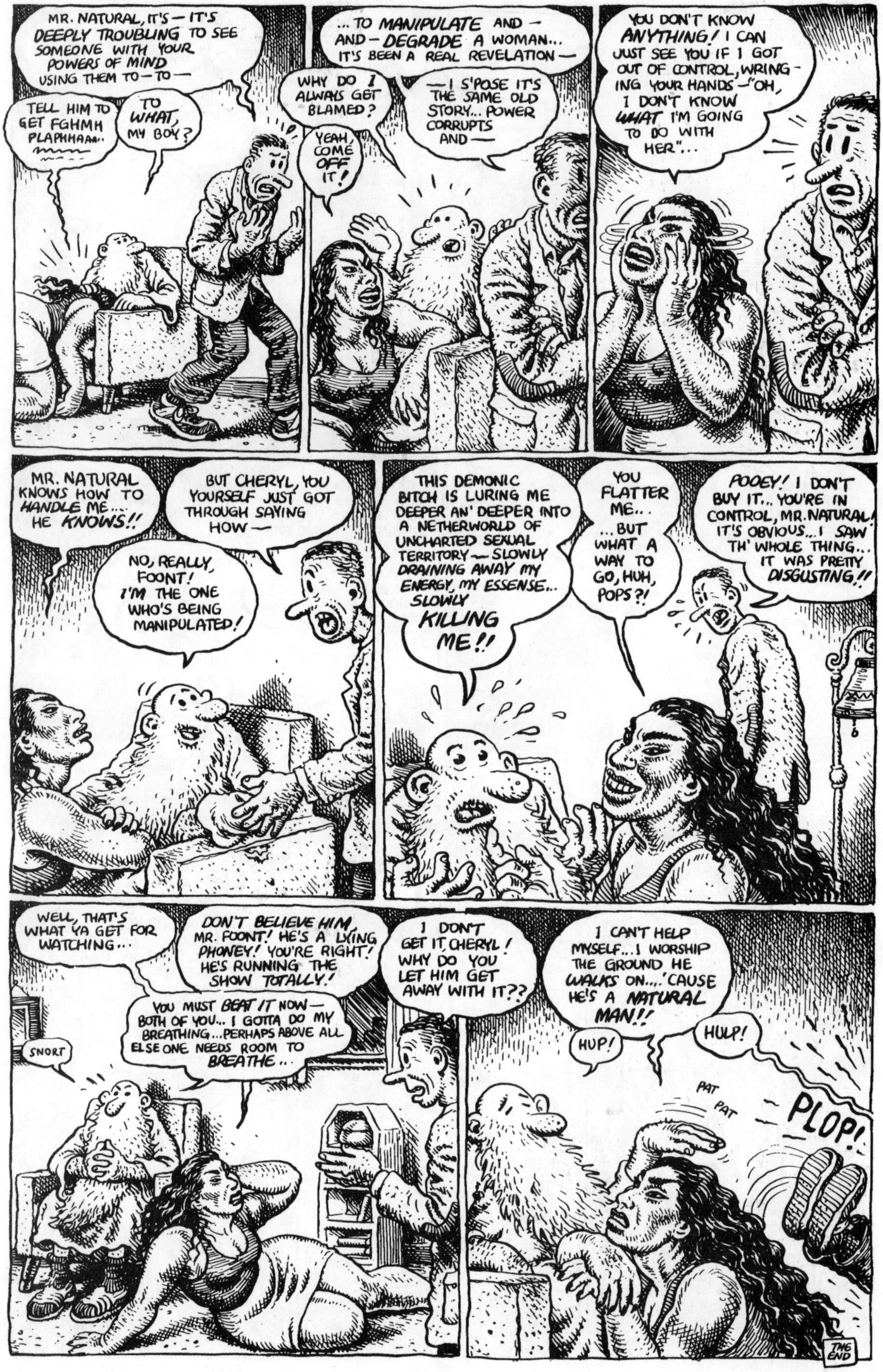
MR. NATURAL, IT'S — IT'S DEEPLY TROUBLING TO SEE SOMEONE WITH YOUR POWERS OF MIND USING THEM TO — TO —
TELL HIM TO GET FGHMH PLAPHHAA...
TO WHAT, MY BOY?
... TO MANIPULATE AND — AND — DEGRADE A WOMAN... IT'S BEEN A REAL REVELATION —
WHY DO I ALWAYS GET BLAMED?
YEAH, COME OFF IT!
— I S'POSE IT'S THE SAME OLD STORY... POWER CORRUPTS AND —
YOU DON'T KNOW ANYTHING! I CAN JUST SEE YOU IF I GOT OUT OF CONTROL, WRINGING YOUR HANDS — "OH, I DON'T KNOW WHAT I'M GOING TO DO WITH HER"...
MR. NATURAL KNOWS HOW TO HANDLE ME... HE KNOWS!!
BUT CHERYL, YOU YOURSELF JUST GOT THROUGH SAYING HOW —
NO, REALLY, FOONT! I'M THE ONE WHO'S BEING MANIPULATED!
THIS DEMONIC BITCH IS LURING ME DEEPER AN' DEEPER INTO A NETHERWORLD OF UNCHARTED SEXUAL TERRITORY — SLOWLY DRAINING AWAY MY ENERGY, MY ESSENSE... SLOWLY KILLING ME!!
YOU FLATTER ME... ... BUT WHAT A WAY TO GO, HUH, POPS?!
POOEY! I DON'T BUY IT... YOU'RE IN CONTROL, MR. NATURAL! IT'S OBVIOUS... I SAW TH' WHOLE THING... IT WAS PRETTY DISGUSTING!!
WELL, THAT'S WHAT YA GET FOR WATCHING...
DON'T BELIEVE HIM, MR. FOONT! HE'S A LYING PHONEY! YOU'RE RIGHT! HE'S RUNNING THE SHOW TOTALLY!
YOU MUST BEAT IT NOW — BOTH OF YOU... I GOTTA DO MY BREATHING... PERHAPS ABOVE ALL ELSE ONE NEEDS ROOM TO BREATHE...
SNORT
I DON'T GET IT, CHERYL! WHY DO YOU LET HIM GET AWAY WITH IT??
I CAN'T HELP MYSELF... I WORSHIP THE GROUND HE WALKS ON... 'CAUSE HE'S A NATURAL MAN!!
HUP!
HULP!
PAT PAT
PLOP!
THE END

MR. NATURAL

"ON THE BANKS OF THAT SILVERY STREAM"

by R. CRUMB ©1991

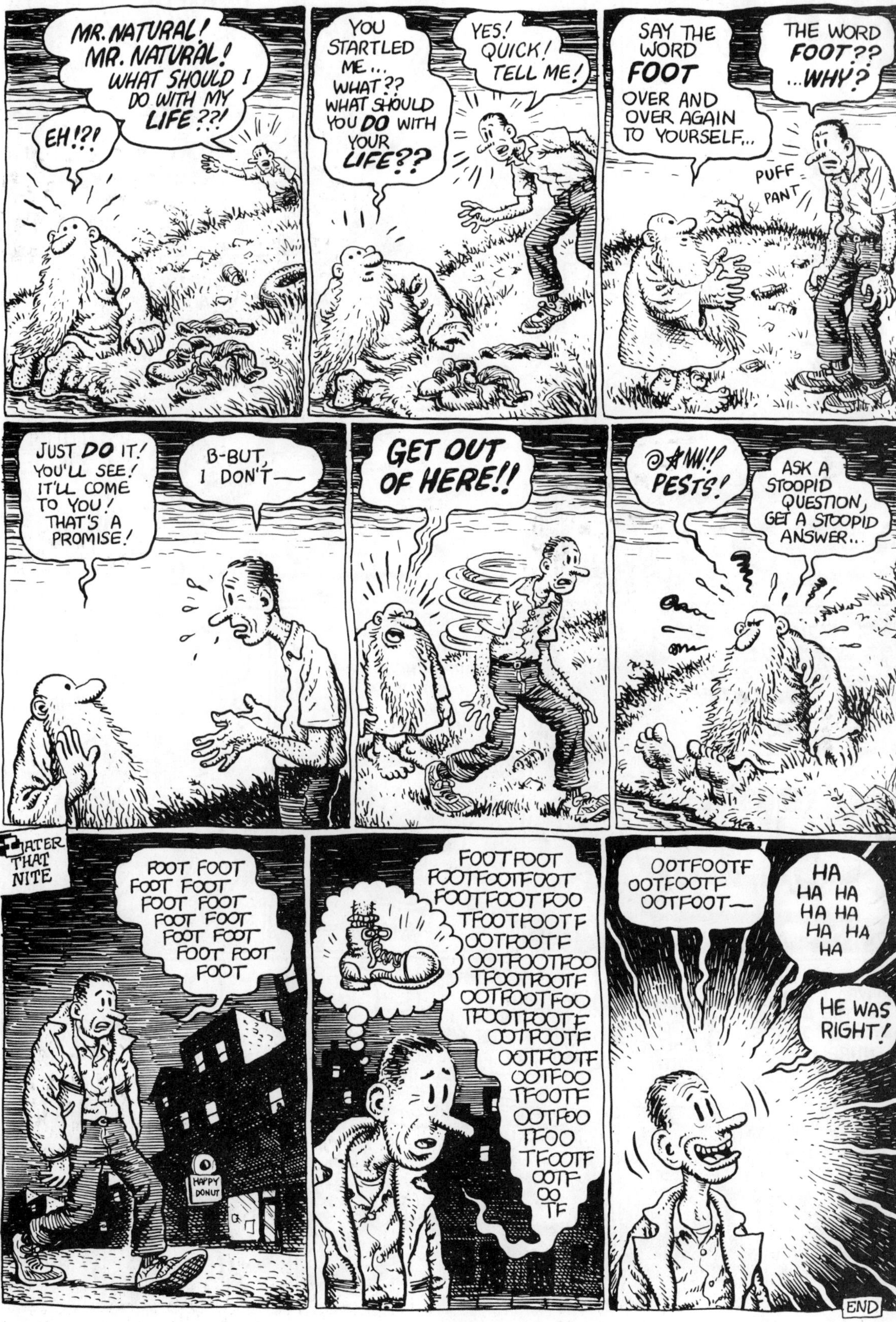

MR. NATURAL! MR. NATURAL! WHAT SHOULD I DO WITH MY LIFE??!
EH!?!
YOU STARTLED ME... WHAT?? WHAT SHOULD YOU DO WITH YOUR LIFE??
YES! QUICK! TELL ME!
SAY THE WORD FOOT OVER AND OVER AGAIN TO YOURSELF...
THE WORD FOOT?? ...WHY?
PUFF
PANT
JUST DO IT! YOU'LL SEE! IT'LL COME TO YOU! THAT'S A PROMISE!
B-BUT, I DON'T—
GET OUT OF HERE!!
PESTS!
ASK A STOOPID QUESTION, GET A STOOPID ANSWER...
LATER THAT NITE
FOOT FOOT FOOT FOOT FOOT FOOT FOOT FOOT FOOT FOOT FOOT FOOT FOOT
HAPPY DONUT
FOOTFOOT FOOTFOOTFOOT FOOTFOOTFOO TFOOTFOOTF OOTFOOTF OOTFOOTFOO TFOOTFOOTF OOTFOOTFOO TFOOTFOOTF OOTFOOTF OOTFOOTF OOTFOO TFOOTF OOTFOO TFOO TFOOTF OOTF OO TF
OOTFOOTF OOTFOOTF OOTFOOT—
HA HA HA HA HA HA HA HA HA
HE WAS RIGHT!
END

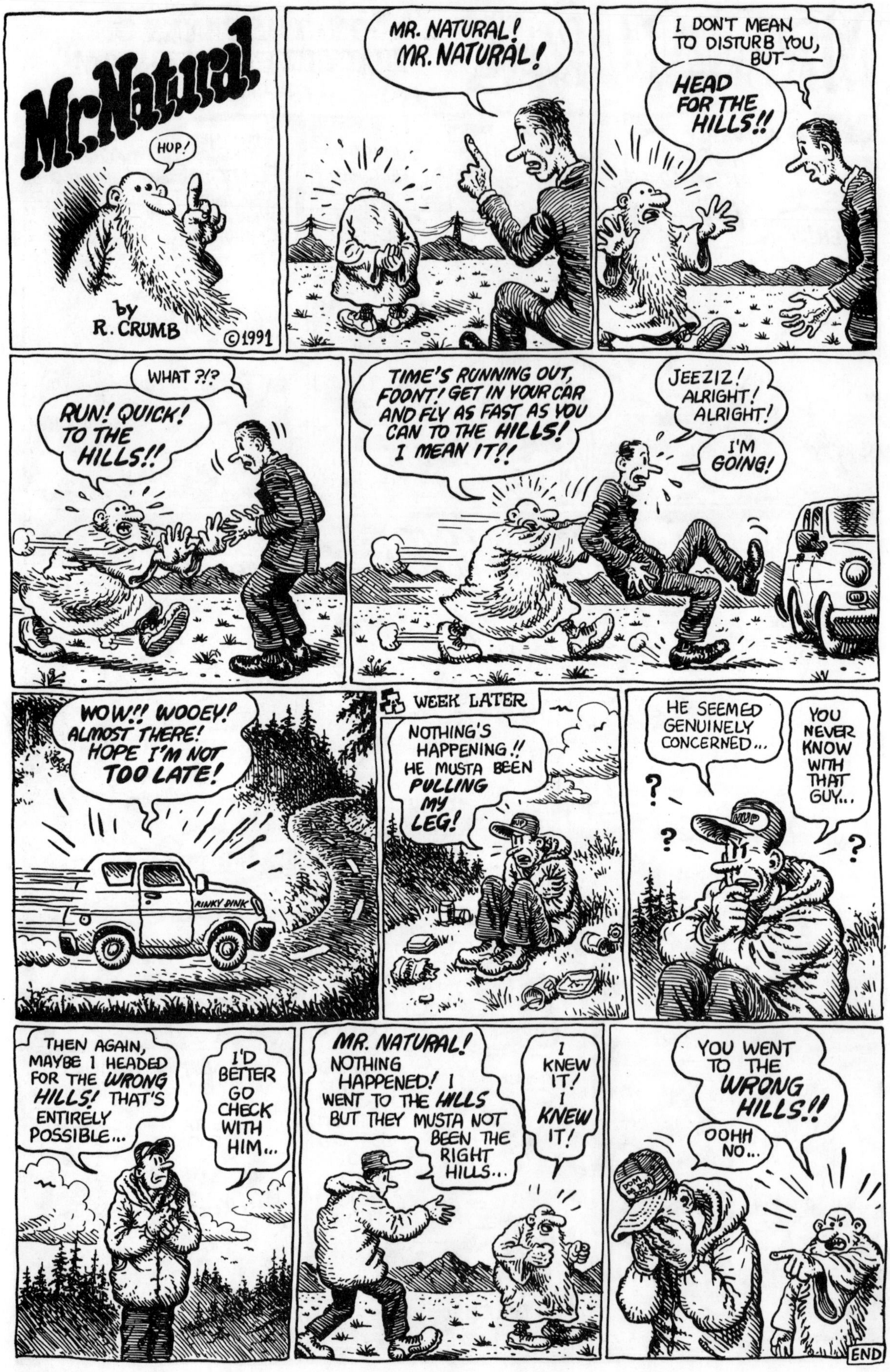
Mr. Natural
HUP!
by R. CRUMB ©1991
MR. NATURAL! MR. NATURAL!
I DON'T MEAN TO DISTURB YOU, BUT—
HEAD FOR THE HILLS!!
WHAT ?!?
RUN! QUICK! TO THE HILLS!!
TIME'S RUNNING OUT, FOONT! GET IN YOUR CAR AND FLY AS FAST AS YOU CAN TO THE HILLS! I MEAN IT?!
JEEZIZ! ALRIGHT! ALRIGHT!
I'M GOING!
WOW!! WOOEY! ALMOST THERE! HOPE I'M NOT TOO LATE!
RINKY DINK
A WEEK LATER
NOTHING'S HAPPENING!! HE MUSTA BEEN PULLING MY LEG!
HUP
HE SEEMED GENUINELY CONCERNED...
YOU NEVER KNOW WITH THAT GUY...
HUP
THEN AGAIN, MAYBE I HEADED FOR THE WRONG HILLS! THAT'S ENTIRELY POSSIBLE...
I'D BETTER GO CHECK WITH HIM...
MR. NATURAL! NOTHING HAPPENED! I WENT TO THE HILLS BUT THEY MUSTA NOT BEEN THE RIGHT HILLS...
I KNEW IT! I KNEW IT!
YOU WENT TO THE WRONG HILLS!!
OOHH NO...
END

Mr. Natural.... DISTRACTIONS DISTRACTIONS!!

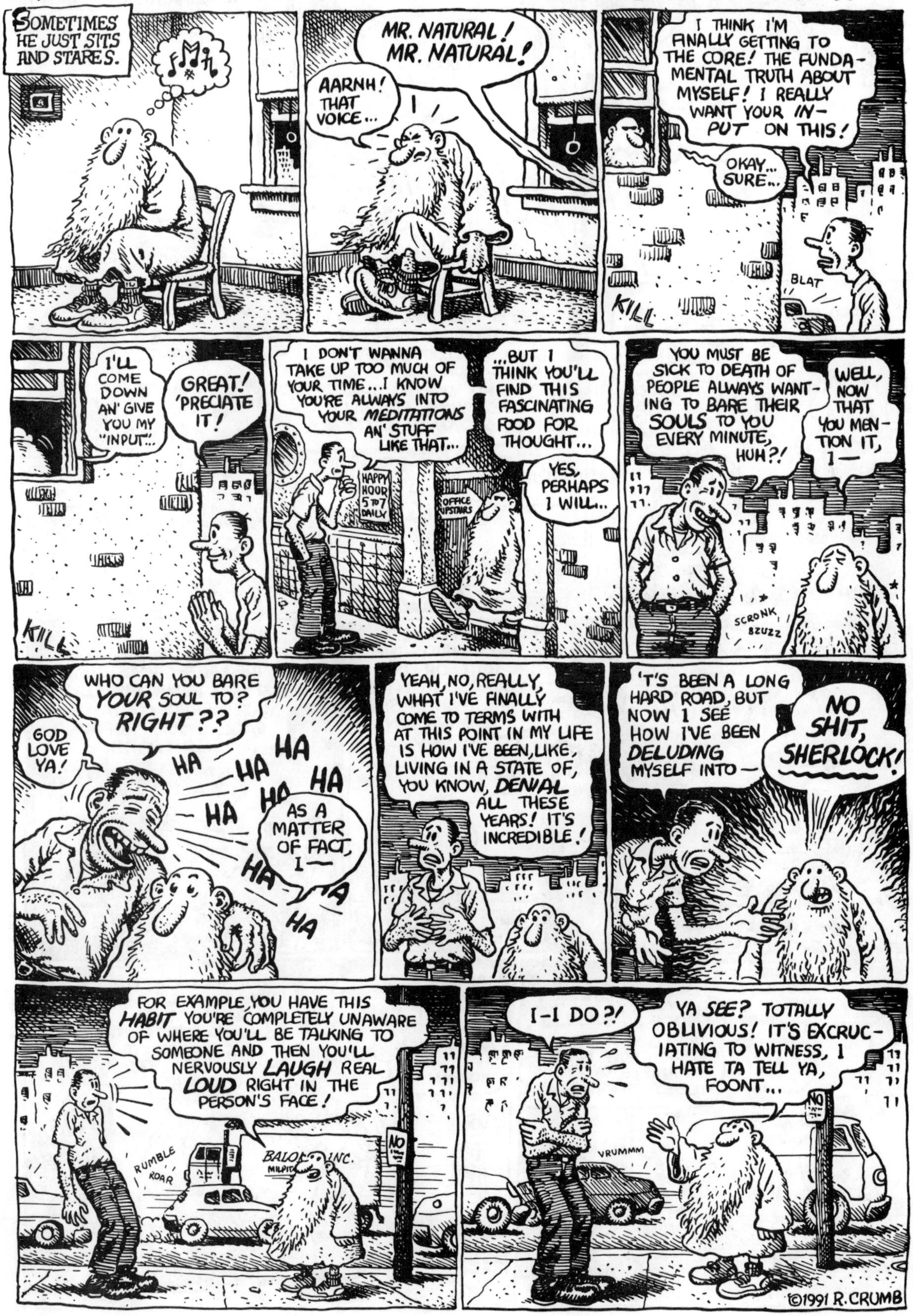

SOMETIMES HE JUST SITS AND STARES.
MR. NATURAL! MR. NATURAL!
AARNH! THAT VOICE...
I THINK I'M FINALLY GETTING TO THE CORE! THE FUNDAMENTAL TRUTH ABOUT MYSELF! I REALLY WANT YOUR INPUT ON THIS!
OKAY... SURE...
BLAT
KILL
I'LL COME DOWN AN' GIVE YOU MY "INPUT"...
GREAT! 'PRECIATE IT!
KILL
I DON'T WANNA TAKE UP TOO MUCH OF YOUR TIME...I KNOW YOU'RE ALWAYS INTO YOUR MEDITATIONS AN' STUFF LIKE THAT...
...BUT I THINK YOU'LL FIND THIS FASCINATING FOOD FOR THOUGHT...
HAPPY HOUR 5 TO 7 DAILY
OFFICE UPSTAIRS
YES, PERHAPS I WILL...
YOU MUST BE SICK TO DEATH OF PEOPLE ALWAYS WANTING TO BARE THEIR SOULS TO YOU EVERY MINUTE, HUH?!
WELL, NOW THAT YOU MENTION IT, I—
SCRONK
BZUZZ
WHO CAN YOU BARE YOUR SOUL TO? RIGHT??
GOD LOVE YA!
HA HA HA HA HA HA HA HA HA
AS A MATTER OF FACT, I—
YEAH, NO, REALLY, WHAT I'VE FINALLY COME TO TERMS WITH AT THIS POINT IN MY LIFE IS HOW I'VE BEEN, LIKE, LIVING IN A STATE OF, YOU KNOW, DENIAL ALL THESE YEARS! IT'S INCREDIBLE!
'T'S BEEN A LONG HARD ROAD, BUT NOW I SEE HOW I'VE BEEN DELUDING MYSELF INTO—
NO SHIT, SHERLOCK!
FOR EXAMPLE, YOU HAVE THIS HABIT YOU'RE COMPLETELY UNAWARE OF WHERE YOU'LL BE TALKING TO SOMEONE AND THEN YOU'LL NERVOUSLY LAUGH REAL LOUD RIGHT IN THE PERSON'S FACE!
RUMBLE ROAR
NO
I-I DO?!
YA SEE? TOTALLY OBLIVIOUS! IT'S EXCRUCIATING TO WITNESS, I HATE TA TELL YA, FOONT...
VRUMMM
NO
©1991 R. CRUMB

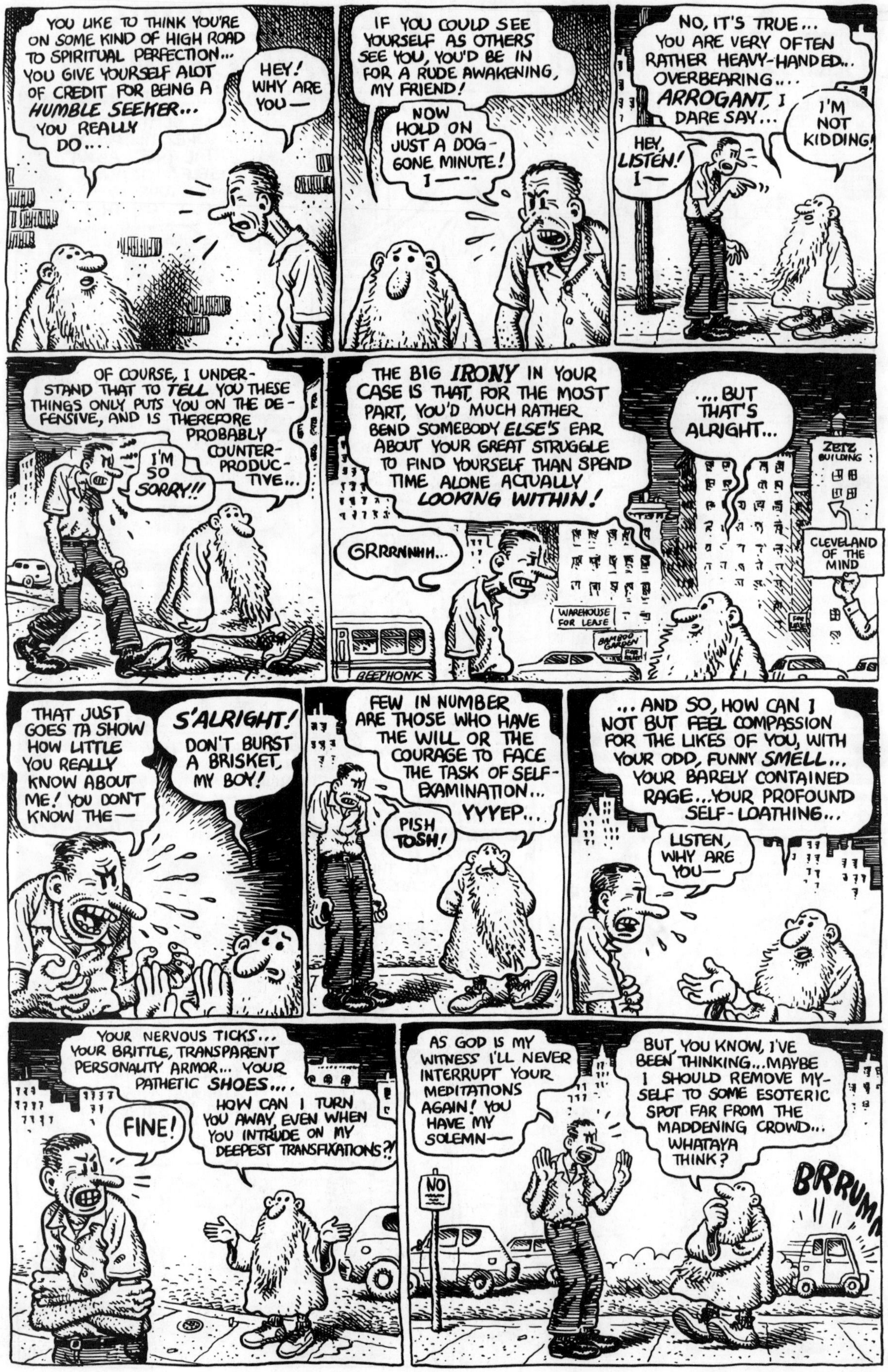

YOU LIKE TO THINK YOU'RE ON SOME KIND OF HIGH ROAD TO SPIRITUAL PERFECTION... YOU GIVE YOURSELF ALOT OF CREDIT FOR BEING A HUMBLE SEEKER... YOU REALLY DO...
HEY! WHY ARE YOU—
IF YOU COULD SEE YOURSELF AS OTHERS SEE YOU, YOU'D BE IN FOR A RUDE AWAKENING, MY FRIEND!
NOW HOLD ON JUST A DOG-GONE MINUTE! I——
NO, IT'S TRUE... YOU ARE VERY OFTEN RATHER HEAVY-HANDED... OVERBEARING... ARROGANT, I DARE SAY...
HEY, LISTEN! I—
I'M NOT KIDDING!
OF COURSE, I UNDERSTAND THAT TO TELL YOU THESE THINGS ONLY PUTS YOU ON THE DEFENSIVE, AND IS THEREFORE PROBABLY COUNTER-PRODUCTIVE...
I'M SO SORRY!!
THE BIG IRONY IN YOUR CASE IS THAT, FOR THE MOST PART, YOU'D MUCH RATHER BEND SOMEBODY ELSE'S EAR ABOUT YOUR GREAT STRUGGLE TO FIND YOURSELF THAN SPEND TIME ALONE ACTUALLY LOOKING WITHIN!
...BUT THAT'S ALRIGHT...
GRRRNNHH...
ZEITZ BUILDING
CLEVELAND OF THE MIND
WAREHOUSE FOR LEASE
BAMBOO GARDEN
BEEPHONK
THAT JUST GOES TA SHOW HOW LITTLE YOU REALLY KNOW ABOUT ME! YOU DON'T KNOW THE—
S'ALRIGHT! DON'T BURST A BRISKET, MY BOY!
FEW IN NUMBER ARE THOSE WHO HAVE THE WILL OR THE COURAGE TO FACE THE TASK OF SELF-EXAMINATION... YYYEP...
PISH TOSH!
...AND SO, HOW CAN I NOT BUT FEEL COMPASSION FOR THE LIKES OF YOU, WITH YOUR ODD, FUNNY SMELL... YOUR BARELY CONTAINED RAGE... YOUR PROFOUND SELF-LOATHING...
LISTEN, WHY ARE YOU—
YOUR NERVOUS TICKS... YOUR BRITTLE, TRANSPARENT PERSONALITY ARMOR... YOUR PATHETIC SHOES...
FINE!
HOW CAN I TURN YOU AWAY, EVEN WHEN YOU INTRUDE ON MY DEEPEST TRANSFIXATIONS?!
AS GOD IS MY WITNESS I'LL NEVER INTERRUPT YOUR MEDITATIONS AGAIN! YOU HAVE MY SOLEMN—
NO
BUT, YOU KNOW, I'VE BEEN THINKING... MAYBE I SHOULD REMOVE MYSELF TO SOME ESOTERIC SPOT FAR FROM THE MADDENING CROWD... WHATAYA THINK?
BRRUMM

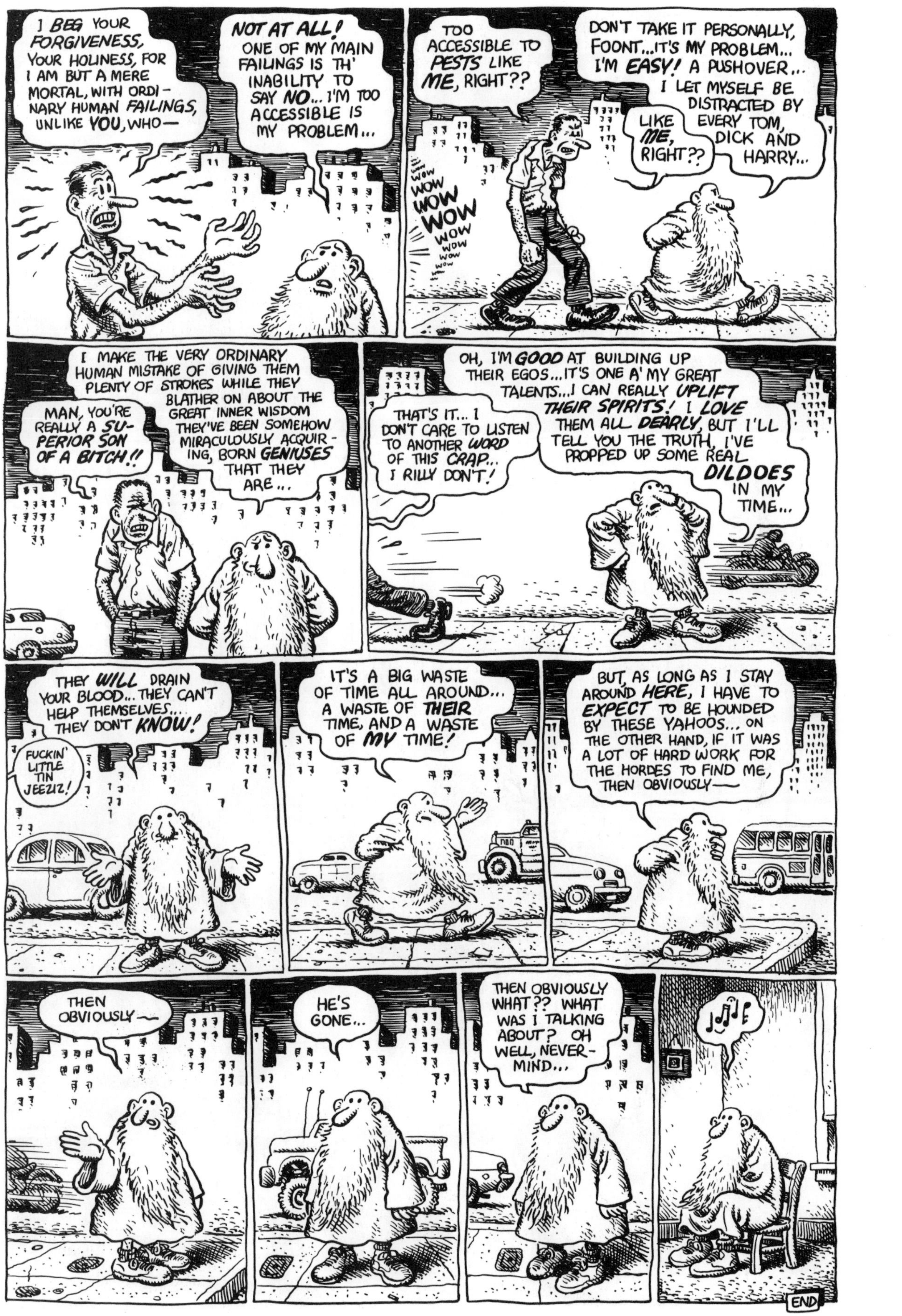
I BEG YOUR FORGIVENESS, YOUR HOLINESS, FOR I AM BUT A MERE MORTAL, WITH ORDINARY HUMAN FAILINGS, UNLIKE YOU, WHO—
NOT AT ALL! ONE OF MY MAIN FAILINGS IS TH' INABILITY TO SAY NO... I'M TOO ACCESSIBLE IS MY PROBLEM...
TOO ACCESSIBLE TO PESTS LIKE ME, RIGHT??
WOW WOW WOW WOW WOW WOW WOW WOW
DON'T TAKE IT PERSONALLY, FOONT...IT'S MY PROBLEM... I'M EASY! A PUSHOVER... I LET MYSELF BE DISTRACTED BY EVERY TOM, DICK AND HARRY...
LIKE ME, RIGHT??
I MAKE THE VERY ORDINARY HUMAN MISTAKE OF GIVING THEM PLENTY OF STROKES WHILE THEY BLATHER ON ABOUT THE GREAT INNER WISDOM THEY'VE BEEN SOMEHOW MIRACULOUSLY ACQUIRING, BORN GENIUSES THAT THEY ARE...
MAN, YOU'RE REALLY A SUPERIOR SON OF A BITCH!!
OH, I'M GOOD AT BUILDING UP THEIR EGOS...IT'S ONE A' MY GREAT TALENTS...I CAN REALLY UPLIFT THEIR SPIRITS! I LOVE THEM ALL DEARLY, BUT I'LL TELL YOU THE TRUTH, I'VE PROPPED UP SOME REAL DILDOES IN MY TIME...
THAT'S IT... I DON'T CARE TO LISTEN TO ANOTHER WORD OF THIS CRAP... I RILLY DON'T!
THEY WILL DRAIN YOUR BLOOD... THEY CAN'T HELP THEMSELVES... THEY DON'T KNOW!
FUCKIN' LITTLE TIN JEEZIZ!
IT'S A BIG WASTE OF TIME ALL AROUND... A WASTE OF THEIR TIME, AND A WASTE OF MY TIME!
BUT, AS LONG AS I STAY AROUND HERE, I HAVE TO EXPECT TO BE HOUNDED BY THESE YAHOOS... ON THE OTHER HAND, IF IT WAS A LOT OF HARD WORK FOR THE HORDES TO FIND ME, THEN OBVIOUSLY—
THEN OBVIOUSLY—
HE'S GONE...
THEN OBVIOUSLY WHAT?? WHAT WAS I TALKING ABOUT? OH WELL, NEVERMIND...
END

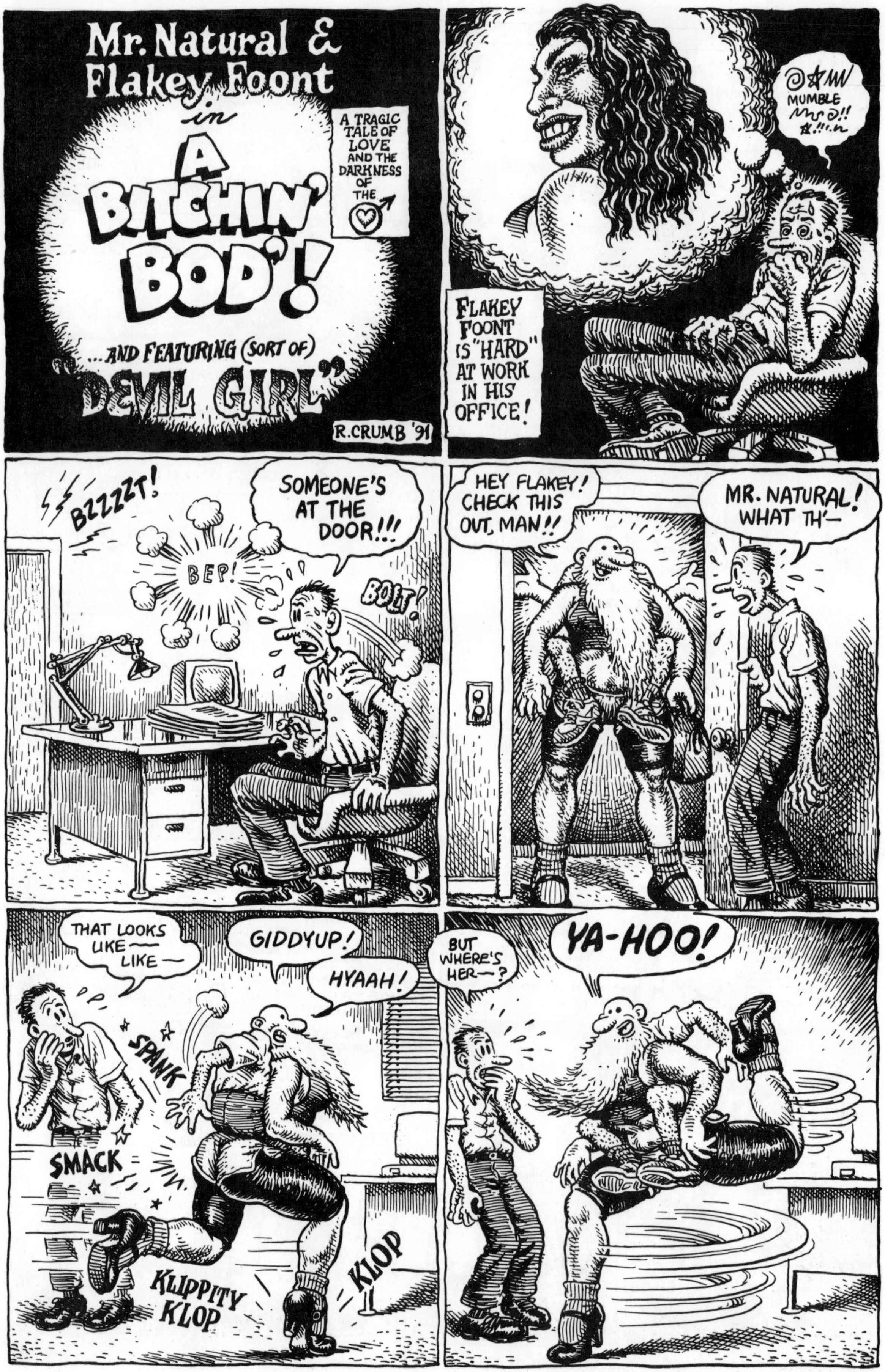
Mr. Natural & Flakey Foont
in
A BITCHIN' BOD'!
A TRAGIC TALE OF LOVE AND THE DARKNESS OF THE
...AND FEATURING (SORT OF) "DEVIL GIRL"
R. CRUMB '91
MUMBLE
FLAKEY FOONT IS "HARD" AT WORK IN HIS OFFICE!
BZZZZT!
SOMEONE'S AT THE DOOR!!!
BEP!
BOLT!
HEY FLAKEY! CHECK THIS OUT, MAN!!
MR. NATURAL! WHAT TH'—
THAT LOOKS LIKE—LIKE—
GIDDYUP!
HYAAH!
SPANK
SMACK
KLIPPITY KLOP
KLOP
BUT WHERE'S HER—?
YA-HOO!

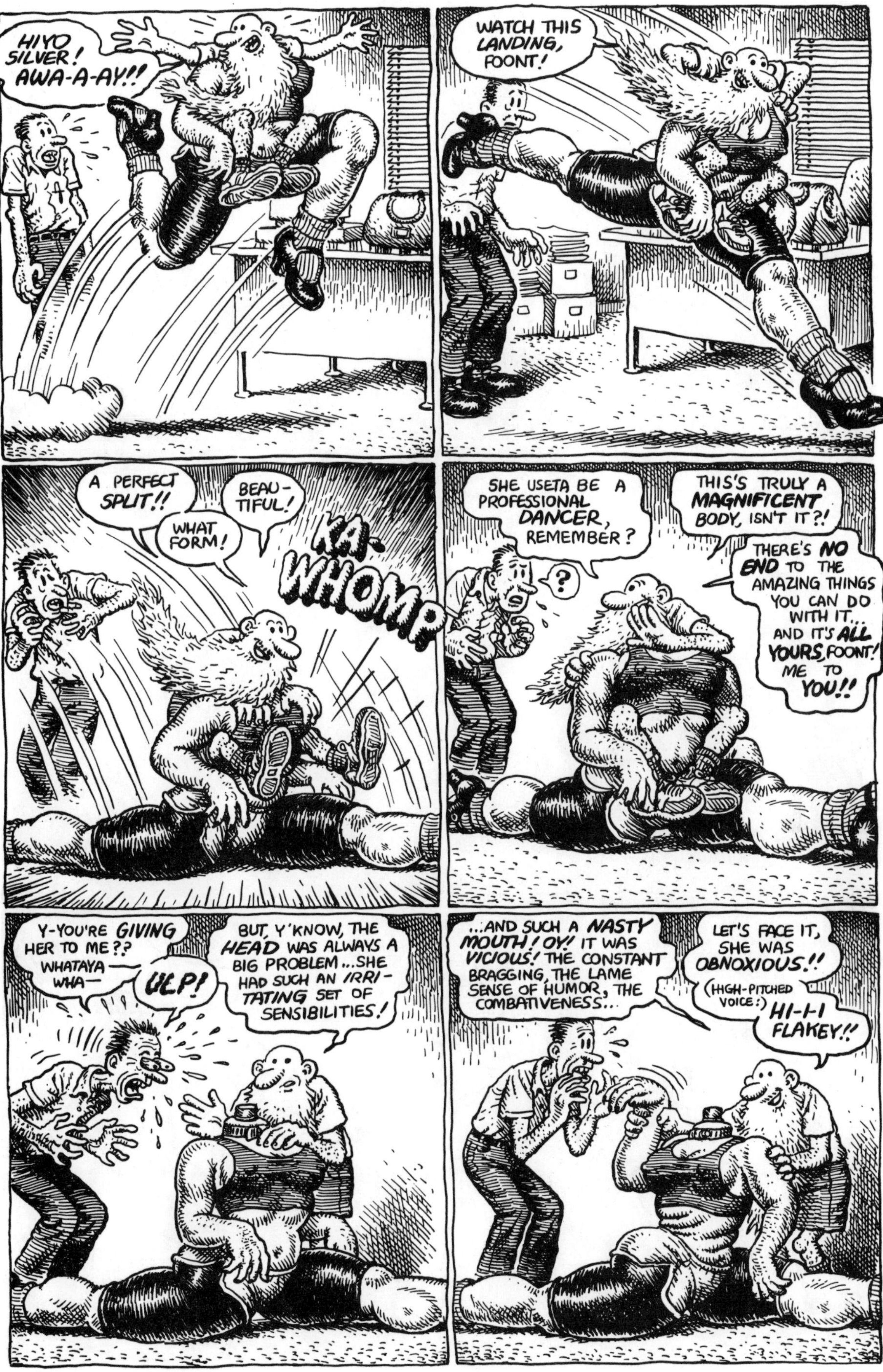
HIYO SILVER! AWA-A-AY!!
WATCH THIS LANDING, FOONT!
A PERFECT SPLIT!!
WHAT FORM!
BEAU-TIFUL!
KA-WHOMP
SHE USETA BE A PROFESSIONAL DANCER, REMEMBER?
?
THIS'S TRULY A MAGNIFICENT BODY, ISN'T IT?!
THERE'S NO END TO THE AMAZING THINGS YOU CAN DO WITH IT... AND IT'S ALL YOURS, FOONT! ME TO YOU!!
Y-YOU'RE GIVING HER TO ME?? WHATAYA— WHA—
ULP!
BUT, Y'KNOW, THE HEAD WAS ALWAYS A BIG PROBLEM... SHE HAD SUCH AN IRRITATING SET OF SENSIBILITIES!
...AND SUCH A NASTY MOUTH! OY! IT WAS VICIOUS! THE CONSTANT BRAGGING, THE LAME SENSE OF HUMOR, THE COMBATIVENESS...
LET'S FACE IT, SHE WAS OBNOXIOUS!!
(HIGH-PITCHED VOICE:) HI-I-I FLAKEY!!

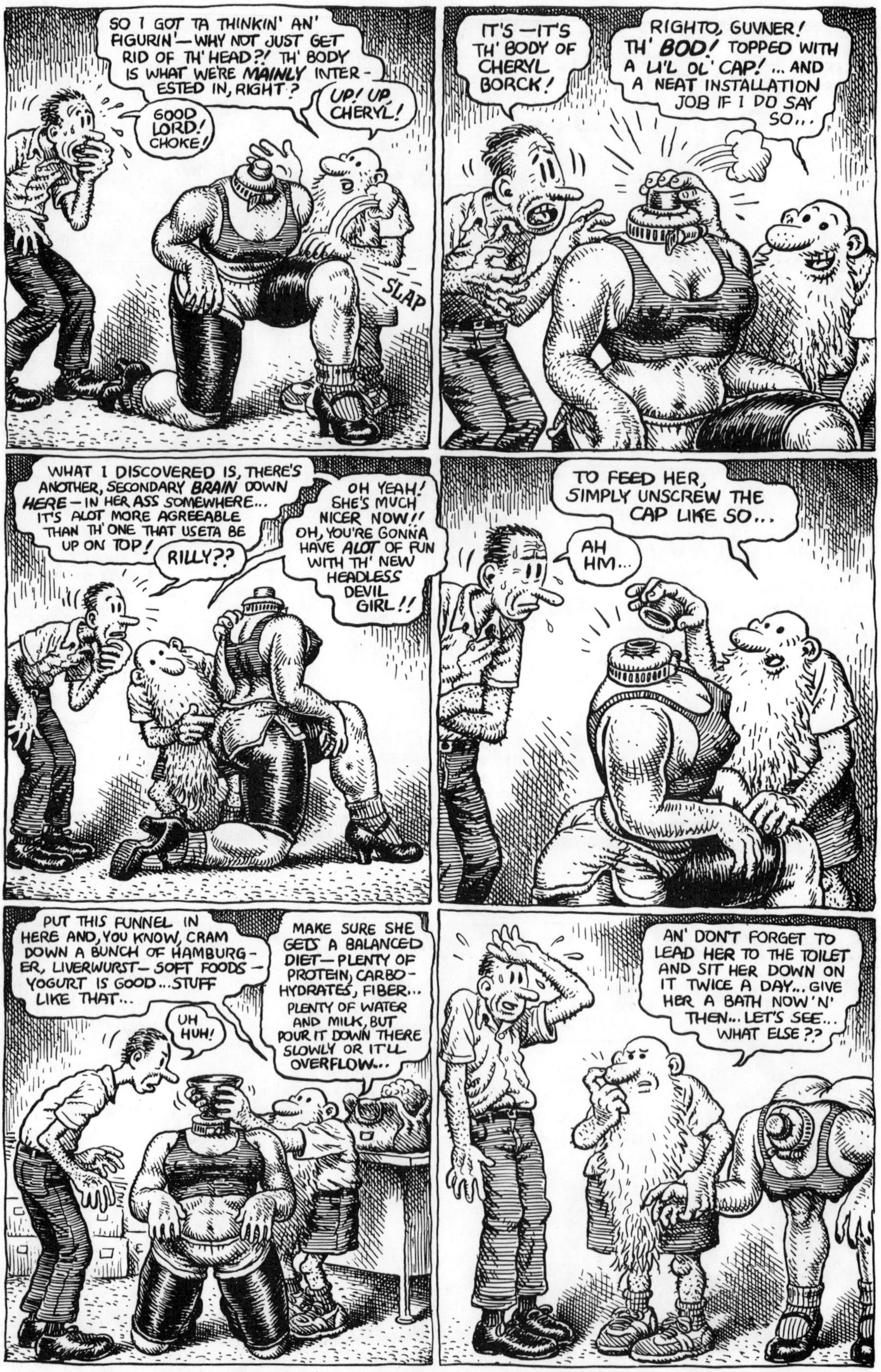
SO I GOT TA THINKIN' AN' FIGURIN'—WHY NOT JUST GET RID OF TH' HEAD?! TH' BODY IS WHAT WE'RE MAINLY INTER-ESTED IN, RIGHT?
GOOD LORD! CHOKE!
UP! UP CHERYL!
SLAP
IT'S—IT'S TH' BODY OF CHERYL BORCK!
RIGHTO, GUVNER! TH' BOD! TOPPED WITH A LI'L OL' CAP! ... AND A NEAT INSTALLATION JOB IF I DO SAY SO...
WHAT I DISCOVERED IS, THERE'S ANOTHER, SECONDARY BRAIN DOWN HERE—IN HER ASS SOMEWHERE... IT'S ALOT MORE AGREEABLE THAN TH' ONE THAT USETA BE UP ON TOP!
RILLY??
OH YEAH! SHE'S MUCH NICER NOW!! OH, YOU'RE GONNA HAVE ALOT OF FUN WITH TH' NEW HEADLESS DEVIL GIRL!!
TO FEED HER, SIMPLY UNSCREW THE CAP LIKE SO...
AH HM...
PUT THIS FUNNEL IN HERE AND, YOU KNOW, CRAM DOWN A BUNCH OF HAMBURG-ER, LIVERWURST—SOFT FOODS—YOGURT IS GOOD...STUFF LIKE THAT...
UH HUH!
MAKE SURE SHE GETS A BALANCED DIET—PLENTY OF PROTEIN, CARBO-HYDRATES, FIBER... PLENTY OF WATER AND MILK, BUT POUR IT DOWN THERE SLOWLY OR IT'LL OVERFLOW...
AN' DON'T FORGET TO LEAD HER TO THE TOILET AND SIT HER DOWN ON IT TWICE A DAY... GIVE HER A BATH NOW 'N' THEN... LET'S SEE... WHAT ELSE??

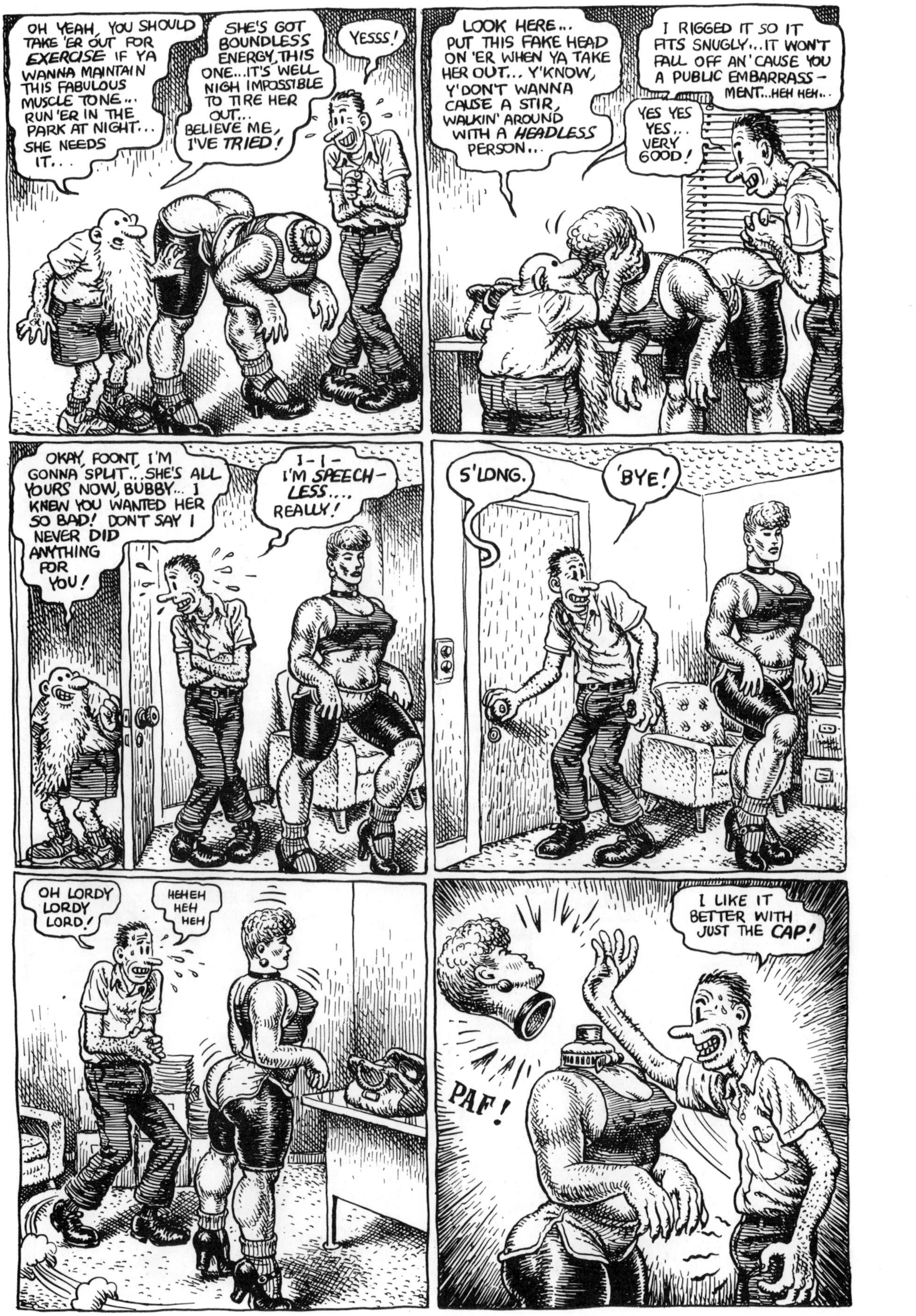
OH YEAH, YOU SHOULD TAKE 'ER OUT FOR EXERCISE IF YA WANNA MAINTAIN THIS FABULOUS MUSCLE TONE... RUN 'ER IN THE PARK AT NIGHT... SHE NEEDS IT...
SHE'S GOT BOUNDLESS ENERGY, THIS ONE... IT'S WELL NIGH IMPOSSIBLE TO TIRE HER OUT... BELIEVE ME, I'VE TRIED!
YESSS!
LOOK HERE... PUT THIS FAKE HEAD ON 'ER WHEN YA TAKE HER OUT... Y'KNOW, Y'DON'T WANNA CAUSE A STIR, WALKIN' AROUND WITH A HEADLESS PERSON...
I RIGGED IT SO IT FITS SNUGLY... IT WON'T FALL OFF AN' CAUSE YOU A PUBLIC EMBARRASS-MENT... HEH HEH...
YES YES YES... VERY GOOD!
OKAY, FOONT, I'M GONNA SPLIT... SHE'S ALL YOURS NOW, BUBBY... I KNEW YOU WANTED HER SO BAD! DON'T SAY I NEVER DID ANYTHING FOR YOU!
I-I- I'M SPEECH-LESS.... REALLY!
S'LONG.
'BYE!
OH LORDY LORDY LORD!
HEHEH HEH HEH
I LIKE IT BETTER WITH JUST THE CAP!
PAF!

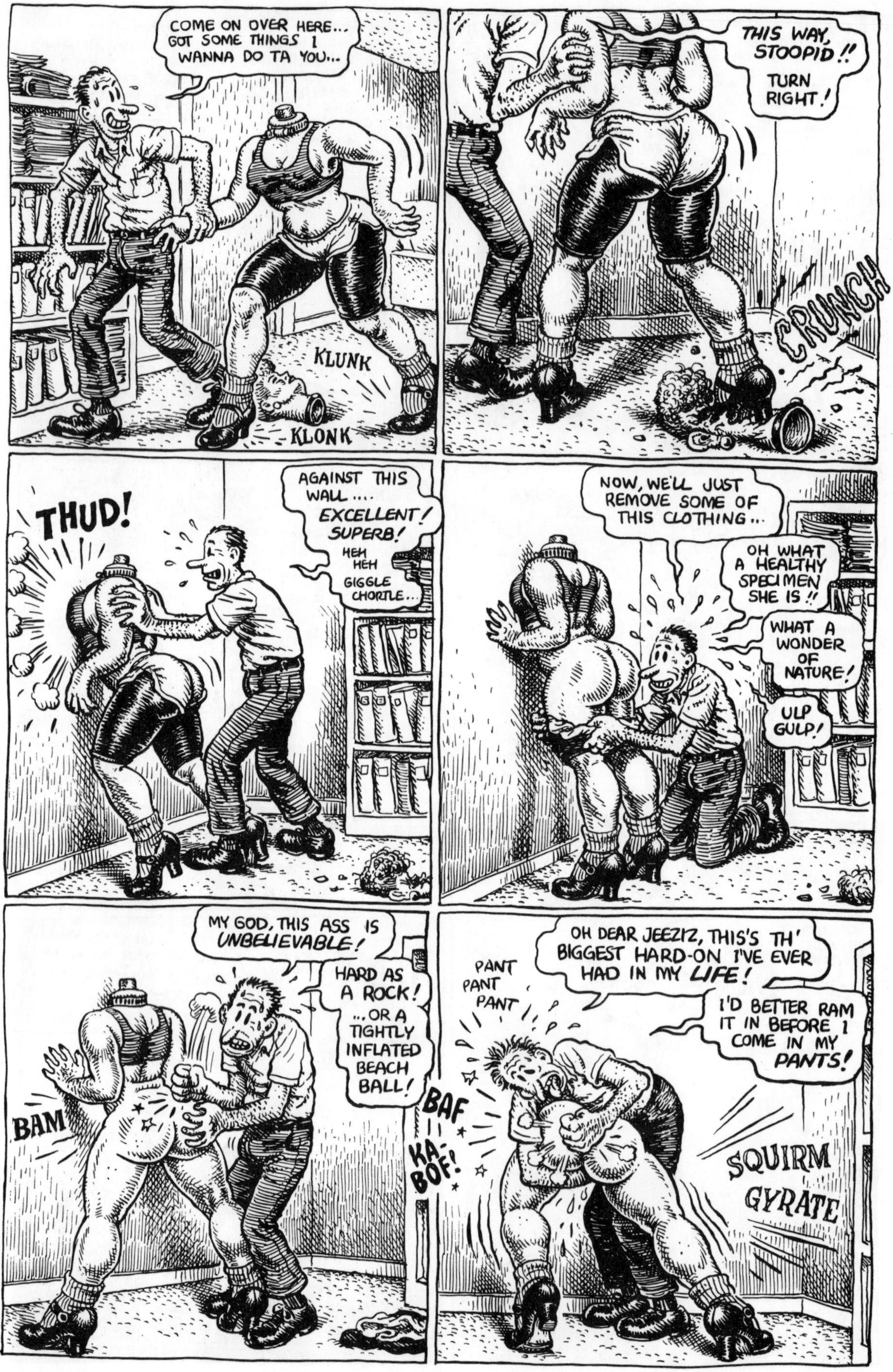

COME ON OVER HERE... GOT SOME THINGS I WANNA DO TA YOU...
KLUNK
KLONK
THIS WAY, STOOPID!!
TURN RIGHT!
CRUNCH
THUD!
AGAINST THIS WALL.... EXCELLENT! SUPERB!
HEH HEH GIGGLE CHORTLE...
NOW, WE'LL JUST REMOVE SOME OF THIS CLOTHING...
OH WHAT A HEALTHY SPECIMEN SHE IS!!
WHAT A WONDER OF NATURE!
ULP GULP!
MY GOD, THIS ASS IS UNBELIEVABLE!
HARD AS A ROCK!
...OR A TIGHTLY INFLATED BEACH BALL!
BAM
PANT PANT PANT
OH DEAR JEEZIZ, THIS'S TH' BIGGEST HARD-ON I'VE EVER HAD IN MY LIFE!
I'D BETTER RAM IT IN BEFORE I COME IN MY PANTS!
BAF
KA-BOF!
SQUIRM
GYRATE

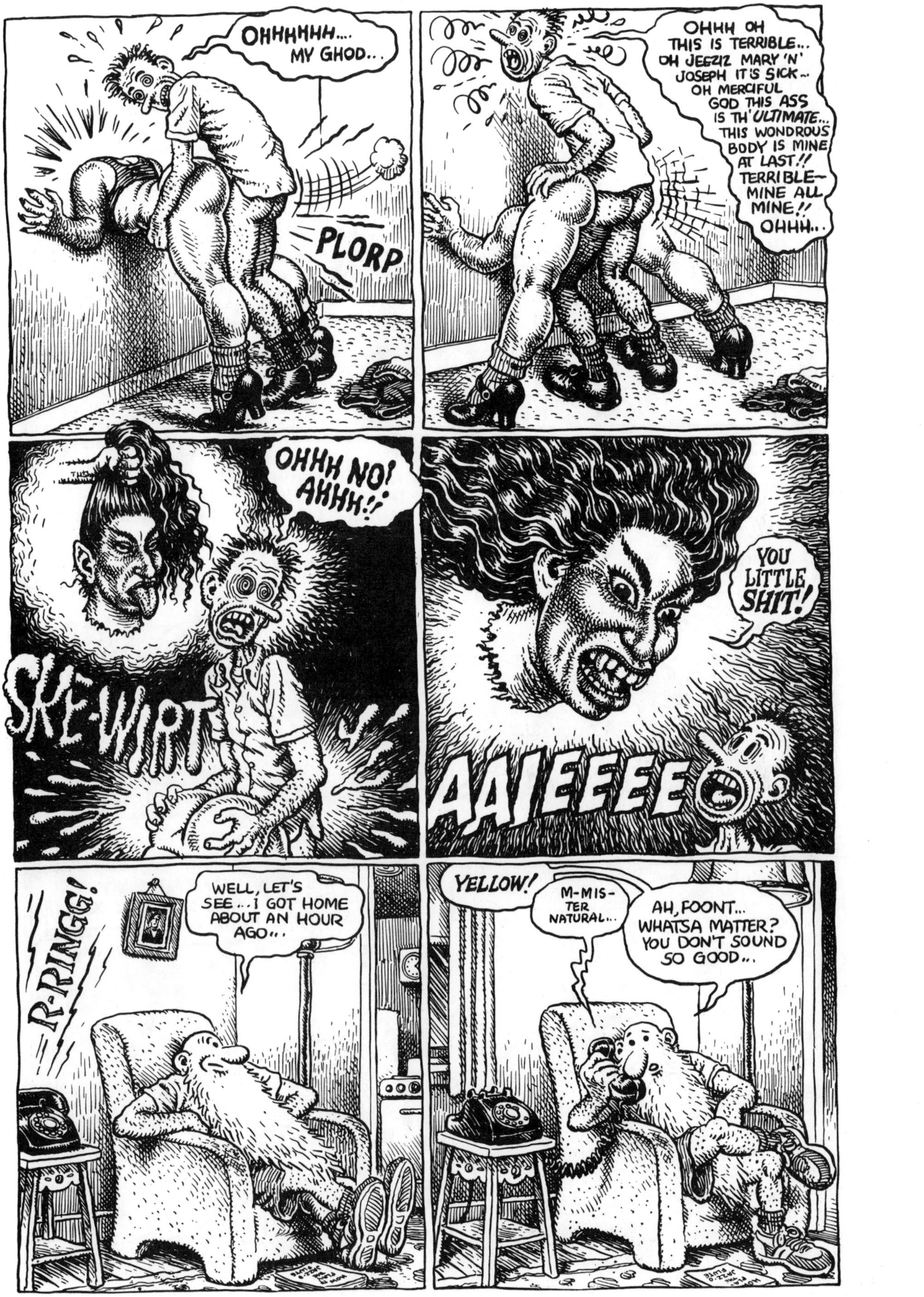
OHHHHHH.... MY GHOD...
PLORP
OHHH OH THIS IS TERRIBLE... OH JEEZIZ MARY 'N' JOSEPH IT'S SICK... OH MERCIFUL GOD THIS ASS IS TH' ULTIMATE... THIS WONDROUS BODY IS MINE AT LAST!! TERRIBLE— MINE ALL MINE!! OHHH...
OHHH NO! AKHH!!
SKE-WIRT
YOU LITTLE SHIT!!
AAIEEEE
R-RINGG!
WELL, LET'S SEE... I GOT HOME ABOUT AN HOUR AGO...
YELLOW!
M-MIS-TER NATURAL...
AH, FOONT... WHATSA MATTER? YOU DON'T SOUND SO GOOD...

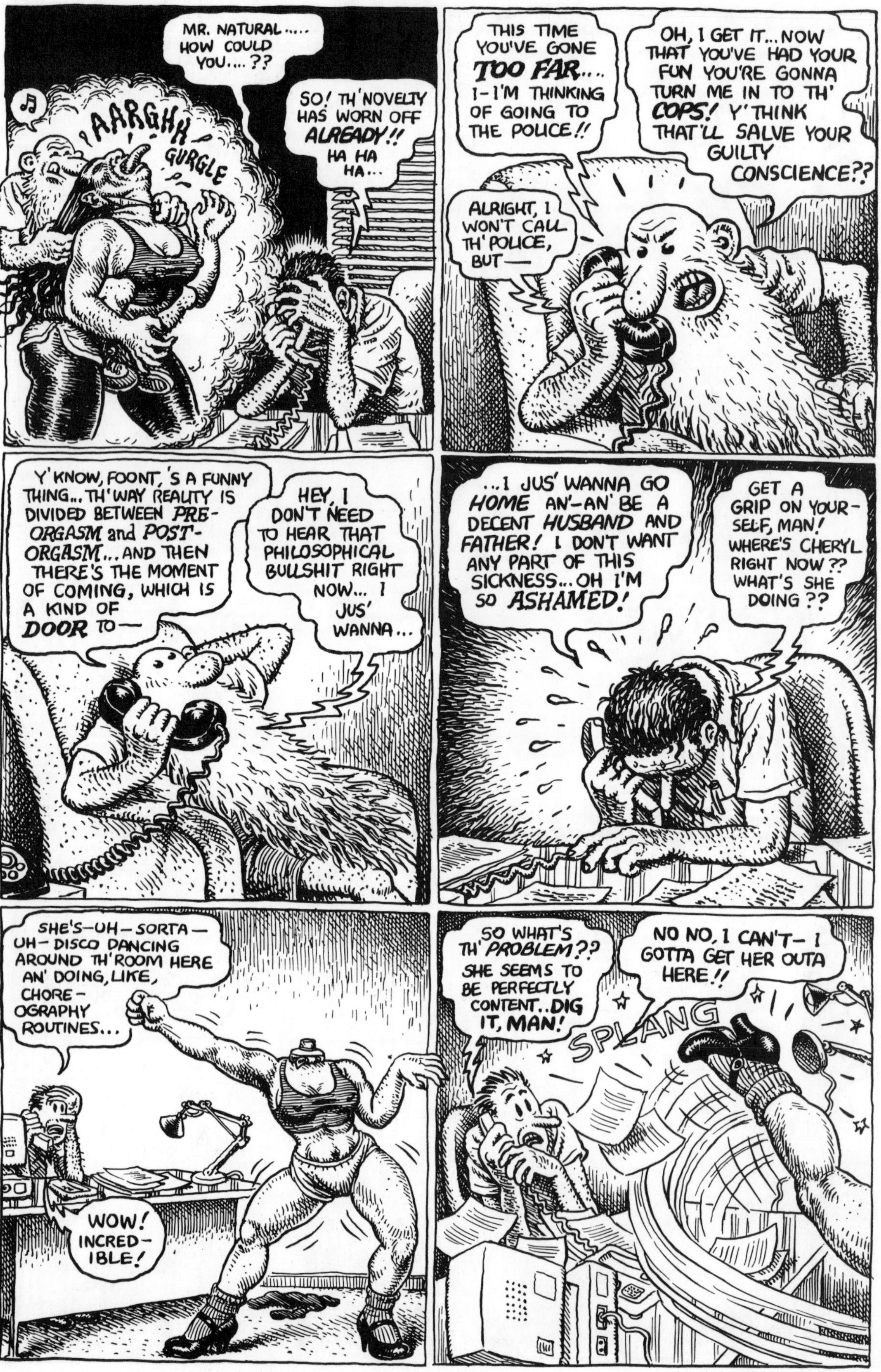
MR. NATURAL..... HOW COULD YOU....??
AARGHH
GURGLE
SO! TH' NOVELTY HAS WORN OFF ALREADY!! HA HA HA...
THIS TIME YOU'VE GONE TOO FAR.... I-I'M THINKING OF GOING TO THE POLICE!!
OH, I GET IT...NOW THAT YOU'VE HAD YOUR FUN YOU'RE GONNA TURN ME IN TO TH' COPS! Y'THINK THAT'LL SALVE YOUR GUILTY CONSCIENCE??
ALRIGHT, I WON'T CALL TH' POLICE, BUT—
Y'KNOW, FOONT, 'S A FUNNY THING... TH' WAY REALITY IS DIVIDED BETWEEN PRE-ORGASM and POST-ORGASM...AND THEN THERE'S THE MOMENT OF COMING, WHICH IS A KIND OF DOOR TO—
HEY, I DON'T NEED TO HEAR THAT PHILOSOPHICAL BULLSHIT RIGHT NOW... I JUS' WANNA...
...I JUS' WANNA GO HOME AN'-AN' BE A DECENT HUSBAND AND FATHER! I DON'T WANT ANY PART OF THIS SICKNESS...OH I'M SO ASHAMED!
GET A GRIP ON YOURSELF, MAN! WHERE'S CHERYL RIGHT NOW?? WHAT'S SHE DOING??
SHE'S—UH—SORTA—UH—DISCO DANCING AROUND TH' ROOM HERE AN' DOING, LIKE, CHOREOGRAPHY ROUTINES...
WOW! INCREDIBLE!
SO WHAT'S TH' PROBLEM?? SHE SEEMS TO BE PERFECTLY CONTENT..DIG IT, MAN!
NO NO, I CAN'T—I GOTTA GET HER OUTA HERE!!
SPLANG

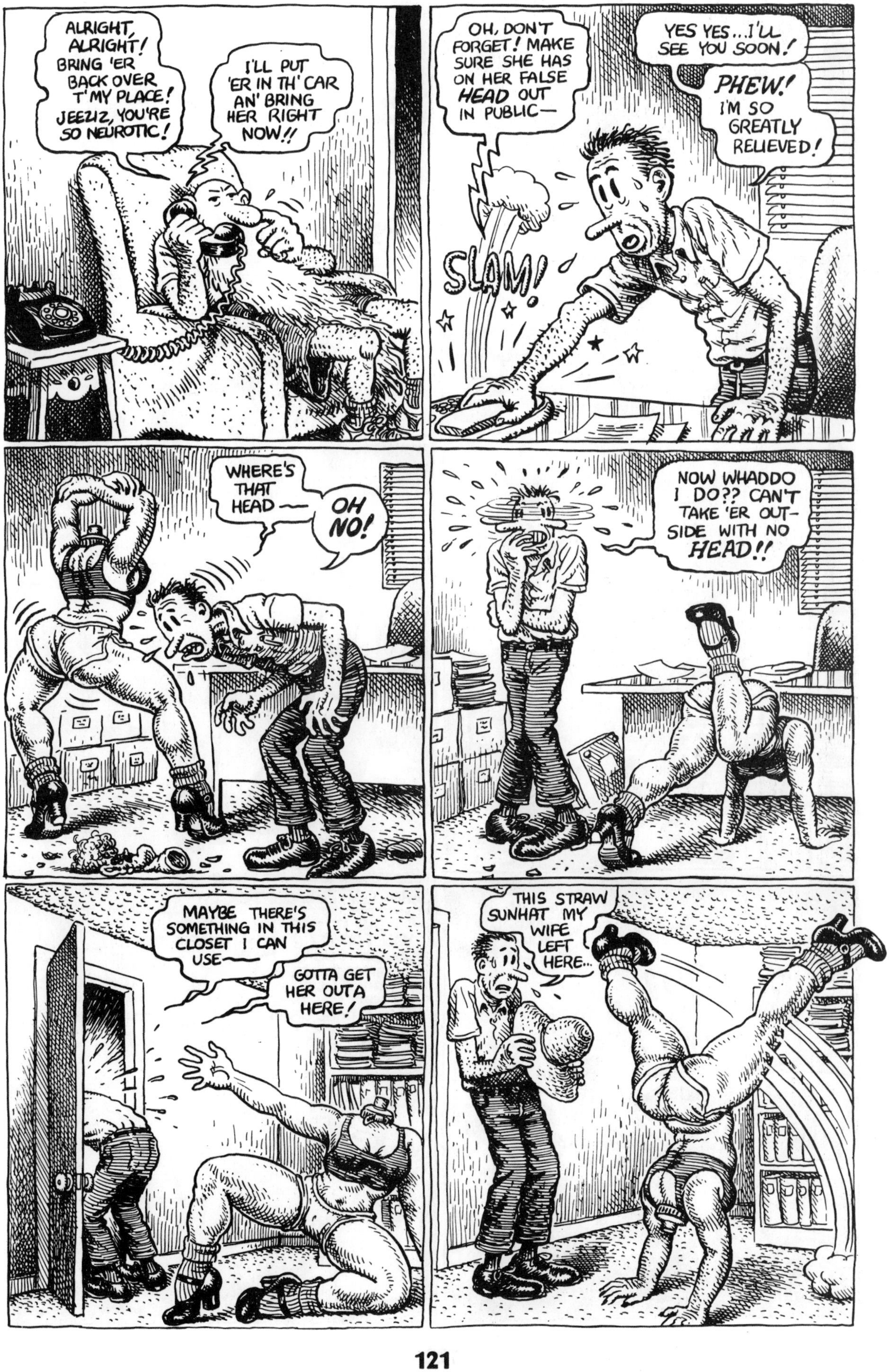
ALRIGHT, ALRIGHT! BRING 'ER BACK OVER T' MY PLACE! JEEZIZ, YOU'RE SO NEUROTIC!
I'LL PUT 'ER IN TH' CAR AN' BRING HER RIGHT NOW!!
OH, DON'T FORGET! MAKE SURE SHE HAS ON HER FALSE HEAD OUT IN PUBLIC—
YES YES... I'LL SEE YOU SOON!
PHEW! I'M SO GREATLY RELIEVED!
SLAM!
WHERE'S THAT HEAD—
OH NO!
NOW WHADDO I DO?? CAN'T TAKE 'ER OUT-SIDE WITH NO HEAD!!
MAYBE THERE'S SOMETHING IN THIS CLOSET I CAN USE—
GOTTA GET HER OUTA HERE!
THIS STRAW SUNHAT MY WIFE LEFT HERE...

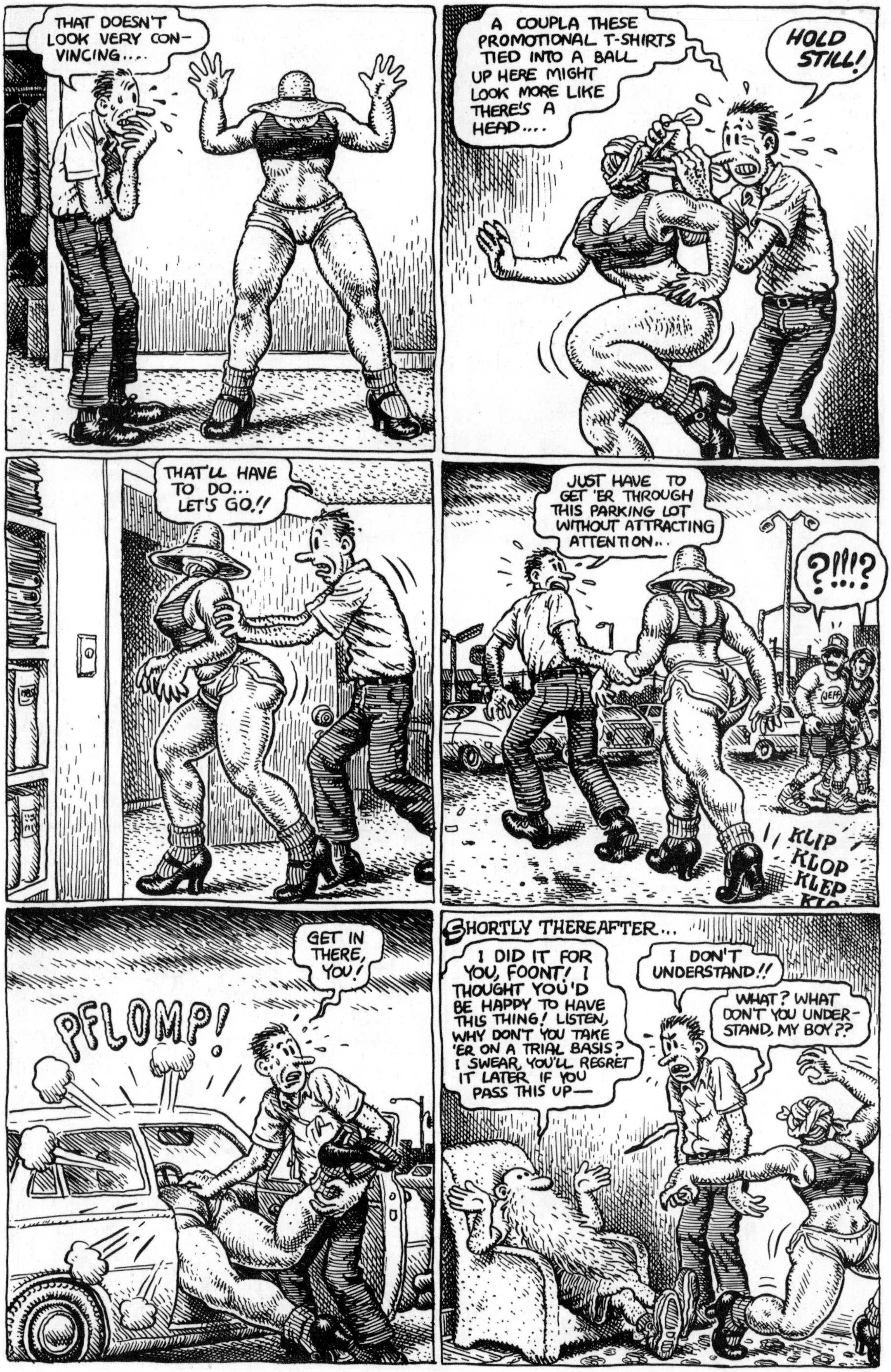
THAT DOESN'T LOOK VERY CON- VINCING....
A COUPLA THESE PROMOTIONAL T-SHIRTS TIED INTO A BALL UP HERE MIGHT LOOK MORE LIKE THERE'S A HEAD....
HOLD STILL!
THAT'LL HAVE TO DO... LET'S GO!!
JUST HAVE TO GET 'ER THROUGH THIS PARKING LOT WITHOUT ATTRACTING ATTENTION...
?!!!?
JEFF
KLIP
KLOP
KLEP
GET IN THERE, YOU!
PFLOMP!
SHORTLY THEREAFTER...
I DID IT FOR YOU, FOONT! I THOUGHT YOU'D BE HAPPY TO HAVE THIS THING! LISTEN, WHY DON'T YOU TAKE 'ER ON A TRIAL BASIS? I SWEAR, YOU'LL REGRET IT LATER IF YOU PASS THIS UP—
I DON'T UNDERSTAND!!
WHAT? WHAT DON'T YOU UNDER- STAND, MY BOY??

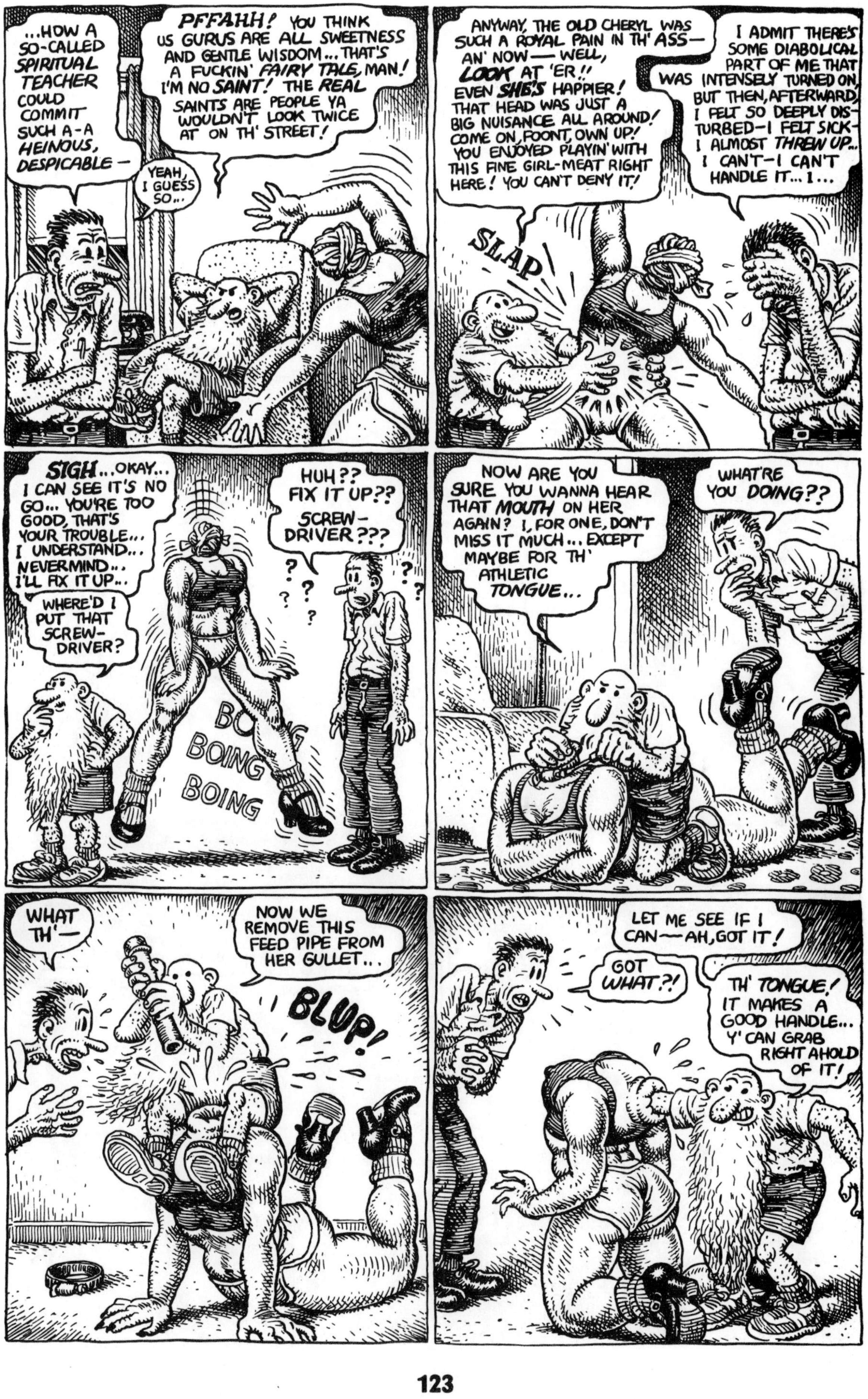

...HOW A SO-CALLED SPIRITUAL TEACHER COULD COMMIT SUCH A-A HEINOUS, DESPICABLE—
PFFAHH! YOU THINK US GURUS ARE ALL SWEETNESS AND GENTLE WISDOM... THAT'S A FUCKIN' FAIRY TALE, MAN! I'M NO SAINT! THE REAL SAINTS ARE PEOPLE YA WOULDN'T LOOK TWICE AT ON TH' STREET!
YEAH, I GUESS SO...
ANYWAY, THE OLD CHERYL WAS SUCH A ROYAL PAIN IN TH' ASS— AN' NOW— WELL, LOOK AT 'ER!! EVEN SHE'S HAPPIER! THAT HEAD WAS JUST A BIG NUISANCE ALL AROUND! COME ON, FOONT, OWN UP! YOU ENJOYED PLAYIN' WITH THIS FINE GIRL-MEAT RIGHT HERE! YOU CAN'T DENY IT!
I ADMIT THERE'S SOME DIABOLICAL PART OF ME THAT WAS INTENSELY TURNED ON, BUT THEN, AFTERWARD, I FELT SO DEEPLY DISTURBED—I FELT SICK— I ALMOST THREW UP... I CAN'T—I CAN'T HANDLE IT... I...
SLAP
SIGH...OKAY... I CAN SEE IT'S NO GO... YOU'RE TOO GOOD, THAT'S YOUR TROUBLE... I UNDERSTAND... NEVERMIND... I'LL FIX IT UP...
WHERE'D I PUT THAT SCREW-DRIVER?
HUH?? FIX IT UP?? SCREW-DRIVER???
BOING BOING BOING
NOW ARE YOU SURE YOU WANNA HEAR THAT MOUTH ON HER AGAIN? I, FOR ONE, DON'T MISS IT MUCH... EXCEPT MAYBE FOR TH' ATHLETIC TONGUE...
WHAT'RE YOU DOING??
WHAT TH'—
NOW WE REMOVE THIS FEED PIPE FROM HER GULLET...
BLUP!
LET ME SEE IF I CAN—AH, GOT IT!
GOT WHAT?!
TH' TONGUE! IT MAKES A GOOD HANDLE... Y' CAN GRAB RIGHT AHOLD OF IT!

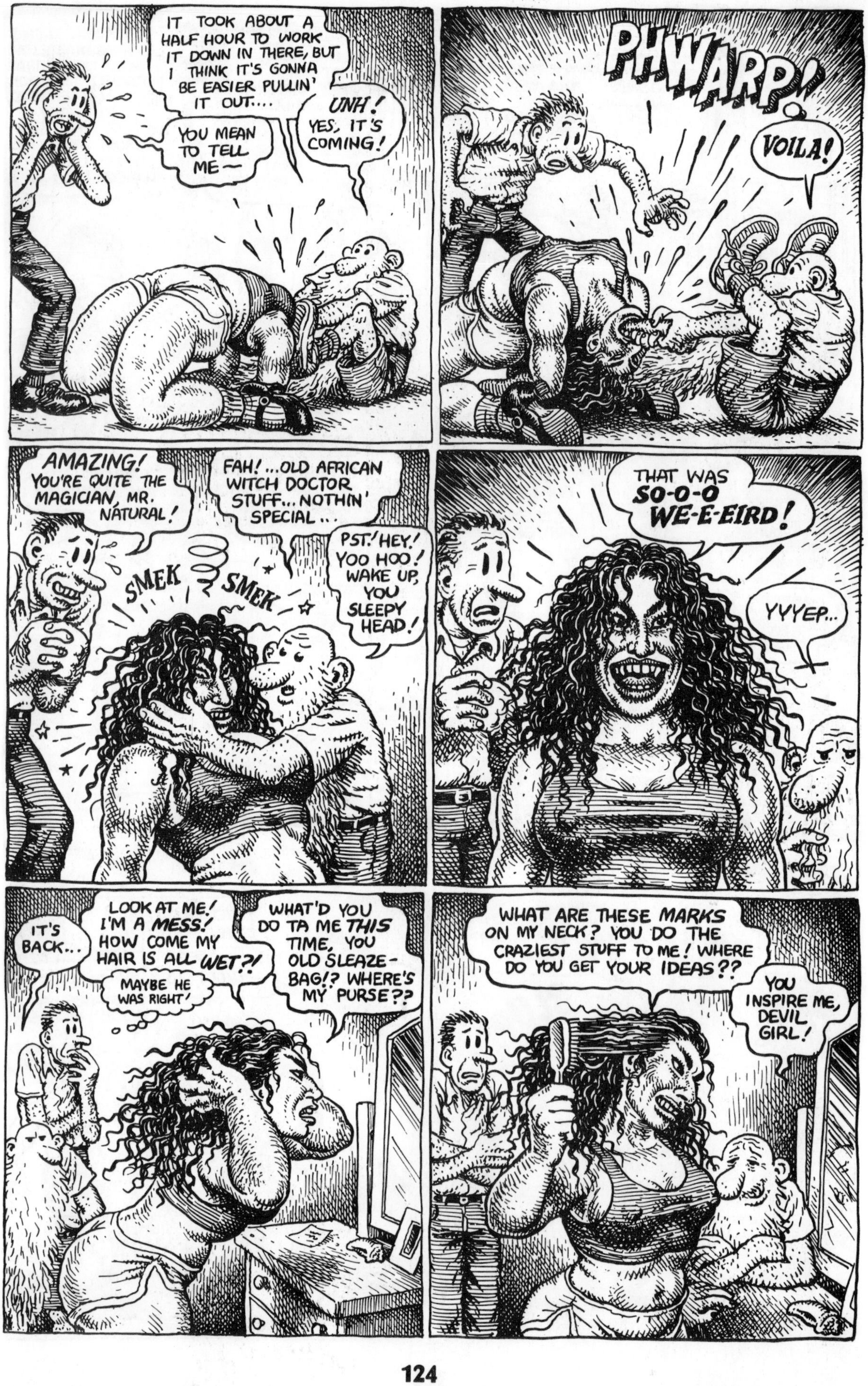

IT TOOK ABOUT A HALF HOUR TO WORK IT DOWN IN THERE, BUT I THINK IT'S GONNA BE EASIER PULLIN' IT OUT....
YOU MEAN TO TELL ME~
UNH! YES, IT'S COMING!
PHWARP!
VOILA!
AMAZING! YOU'RE QUITE THE MAGICIAN, MR. NATURAL!
FAH! ...OLD AFRICAN WITCH DOCTOR STUFF... NOTHIN' SPECIAL...
SMEK
SMEK
PST! HEY! YOO HOO! WAKE UP, YOU SLEEPY HEAD!
THAT WAS SO-O-O WE-E-EIRD!
YYYEP...
IT'S BACK...
LOOK AT ME! I'M A MESS! HOW COME MY HAIR IS ALL WET?!
MAYBE HE WAS RIGHT!
WHAT'D YOU DO TA ME THIS TIME, YOU OLD SLEAZE-BAG!? WHERE'S MY PURSE??
WHAT ARE THESE MARKS ON MY NECK? YOU DO THE CRAZIEST STUFF TO ME! WHERE DO YOU GET YOUR IDEAS??
YOU INSPIRE ME, DEVIL GIRL!

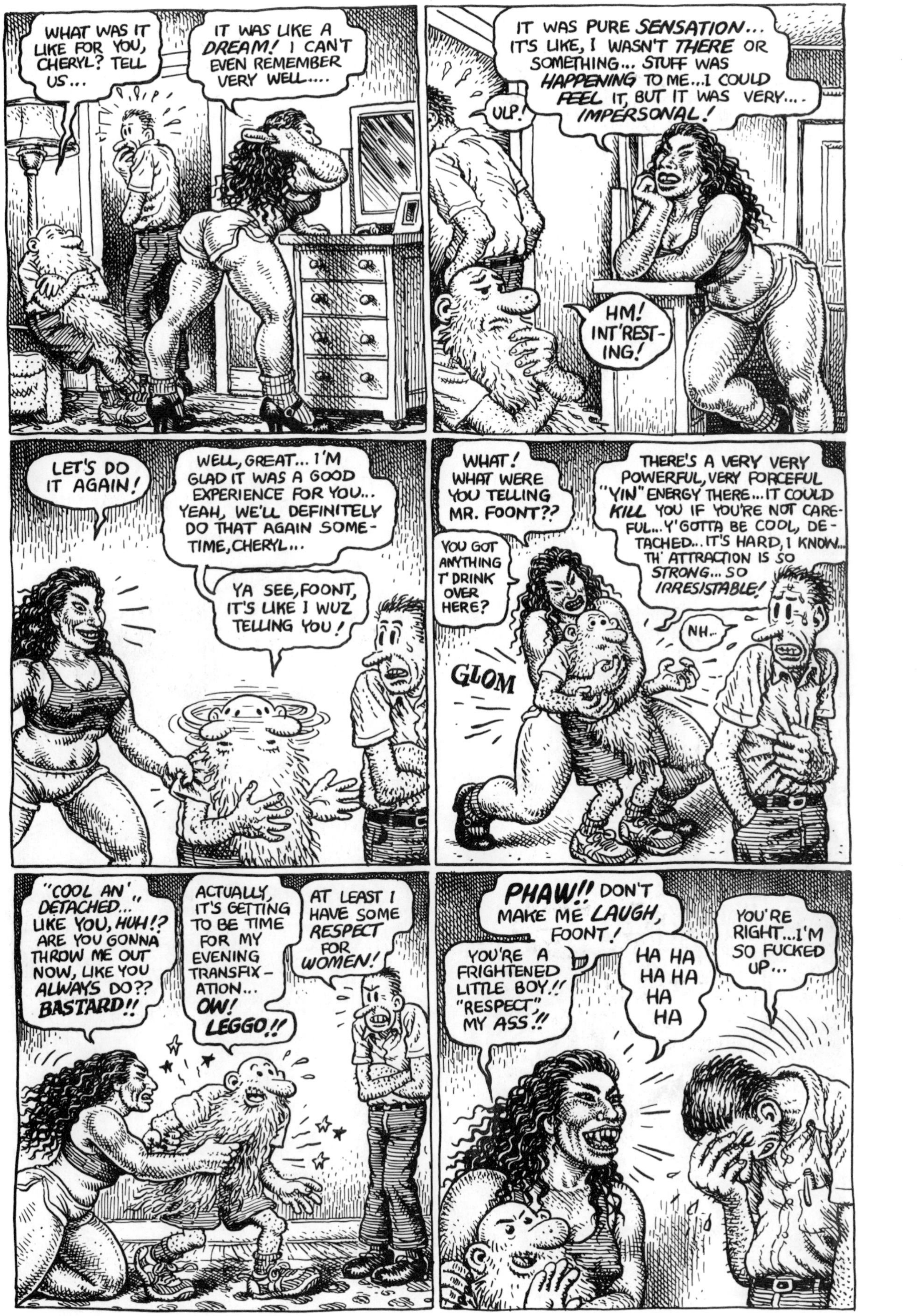

WHAT WAS IT LIKE FOR YOU, CHERYL? TELL US...
IT WAS LIKE A DREAM! I CAN'T EVEN REMEMBER VERY WELL....
ULP!
IT WAS PURE SENSATION... IT'S LIKE, I WASN'T THERE OR SOMETHING... STUFF WAS HAPPENING TO ME...I COULD FEEL IT, BUT IT WAS VERY... IMPERSONAL!
HM! INT'REST-ING!
LET'S DO IT AGAIN!
WELL, GREAT... I'M GLAD IT WAS A GOOD EXPERIENCE FOR YOU... YEAH, WE'LL DEFINITELY DO THAT AGAIN SOME-TIME, CHERYL...
YA SEE, FOONT, IT'S LIKE I WUZ TELLING YOU!
WHAT! WHAT WERE YOU TELLING MR. FOONT??
THERE'S A VERY VERY POWERFUL, VERY FORCEFUL "YIN" ENERGY THERE... IT COULD KILL YOU IF YOU'RE NOT CARE-FUL... Y'GOTTA BE COOL, DE-TACHED... IT'S HARD, I KNOW... TH' ATTRACTION IS SO STRONG... SO IRRESISTABLE!
YOU GOT ANYTHING T' DRINK OVER HERE?
NH...
GLOM
"COOL AN' DETACHED"... LIKE YOU, HUH!? ARE YOU GONNA THROW ME OUT NOW, LIKE YOU ALWAYS DO?? BASTARD!!
ACTUALLY, IT'S GETTING TO BE TIME FOR MY EVENING TRANSFIX-ATION... OW! LEGGO!!
AT LEAST I HAVE SOME RESPECT FOR WOMEN!
PHAW!! DON'T MAKE ME LAUGH, FOONT!
YOU'RE A FRIGHTENED LITTLE BOY!! "RESPECT", MY ASS!!
HA HA HA HA HA HA
YOU'RE RIGHT...I'M SO FUCKED UP...

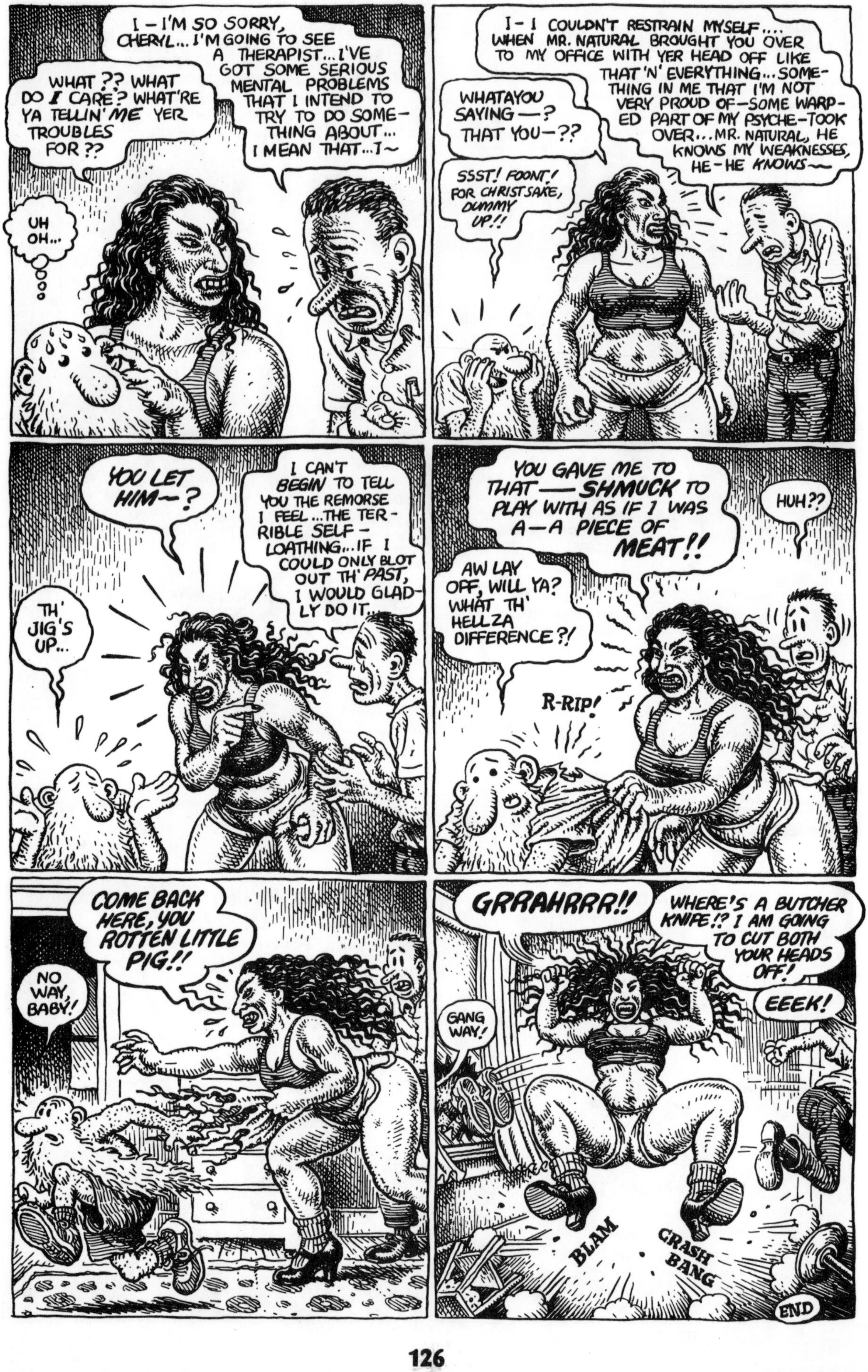
I – I'M SO SORRY, CHERYL... I'M GOING TO SEE A THERAPIST... I'VE GOT SOME SERIOUS MENTAL PROBLEMS THAT I INTEND TO TRY TO DO SOMETHING ABOUT... I MEAN THAT... I~
WHAT ?? WHAT DO I CARE? WHAT'RE YA TELLIN' ME YER TROUBLES FOR ??
UH OH...
I – I COULDN'T RESTRAIN MYSELF.... WHEN MR. NATURAL BROUGHT YOU OVER TO MY OFFICE WITH YER HEAD OFF LIKE THAT 'N' EVERYTHING... SOMETHING IN ME THAT I'M NOT VERY PROUD OF — SOME WARPED PART OF MY PSYCHE — TOOK OVER... MR. NATURAL, HE KNOWS MY WEAKNESSES, HE – HE KNOWS~
WHATAYOU SAYING —? THAT YOU —??
SSST! FOONT! FOR CHRISTSAKE, DUMMY UP!!
YOU LET HIM—?
I CAN'T BEGIN TO TELL YOU THE REMORSE I FEEL... THE TERRIBLE SELF-LOATHING... IF I COULD ONLY BLOT OUT TH' PAST, I WOULD GLADLY DO IT...
TH' JIG'S UP...
YOU GAVE ME TO THAT — SHMUCK TO PLAY WITH AS IF I WAS A — A PIECE OF MEAT!!
HUH??
AW LAY OFF, WILL YA? WHAT TH' HELLZA DIFFERENCE?!
R-RIP!
COME BACK HERE, YOU ROTTEN LITTLE PIG!!
NO WAY, BABY!
GRRAHRRR!!
WHERE'S A BUTCHER KNIFE!? I AM GOING TO CUT BOTH YOUR HEADS OFF!
EEEK!
GANG WAY!
BLAM
CRASH
BANG
END

Other works of R. Crumb available from Fantagraphics:

The Complete Crumb Comics, Vol. 1-11

R. Crumb Sketchbook, Vols. 1-5

The Life and Death of Fritz the Cat

Self-Loathing Comics
(with Aline Kominsky)

For a free 64-page color catalog of
Fantagraphics Books' publications, write:
7563 Lake City Way NE
Seattle, WA 98115